学术英语课程
设计、研究与实践范例

——国际交流能力与批判性学术素养培养

主编 ◎ 杨　苗
主审 ◎ 蔡基刚

北京大学医学出版社

XUESHU YINGYU KECHENG SHEJI、YANJIU YU SHIJIAN FANLI——GUOJI JIAOLIU NENGLI YU PIPANXING XUESHU SUYANG PEIYANG

图书在版编目（CIP）数据

学术英语课程设计、研究与实践范例：国际交流能力与批判性学术素养培养/杨苗主编. —北京：北京大学医学出版社，2023.11

ISBN 978-7-5659-2449-1

Ⅰ. ①学… Ⅱ. ①杨… Ⅲ. ①英语－教学研究－高等学校 Ⅳ. ①H319.3

中国版本图书馆 CIP 数据核字（2021）第 129283 号

学术英语课程设计、研究与实践范例——国际交流能力与批判性学术素养培养

主　　编：杨　苗
出版发行：北京大学医学出版社
地　　址：(100191) 北京市海淀区学院路 38 号　北京大学医学部院内
电　　话：发行部 010-82802230；图书邮购 010-82802495
网　　址：http://www.pumpress.com.cn
E - mail：booksale@bjmu.edu.cn
印　　刷：北京信彩瑞禾印刷厂
经　　销：新华书店
策划编辑：赵　欣
责任编辑：王　霞　　责任校对：靳新强　　责任印制：李　啸
开　　本：787 mm×1092 mm　1/16　　印张：11.25　　字数：288 千字
版　　次：2023 年 11 月第 1 版　2023 年 11 月第 1 次印刷
书　　号：ISBN 978-7-5659-2449-1
定　　价：65.00 元

版权所有，违者必究

（凡属质量问题请与本社发行部联系退换）

编委名单

(按姓名汉语拼音排序)

主　编　杨　苗

主　审　蔡基刚

副主编　李晓玲　林常敏　谢黎嘉

编　委　蔡　珩　赖佩芳　刘佳佳　余　凡

秘　书　蔡晓冬

序

《学术英语课程设计、研究与实践范例——国际交流能力与批判性学术素养培养》一书在汕头大学医学院英语教师团队的努力下即将问世出版，可喜可贺。

学术英语教学在国内最早是在上海市高校中大规模开展的。2013年秋季，上海26所高校在上海市教育委员会和上海高校大学英语教学指导委员会领导下，开始了由通用英语教学向学术英语教学转移的改革。尽管上海市教委沪教委高〔2013〕2号文件要求上海市高校开展"以学术英语为核心"的大学英语教学改革试点，培养大学生能用英语直接从事自己的专业学习、研究和今后工作，在自己专业领域具有较强的国际交往能力，但是改革的道路并不平坦。学科特点不同，理解认识不同，课程设置不同，决定了改革的成效不同。

这本书不仅仅是一部学术著作，更重要的是一所学校，尤其是医科高校改革成果的展示。书中介绍的汕头大学医学院（以下简称"汕医"）的学术英语课程也是启动于2013年，试行3年后，于2016年作为大学英语后续课程正式纳入英语课程体系。该学术英语课程设置、教案设计、活动方式、评估框架和教学反馈大大丰富了我国学术英语教学和研究实践。其中令人印象最深刻或最有成效的是从需求中来到需求中去，即课程设置和教学实践都基于需求分析，以成果为导向，最终服务和满足学生的医学专业学习和研究需求。

中国学术英语教学研究会从2015年起举办了5届中国大学生学术英语教学研讨会和3届中国大学生5分钟科研英语演讲比赛。这两个活动都要求大学生（本科生和研究生）以学科专业的问题为导向设计一篇小论文或科研报告，通过文献回顾，发现可以进一步解决的问题或研究空白，以此设计方法、收集数据、汇报研究结果。小论文写成后，学生还要把它们转换成口头陈述稿，向大学生同行演讲。这个过程大大激发了学生进行学术英语学习的热情，也满足了提高大学生的国际书面和口头交流能力的需求。而这种需求与汕医的英语教学改革目标不谋而合。这两项赛事为汕医的学生提供了展示课程学习成果的舞台，也进一步推动了课程改革。

这几年来，汕医的学生积极参加这两项赛事，每年特等奖或一等奖的获奖名单都会出现汕医学生的名字。以"中国大学生5分钟科研英语演讲比赛"为例，汕医学生在2018到2020年的3届赛事中，共获得6项特等奖、12项一等奖、22项二等奖、9项三等奖的优异成绩。根据汕医教务处统计，自 2018 年以来，完成学术英语课程学习的本科生以第一作者发表 SCI 国际期刊论文多达 27 篇，总影响因子达到了 84.554。这从一定程度证明了基于需求分析、以成果为导向的学术英语教学改革的成功。

我们相信这本书的出版对于推动我国高校各学科开展学术英语教学将做出极大的贡献，是为序。

蔡基刚

2021 年 6 月 8 日

前　言

本书是汕头大学医学院 2016 校级精品资源共享课程和 2018 年省级在线开放课程的教学成果，也是 2017 年教育部人文社会科学研究规划基金项目"批判教育视角下英语学术素养理论建构与实证研究（17YJA740063）"的研究成果。

本书第一部分"理论阐述与课程设计"包括两章，首先从学术英语课程的理论框架入手（第一章），分析构成学术英语学习的几大要素，以便一线的英语教师能先从理论的层面充分理解该课程的设计思路，并将此课程思路融会贯通到教学实践里。课程的具体设计、实施和教学方法部分（第二章）为读者描述了课程在汕头大学医学院（以下简称"汕医"）具体执行的概貌，体现了课程的整体设置。第二部分"教学实践案例"（第三章至第十五章）共分学术听说、学术读写和综合能力训练三大模块。这些章节都按照理论—实践—反馈的思路撰写。理论部分主要解读相关教学主题和教学思路，并阐明与教学内容相关的重要概念。实践部分主要介绍具体的教学目标、教学内容、课堂和课后任务，以及学生课后作业范例点评，以便使用本书的教师对每章的教学主题在课堂的具体运行与学生表现有清晰的了解。我们在完成每个阶段的教学之后两周内，都会通过问卷收集学生对课程的反馈意见。问卷主要使用李克特 5 分量表询问学生对每个授课内容的看法，包括他们对授课内容的作用、兴趣度、难度、投入程度和收获等方面的评分。教师对课程的反馈信息主要聚焦在备课和授课的难点、学生的课堂表现和学习任务评价等方面。需要说明的是我们在每章援引问卷所得数据时，因学生批次不同，参与总人数时有变化。学生反馈和教师反馈部分能促使阅读本书的教师对教学内容的适用性和教学效果进行思考，使课程与本校的具体情况和学生的实际水平结合起来。本书的第三部分是课程评估（第十六章），介绍了课程的评估框架和相关研究，对课程的教学效果进行初步评价。

本书总结了汕医外语教研室自 2013 年以来对大学英语课程进行第二轮改革之后所取得的成果，是教学团队多年协同努力的结果。值此书出版之际，我们的慕课《学术英语与学术素养》已在中国大学慕课和学堂在线同步上线，同时，基于此慕课开展的《学术英语》课程获广东省教育厅认定为省级线上线下混合式一流本科课程，并在第二届全国高校混合式教学设计创新大赛中荣获三等奖。

在多年的课程建设过程中，我们始终坚持这样的课程建设理念：学术英语课程应该以学术英语能力、批判性思维能力和信息管理能力三位一体的英语学术素养概念作为课程的理论框架，以人文性目标为本，以满足专业要求的工具性目标为导向，通过高度模拟学术研究和交流活动，帮助学生在身体力行中接受学术挑战、塑造科研人格，同时有机融合学术英语语言技能和专业知识的运用，使学生具备科研思维、树立科研自信、拥有学术素质、建立"外语学习者＋研究者"身份认同。我们深信即使存在不同的学科特点和对专业人才的不同需求，但这些核心的课程建设理念能够适用于我国高等教育阶段各个学科的学术英语课程改革。期待与其他院校的同行展开深入的探讨，共同推动我国学术英语课程改革与研究！

在此，我们衷心感谢本书主审蔡基刚教授对每个章节提出的宝贵的修改意见，衷心感谢所有为课程提供反馈意见的老师，衷心感谢汕头大学医学院所有参与课程学习并积极提供反馈意见的学生，衷心感谢无私贡献出自己的习作作为分析素材的学生。

本书编者合照

杨　苗

2021 年 6 月 8 日

目　录

第一部分　理论阐述与课程设计

第一章　课程理论构建 ··· 3
第二章　课程设计、实施与教学法 ··· 7

第二部分　教学实践案例

第一篇　学术听说模块

第三章　学术思维语言 ·· 14
第四章　学术口头报告 ·· 24
第五章　学术听力基本技巧 ··· 33
第六章　批判性学术听力 ·· 41

第二篇　学术读写模块

第七章　学术书面语特点 ·· 50
第八章　研究论文结构分析 ··· 60
第九章　多文本阅读技巧 ·· 67
第十章　同义转化技巧 ·· 81
第十一章　文献概述技巧 ·· 90

第三篇　综合能力训练：专业情境化任务

第十二章　综述写作（上）——文献汇总与思路形成 ···································· 101
第十三章　综述写作（下）——表述己见 ··· 113
第十四章　研究计划书 ·· 124
第十五章　学术壁报 ·· 139

第三部分　课程评估

第十六章　课程评估 ·· 163

第一部分

理论阐述与课程设计

第一章　课程理论构建

杨　苗　林常敏

本章主要从理论的角度介绍学术英语的课程框架,在论述学术英语的多维化概念之后,引入元素养的概念,提出信息、思维和语言能力"三位一体"的批判性英语学术素养课程理论框架。

一、学术英语多维化概念

非英语国家对大学生,尤其是研究生在国际期刊发表论文的要求,使得学术英语课程得到空前重视(Huang,2017)。学界对如何教好学术英语已有很多深入的讨论,可见于Hyland(2006)、Jenkins(2014)和Tribble(2009,2017)等名家的论著。根据Hyland(2006)的梳理,从历史的角度看,学术英语教学法共出现了学习技能(study skills)、学科社会化(disciplinary socialization)和学术素养(academic literacies)三大流派,代表了由基于技能和文本的教学向基于场景和实践的教学的转变。学术素养教学法认为学术素养植根于社会文化场景(Lea及Street,2006),培养了学生对学术界的认识,尤其是了解学科知识的建构方式(Curry,2015)。对学术语言的本位视角和批判性解读拓宽了我们对学术语言和学术素养的理解。Snow及Uccelli(2009)认为学术素养必须包括四大维度的学习内容:语言技能、体裁特点、思辨策略和学科知识。

但是,我们对学术素养内涵的多维度理解,还未能在实践层面形成清晰的教学方法(Hyland,2006)。传统的学术英语课堂仅注重教授专业术语、句式和体裁,认为这样就能培养学习者参与学术活动的能力。对学术圈新手作者的论文稿进行的研究,也多数停留于遣词造句或文本层面的抄袭等表层问题(Huang,2017)。Snow及Uccelli(2009)认为必须把学科知识纳入学术素养的学习内容,但事实上,在许多学术英语课程中,专业信息与学术写作课是被割裂开的。谁更能胜任学术写作课,是英语老师还是专业老师？这是一个一直未能解决的难题。Huang(2017)的研究表明专业老师比较注重论文里的思辨,英语老师则注重语言表述。但现实教学中两个团队鲜有合作教学的尝试,其结果是专业信息被当成独立存在、可以通过检索获取的知识,但没有融入语言训练,因而学术写作课往往脱离专业语境。如何将专业信息和学科要求与学术英语课程结合起来,如何寓思维训练于语言训练,从而满足数字信息时代学习者的专业发展需求,是学术英语课程亟须解决的问题。

二、信息素养与元素养

越来越多的学者认为学术英语素养的培养应该与专业实践紧密联系,尤其是学科传承下来的规范与思维。有一些学者已经做过尝试,如在教学中关注科学写作规范(Parkinson et al.,2007),强调科学学习策略(Soules et al.,2014),或者注重批判性思维(Hayes及Williams,2016),但这些尝试仍未能体现学术素养的多维度培养内容,也未能形成连贯的课程体系。

我们找到了能够将学术素养的多维内容统整起来的概念,即元素养(metaliteracy,ML),并将之运用到课程设置。元素养的概念起源于图书管理学的信息素养理论。早期的信息素养被界定为一系列检索与发现信息、评价与使用信息的能力(American Library Association,1989),但这些能力是离散的。在 Mackey 及 Jacobson(2014)将批判性思维和元认知学习引入信息素养的概念,创建了"元素养"理念之后,信息素养具备了更丰富、更复杂的核心理念,更强调动态性、灵活性、个人成长和团体学习。信息素养包括对信息的反思性发现,对信息如何产生和评价的理解,以及利用信息创造新知识并合理参与学习(学术)团体的综合能力(ACRL,2015,p.2)。作为信息素养的核心概念,"元素养"是指学生作为信息消费者和创造者成功参与实践共同体(community of practice)所需的综合能力,它要求学习者从行为上、情感上、认知上及元认知上都参与到信息生态系统的建构中(Mackey 及 Jacobson,2014)。几位美国学者尝试将元素养理念融入课堂教学,包括专业写作、戏剧、图书管理、信息素养等课程,结果发现这样的课程既能够提高学生对信息生态系统的动态发展的认识,又能够促使他们批判性地反思自己运用信息、分析数据和分享学术成果的过程(Jacobson 及 Mackey,2016)。

元素养所倡导的积极使用信息、创造信息,并进行批判性反思,与 Scriven 及 Paul(2004)对"批判性思维"的定义高度一致:

The intellectually disciplined process of actively and skillfully conceptualizing, applying, analyzing, synthesizing, and/or evaluating information gathered from, or generated by, observation, experience, reflection, reasoning, or communication, as a guide to belief and action.

在这个定义里,批判性思维是主动和技巧处理信息的过程,既包括"理解""应用""分析""综合"和"评价"等思维活动,也包括"观察""体验""反思""推理"和"交流"等实践行动,充分体现了信息管理与批判性思维之间的联系。再结合英语在国际学术界的通用程度,我们可以看到英语语言能力在处理信息时的重要性,因而,我们认为"元素养"这个概念能够统整多维度的学术英语素养概念,即语言、思维和信息等层面的能力要求,是学术英语课程框架的核心概念。

三、批判性学术素养理论框架

随着信息时代的到来,专业信息管理能力逐步成为专业能力评估的关键指标。数字信息技术时代的专业信息不再是静态和被分割的,因此专业信息素养不只包含对专业信息的检索、获取和理解,还强调学习者对特定专业体系内的信息流通和思维模式的深刻理解,对自身素养水平和学习过程的反思意识,以及重塑与产出信息的能力(Elmborg,2006;Mackey 及 Jacobson,2014;Jacobson 及 Mackey,2016;Tewell,2015)。数码信息时代的信息素养标准蕴含了对学习者的批判性思维能力、专业信息管理能力和语言运用能力的多重要求(ACRL,2015)。

基于这样的时代背景与要求,我们认为英语学术素养培养应该将语言技能训练嵌入学术任务(skills-embedded),以专业信息为依托(discipline-based),同时聚焦批判性思维发展(thinking-focused),而融合了信息、思维和语言能力三者的核心概念就是批判性英语学术素养。批判性英语学术素养集中体现了数字信息科技时代语言、专业知识和思辨能力的互联性(inter-connectivity),以及个体学习者与学科情境乃至社会文化情境的互动性(inter-activity)。它并非三者简单的叠加,而是依托动态的专业信息管理过程将多元能力进行整合运用。我们依据此核心理念构建的学术英语课程理论框架以"元素养"(metaliteracy)为信息、思维和语言三种能力的交汇点,注重培养学生使用信息(information consuming)和创造信息(information creating)的能力(图1.1)

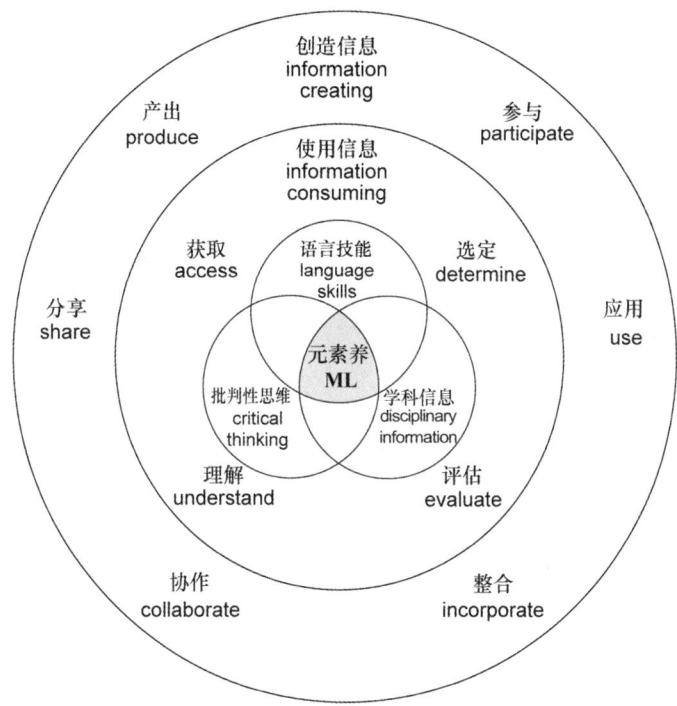

图 1.1　以批判性英语学术素养为核心的课程框架

依据此课程框架,学术英语课程的具体实施,从学习需求分析、课程内容设计和教学到学习评价,都以专业信息、语言技能和思维训练的整合为导向。此课程模式既契合目前国际语言主流教学模式,即课语整合式学习(content language integrated learning),又符合以学科知识为依托培养信息素养和思维能力的思路(Elmborg,2006;Kong,2014)。更为重要的是,此课程模式既能有效评价整合课程的学习效果,又能为评价思维能力和信息素养提供更动态、客观的评价模式。

本章主要从理论的角度介绍课程框架,下一章将讲述具体的课程设计与教学法。

参考文献

American Library Association,1989. American Library Association Presidential Committee on information literacy,Final report. Chicago:ALA.

Association of College & Research Libraries,2015. Framework for information literacy for higher education. Chicago:ALA.

Curry MJ,2015. UCLA Community College Review:Academic literacy for English language learners. Community College Review,32(2):52-68.

Elmborg J,2006. Critical information literacy:Implications for instructional practice. The Journal of Academic Librarianship,32(2):192-199.

Hayes SM, Williams JL, 2016. ACLT 052: Academic literacy—an integrated, accelerated model for developmental reading and writing. NADE Digest, 9(1): 13-22.

Huang JC, 2017. What do subject experts teach about writing research articles? An exploratory study. Journal of English for Academic Purposes, 25: 18-29.

Hyland K, 2006. English for academic purposes: An advanced resource book. London: Routledge.

Jacobson TE, Mackey TP, 2016. Metaliteracy in practice. Chicago: ALA Publishing.

Jenkins J, 2014. English as a lingua franca in the international university: The politics of academic English language policy. Abingdon: Routledge.

Kong SC, 2014. Developing information literacy and critical thinking skills through domain knowledge learning in digital classrooms: An experience of practicing flipped classroom strategy. Computers & Education, 78: 160-173.

Lea MR, Street B, 2006. The 'academic literacies' model: theory and applications. Theory into Practice, 45(4): 368-377.

Mackey TP, Jacobson TE, 2014. Metaliteracy. Chicago: ALA Publishing.

Parkinson J, Jackson L, Kirkwood T, et al., 2007. A scaffolded reading and writing course for foundation level science students. English for Specific Purposes, 26: 443-461.

Scriven M, Paul R, 2004. Defining critical thinking [2019-12-10]. http://www.criticalthinking.org.

Snow CE, Uccelli P, 2009. The challenges of academic language. // Olson DR, Torranace N. The Cambridge Handbook of Literacy. Cambridge: Cambridge University Press, 112-133.

Soules A, Nielsen S, LeDuc D, et al., 2014. Embedding multiple literacies into stem curricula. College Teaching, 62: 121-128.

Tewell E, 2015. A decade of critical information literacy: A review of literature. Communications in Information Literacy, 9(1): 24-43.

Tribble C, 2009. Writing academic English-A review of current published resources. English Language Teaching Journal, 63: 400-441.

Tribble C, 2017. ELFA vs. Genre: A new paradigm war in EAP writing instruction? English for Academic Purposes, 25: 30-44.

第二章　课程设计、实施与教学法

杨　苗

第一章介绍了学术英语课程的理论框架,以"元素养"统整语言能力、信息素养和批判性思维能力三方面的能力,构建批判性英语学术素养理论框架。本章介绍课程的具体设计、实施方案和主要教学方法。

一、学术英语课程设计

我们将学术英语课程纳入大学英语课程时数中,本科生在一年级修通用英语课程,二年级和三年级修学术英语课程。两个层次的学术英语课程各安排在两个学期,每学期20课时,一共80课时。我们参照社会认知的视角下的大学英语语言能力描述维度及其组成要素(赵雯 等,2014),以及通用英语与专用英语的分类目标(文秋芳,2014),从工具性和人文性两方面描述学术英语的课程目标(表2.1)。

表 2.1　学术英语课程能力目标培养体系

学习阶段		本科第二及第三学年
学习时间		80学时(每学期各20学时)
课程目标	工具性	✓ 培养运用英语进行专业学习的能力,如听讲座、做笔记、查找文献 ✓ 培养国际学术交流能力,如学术报告和壁报等 ✓ 提高运用英语从事专业工作的能力,如阅读英语文献、撰写研究计划书、文献综述和研究论文等
	人文性	✓ 提高思辨能力 ✓ 提高专业自主学习能力 ✓ 通过对中西方医学教育制度、卫生保健体系和医学伦理的对比学习,提高医学人文素养 ✓ 通过学术思维和科研思维的培养,提高学术素养 ✓ 通过学术研究活动,培养科研自信,建立二语学习者和新手研究者的身份认同

在具体学科中,重要的概念、说理的方法、意义的协商,以及专业知识的建构,都离不开语言,因此学术英语必须在特定的情景下为完成特定的任务而使用(Hyland,2006),专业情景化的教学是学术英语课程的重要特色。在前期研究阶段,我们在医科生和临床医生中进行英语学习需求分析(杨苗,2017),确定了一系列的专业学习需求和应用场景,设计成基于项目的课程任务,与听说读写等学术英语技巧结合起来,形成螺旋式上升、由易到难的学习内容(表2.2)。

为了既达到依托专业信息的课程目的,又能帮助英语教师团队胜任本课程,我们主要采用两种策略。一种策略是向医学专业教师请教,大至教学设计和教材选用,小至文本理解和分析(比如对专业术语或研究方法的理解),都进行了广泛的探讨,以增强对学生专业的理解。我们甚至和专业教师进行跨界合作,共同指导学生的科研英语演讲比赛、研究计划书、研究论文和壁报比赛,并在全国竞赛中获得优异成绩。英语教师和医学教师还合作开展教学研究并发表科研论文(杨苗,林常敏,2017;Yang et al.,2019)。另一种策略是在课程中有意识地选择医学人文研究领域的文献作为教材的主体,同时配合学生的专业课程选择少量的医学专业性较强的文献。在课程启动之前,我们在医学生和医学教师中进行调研,确定了六大医学人文研究主题:卫生保健、医学伦理、医学教育、健康教育、死亡教育和生命教育。教师团队对每个研究主题中可能出现的研究话题进行梳理,至少需要找到一个热点话题和10~15篇与之相关的、在国际知名期刊发表的学术论文(包括综述和研究论文),建立了一个简单的文献库,提供备课和设计教学活动所需的素材,如需要学生阅读、分析、点评并写综述的文献。在经过两轮的课程之后,这个文献库得到更新和增长,将学生自发检索的、老师们备课时获取的,以及医学教师推荐的文献不断补充进来。从研究内容来看,医学人文话题的医学专业性相较其他医学专业弱一些,英语教师更容易理解;从研究方法来看,医学人文话题的研究属于社科类研究,多数研究方法是英语教师所熟悉的。这些专业信息既不会对授课造成太大的困难,还能够达到有效培养学生的学术思维和医学人文素养等人文类课程目标。

表 2.2 学术英语课程各阶段的学习内容和专业情境任务

学年	学期	重点技巧	主要教学内容	专业情境任务
第二学年	1	学术听说能力	学术语言与思维特点、学术听力与口头报告技巧	学术口头报告
第二学年	2	学术读写能力	学术阅读技巧、学术体裁与结构、学术写作基本技巧	学术壁报报告
第三学年	1	学术读写与研究思维	研究思维与方法、多文本阅读技巧、学术书面语特点	文献综述
第三学年	2	学术读写与研究思维	文献阅读与评估、学术研究与写作规范	研究建议书、研究壁报/论文

上述两种策略的采用既降低了医学专业内容对英语教师的挑战,又促进了英语教师和其他学科教师的跨界合作,这也是大学英语教师积极应对行业更新和外界挑战,寻求更大的事业发展空间的良好举措。

二、批判实用性的学术英语教学法

本课程以体裁教学法(genre-based pedagogy)为主要的教学方法,同时兼顾过程教学法(process approach)所倡导的学生的自主思考、互动、反馈和修改等元素,尤其是将"语域"(register)的概念与批判教育学的教学思维紧密联系,充分体现了集批判性和实用性于一体的学术英语教学法(the critical pragmatic approaches to EAP)(Lin,2016)。

语言是思想最重要的媒介(Vygotsky,1987)。许多专业体裁与特定的认知和思维密切联系,因而在运用这些体裁时相应的思维模式和认知发展就会逐渐形成(Bazerman,2012)。传统意义上,体裁是指根据不同的形式、风格、特点和情节等对文学作品进行的分类(Johns,

2003),近年来体裁多用于不同的教学情境中,用来指"日常生活中、学术领域里或文学作品中由特定文化产生的、反复出现的、可辨识的语言模式"(Hammond 及 Derewianka,2001:p186),这从理论上重新界定了体裁的概念,使话语类型中语言表达的规律性与语言在更广泛的社会和文化背景中的使用产生联系。Hyon(1996)将体裁理论分成三个既相互独立又彼此联系的学派:系统功能语言学派、新修辞学派和专门用途英语学派。这三个学派都认为人类行为最大的特点是语言的使用,而语言正是通过体裁来构建意义和社会环境的。三个学派在理论根源、教学背景和教学重点方面略有差异,如系统功能语言学派强调对语域和体裁的微观分析,注重课堂教学,多用于中小学和成人教育;新修辞学派则侧重语篇所能实现的社会行为和目的,多用来帮助大学生和从事某一职业的新人了解特定体裁的社会功能及其使用场合;而专门用途英语学派通过对专门用途英语的语篇进行体裁分析,引导学生掌握谋篇布局的机制及其文体特征。随着体裁研究的逐步深入,人们发现在教学实践中这三个学派完全可以互补和融合(Swales,2011)。

我国语言教学界对体裁教学法的理论价值非常推崇,但在实践中运用甚少(孙厌舒,王俊菊,2015)。我们在汕头大学医学院的英语课堂,尤其是写作课堂,大量使用体裁教学法(Yang,2010;杨苗,2013)。在学术英语课程中更是集众家之长,在体裁的宏观分析方面由新修辞学派所倚重的体裁的社会功能和使用场合入手,微观分析时则大量使用专门用途英语学派所提倡的学术体裁语步分析及其相关研究成果(Swales,1990;Swales 及 Feak,1994;Swales 及 Feak,2012),在体裁教学方面采用系统功能语言学派的教学模式,以"解构范文""共同建构文本"和"独立建构文本"为三大教学步骤(Martin,1999)。

在具体运用体裁教学法时,本课程将批判教育学思维融入体裁教学的步骤,帮助学生批判性地思考专业知识的传播是如何产生和发生变化的。每介绍一种核心学术任务,老师都会按照 why、what 和 how 三大环节引导学生对学术任务所涉及的体裁进行解构。"Why"环节主要介绍为什么使用该体裁,即使用该体裁的学术场景。在这一环节,老师重点对体裁进行情景分析,即 So(2005)所使用的 contextual analysis,借助 Halliday 及 Hasan(1989)的语域理论(register theory)分析使用该体裁的语场(field)、语式(mode)和语旨(tenor),突出交流目的。"How"环节主要分析该体裁如何谋篇布局,以达到相应的交流目的,即 analysis of schematic structure。"What"环节主要分析该体裁的遣词造句,即 analysis of linguistic features。这样由大至小,层层剖析解构之后,就进入"共同建构"阶段,一般设计为在课堂里完成的小任务,在此环节老师借助题目设计,如提问的方式,主要起脚手架(scaffolding)的作用,辅助学生一步步构建文本。在"独立建构文本"阶段,学生完成相应的课后作业,提交电子版初稿。这一阶段的任务完成后,"过程写作法"所提倡的注重写作过程的反思、反馈和修改开始融入课程。老师会在初稿上点评,将意见反馈给学生,同时组织学生在课堂上或课外交换作业,互相点评。学生的终稿一般都会经过两轮修改。

参考文献

Bazerman C,2012. Writing with concepts: Communal, internalized and externalized. Mind, Culture and Activity,19(3):259-272.

Halliday MAK, Hasan R,1989. Language, context, and text: Aspects of language in a social-semiotic perspective. 2nd edition. Oxford: Oxford University Press.

Hammond J, Derewianka B,2001. Genre. // Carter R, Nunan D. The Cambridge guide to teaching English to speakers of other languages. Cambridge: Cambridge University Press: 186-193.

Hyland K, 2006. English for academic purposes: an advanced resource book. New York: Routledge.

Hyon S, 1996. Genre in three traditions: Implications for ESL. TESOL Quarterly, 30(4): 693-722.

Johns AM, 2003. Genre and ESL/EFL composition instruction. // Kroll B. Exploring the dynamics of second language writing. Cambridge: Cambridge University Press: 195-217.

Lin A, 2016. Language across the curriculum & CLIL in English as an additional language (EAL) context: Theory and practice. Singapore: Springer.

Martin JR, 1999. Mentoring semogenesis: "genre-based" literacy pedagogy. // Christie F. Pedagogy and the shaping of consciousness: Linguistic and social process. London: Continuum: 123-155.

So BC, 2005. From analysis to pedagogic applications: Using newspaper genres to write school genres. Journal of English for Academic Purposes, 4: 67-82.

Swales JM, 1990. Genre analysis: English in academic and research settings. Cambridge: Cambridge University Press.

Swales JM, 2011. Coda: Reflections on the future of genre and L2 writing. Journal of Second Language Writing, 20: 83-87.

Swales JM, Feak CB, 1994. Academic writing for graduate students. Ann Arbor: University of Michigan Press.

Swales J, Feak C, 2012. Academic writing for graduate students: Essential tasks and skills. 3rd ed., Michigan series in English for academic & professional purposes. Ann Arbor: University of Michigan Press.

Vygotsky LS, 1987. Thinking and speech. New York: Plenum.

Yang M, 2010. A process-genre approach to teaching writing to medical science graduate students. // Kasten S. Effective second language writing. Alexandria: TESOL Inc: 77-87.

Yang M, O'Sullivan PS, Irby DM, et al., Challenges and adaptations in implementing an English-medium medical program: a case study in China. BMC Medical Education, 19(15) [2019-01-09]. https://doi.org/10.1186/s12909-018-1452-3.

孙厌舒,王俊菊,2015.二语写作体裁教学研究的回顾与反思.解放军外国语学院学报.(1):44-50.

文秋芳,2014.大学英语教学中通用英语与专用英语之争:问题与对策.外语与外语教学.(1):1-8.

杨苗,2013.概念构建和学习收获:体裁教学法在医学英语课堂中的实证研究.中国ESP研究.(1):16-28.

杨苗,2017.体裁教学法课程框架中的医学英语扩展式学习:一项基于批判性学习需求分析的介入研究.北京:高等教育出版社.

杨苗,林常敏,2017.医学院校大学英语教学中依托信息管理的批判性学术素养培养实证研究.复旦教育论坛.15(4):107-112.

赵雯,王海啸,余渭深,2014.大学英语"语言能力"框架的建构.外语与外语教学.(1):15-21.

第二部分

教学实践案例

第一篇

学术听说模块

第三章　学术思维语言

杨　苗　蔡　珩

一、对教学主题和教学思路的解读

本章是本学术英语课程的开宗明义之作，主要向学生阐述学术语言的内涵及学术思维与学术语言的紧密联系，使学生意识到语言不仅是交流和表述的工具，更是帮助他们建立起和未来专业联系的媒介。本章借用 Zwiers（2008）书中的章节标题"Language for Academic Thinking"，将其翻译为学术思维语言，在阐述教学主题时，突出学术语言和学术思维两个概念及其内在联系。

（一）教学主题——学术语言与学术思维

率先提出学术语言（academic language）概念的是加拿大双语教育学者 Cummins（1979），他将基础人际沟通能力（basic interpersonal communicative skills，BICS）与认知学术语言能力（cognitive academic language proficiency，CALP）区分开来，认为学校应该有意识地培养学生认知学术语言的能力，才能帮助他们成功完成学业。但长期以来，很多人对学术语言的理解仅限于学术词汇，即某一学科领域的专业词汇，以及某些特定的表达法和句式，往往忽略语言在学术思维过程中的重要作用。

Dutro 及 Moran（2003）将学术语言能力定义为从口头和书面语言构建意义、理解复杂的概念和信息、区分不同体裁的特点、运用多种语言策略进行交流等方面的能力。Diaz-Rico 及 Weed（2002）的定义更为简洁：学术语言能力包含了一系列的思维能力和语言能力，用于理解和表述复杂的概念。Zwiers（2008）认为学术语言必须发挥三种作用：描述复杂的概念、描述高级思维过程（包括对知识的评估、分析、综合和运用）、描述抽象的概念，因此将学术语言能力定义为能发挥这三种作用的特定的词汇、语法和语篇组织策略。

由此可见，在学术英语课程中，学生要学习的不仅是特定学术情景里的语言交流能力，还有从复杂、抽象的学科知识中构建意义，用于更新和综合知识的思维能力。本章设计的教学活动，均为了加深学生在这方面的理解，并帮助他们了解后面各章节的学习目标。因本章是总起之作，仅对批判性思维做简单介绍，在与批判性思维紧密相关的教学主题（如第六章"批判性学术听力"和第九章"多文本阅读技巧"）中，我们侧重讲述整合批判性思维与语言技能的技巧。本章对学术语言的特点也仅做简单呈现，第四章"学术口头报告"和第七章"学术书面语特点"均有更详细的教学内容。

（二）教学思路

为帮助学生理解学术语言的概念，本节先由理论入手，介绍批判性思维的概念及其与语言学习的关系，从而引入学术语言的概念。之后，由理论进入实践，借用 Gibbons（1998）所列举的不同学习场景下的语言范例和 Halliday 及 Hasan（1985）的语域理论，解释交流场景（field）、交流方式(mode)和交流者(tenor)三大因素如何影响语言的使用。另外，还引用两个医学场景中的文本，即患者口述病情和医生的病历报告，进一步呈现语域如何受上述三大交流因素的影响。之后学生完成第一个学习任务：对比分析三种书面文本。本节理论阐述的第二部分是学术语言五个层次的能力要求(语音、词汇、语法、语篇发展和认知能力)，之后学生完成第二个学习任务：对学术论文的前言部分进行语言分析和语步分析(move analysis)(Swales，1990)，进一步理解语言与思维的密切联系。

二、教学案例设计

(一) 教学目标

1. 学生能够初步了解学术思维与学术语言的联系，并根据具体的学术场景和交流因素判断如何恰当地使用不同的学术体裁(如学术口语与书面语)。

2. 学生能够理解研究的思维如何与具体的学科内容和语言表述结合起来，并能够基于特定的文献进行语言分析与思路分析。

(二) 教学内容

1. Critical thinking in language usage

教学内容	注解
❖ **Critical thinking: what is it?** ✓ John Dewey (1909): active and reflective thinking ✓ Edward Glaser (1941): attitude (to be thoughtful about problems); Knowledge (to know methods of logical enquiries & reasoning); Skills (to apply these methods) ✓ Scriven & Paul (2003): the process of actively and skillfully conceptualizing, applying and analyzing, synthesizing, and evaluating information to reach an answer or conclusion	这里我们由 John Dewey 的定义入手，以 Scriven 及 Paul(2003)的定义总结。Scriven 及 Paul(2003)对批判性思维的定义最能够体现学术语言的思维要求，正如 Fisher 及 Scriven(1997)先前指出的，"critical thinking is an academic competency akin to reading and writing"。它突出了信息在思维过程中的运用。这个定义成为指导本课程的工作定义
❖ **A critical perspective to language education** ✓ Critical Education: a form of education in which students are encouraged to question dominant or common notions of meaning and form their own understanding of what they learn; a praxis-oriented educational approach (Castells, et al., 1999) ✓ Traditional EAP: emphasize language (lexis, grammar and register), skills, discourse appropriate to academic activities ✓ A critical perspective to language education: language is not simply a means of expression or communication; rather, it is a practice that constructs, and is constructed by the way language learners understand themselves, their social surroundings, their stories, and their possibilities for the future. (Norton & Toohey, 2004, p. 1)	这部分从批判教育学与批判性语言学习的角度入手，讲述语言学习中的批判性思维，强调应该突破传统学术英语课程以文本为基础(text-based focus)(Hyland, 2006)的局限性，将高阶思维和理智德性引入对学术语言的要求

(续表)

教学内容	注解
✓ A critical perspective to EAP: language skills ＋ higher order thinking needed in academic activities ＋ intellectual virtue (the habit of critical reflection on one's own and other's problematic assumption and the valuing of reasoned support for beliefs and actions) (Bensch, 2009)	

2. Contextualizing academic English

教学内容	注解
❖ **The differentiation of two kinds of language skills** (**Cummins**, 1979) ✓ Social language: basic interpersonal communication skills (BICS) ✓ Academic language: cognitive academic language proficiency (CALP)	以 Cummins (1979) 对基本人际交流能力和认知学术语言水平两种语言能力的区分引入学术语言的概念
❖ **What is academic language**? ✓ The set of words, grammar, and organizational strategies used to describe complex ideas, higher-order thinking processes, and abstract concepts. (Zwiers, 2008)	
❖ **Contextualize academic language** ✓ Four texts illustrating the mode continuum of casual, informal register to formal register (Gibbons, 1998) ✓ Two texts illustrating language usage in different medical contexts	讨论环节： 这部分以两组文本为例呈现交流场景、交流方式和交流者三大因素如何影响语言的使用，从而强调学术语言与专业使用情景的紧密联系。第一组例子侧重从非正式语域到正式语域的语言变化。第二组例子侧重不同学术场景中的语言变化。文本范例见附录3.1课堂讨论 此讨论结束后，学生完成任务一
❖ **Types of knowledge needed to foster academic English** ✓ Understanding of the phonological features of English ✓ Lexical knowledge ✓ Grammatical competence ✓ Discourse ✓ Cognition	此部分介绍学术语言蕴含的五个层面的知识要求(Scarcella, 2003)，之后学生完成任务二，以此进一步了解抽象、复杂的学术思路如何通过学术语言来表述

(三) 学习任务

任务一

任务内容 学生依据交流场景、交流目的、交流者和交流方式，对比分析三个与母乳喂养相关的文本，这些文本分别取自一个访谈节目(对话已转写)、一个科普节目的文稿和一篇正式发表的学术论文的前言部分。

任务要点　学生快速阅读三个文本,判断文本使用的场景和交流目的、所涉及的交流者和使用的交流方式,对比分析同样的信息如何由口头语表述转向学术性最强的书面语,并分析产生语言表述差异的原因,完成相关表格。

任务完成形式/师生互动形式　学生独立完成任务,之后老师以提问的形式检查任务完成情况,引导学生思考影响语言运用的语域因素。

任务二

任务内容　学生详细阅读第三个文本(即一篇学术论文的前言),分析其语步以及所使用的语言策略。

任务要点　学生通过对前言进行"语步分析",理清其语篇发展的思路,同时重点关注连接词、用于引用的动词(reporting verbs)和句式等遣词造句的方法如何清晰地表述该思路。

任务完成形式/师生互动形式　学生独立完成任务,之后老师以提问的形式检查任务完成情况。老师通过介绍 John Swales (1990)的"创建研究空间模式(create a research space model, CARS)"总结本次练习。

课堂学习任务讲义见附录 3.2。

(四) 课后作业

Read the following two texts and figure out the linguistic differences between them. Use contextual factors (e. g. communicative purposes, modes and audience) to analyze the differences.

Text 1

Jack Springer maintains that the government should allow people the right to own a gun. This position asserts that the government is infringing on our democratic rights when it restricts gun ownership. Most people who own guns, so the argument goes, are responsible citizens who keep guns for sport and recreation. It is further contended that because the police are unable to prevent violent crime, people need guns to protect themselves. However, as Josephine Bluff states, guns lead to increased violence. This is especially the case since many of the guns that individuals store in their homes are used in domestic disputes and teenage suicides. Lives are worth more than guns.

Text 2

Jack Springer thinks that the government should allow people the right to own a gun. But I don't agree with him. People like him sort of think that the government limits our rights when it restricts gun stuff. They kind of think that most people who own guns are responsible guys who keep the guns for sport and recreation. They also think that the police are unable to stop violent crime and we need guns to protect ourselves. But I think he is wrong. I agree with Josephine Bluff who thinks that guns increase the amount of violent crime in the community. And I also think that many of the guns that are kept around the house would be ended up being used in violent domestic disputes or teenage suicides. I also think that human life is worth more than giving shooters the right to go shooting on the weekend.

(Adapted from Bill Daly, 1997, at http://www.doc88.com/p-0012453410385.html)

(五) 学生作业点评

作业范例与点评 1

The two passages have linguistic differences on contexts, mode of communication, interaction, words, grammar and purpose. Here are the details of every aspect.

About contexts, text 1 is the written one, which can be confirmed by the usage of "Jack Springer maintains" and "Jack Springer states", while text 2 is the oral one. It is stated in the first-person perspective, beginning with "I don't agree" "I agree" "I also think", etc..

As for the mode of communication, text 1 is more likely reported on newspaper or magazines. Text 2 is more likely told in daily conversation or interview. Because of the difference in mode of communication, text 2 is more instantaneous than text 1. Examples here are the same as those for the previous paragraph.

As for the words, text 1 uses the ones which are more formal and professional, such as "maintain" "This position asserts" "infringing on our democratic rights". However, words in text 2 are simpler. For examples, it uses "think" rather than "maintain", and uses "limits our rights" rather than "infringing on our democratic rights".

On the aspect of grammar, the sentences in text 1 are more complicated than those in text 2. The author also uses a lot of subordinate clauses to make the text more organized, such as "maintains that" "It is further contented that" and "This is especially the case since". However, the sentences in text 2 are simpler and the sentence structures are looser.

Last but not least, text 1 is more objective. It is written to state different existing views, while text 2 seems subjective with only personal opinion.

点评：该学生能运用课堂学到的语域知识分析文本的语言特点，所找到的文本之间的语言差异也比较完整。不足之处在于学生没有厘清不同交际情景与语言差异之间的因果关系，这一点可以从作业第一句话和作业的整体结构看出。该学生将交际情景和模式与语法、用词等语言差异并列，所用例子出现许多重复之处。

作业范例与点评 2

Text 1 is more formal than text 2. Some words used in the two passages shows the difference. For example, some verbs in text 1, like "maintain" "restrict" "assert", etc. What's more, there are no abbreviation in text 1. Text 1 is also more objective than text 2, because there are no "I" in text 1.

点评：该学生的作业证实了我们从课后学生对课程的反馈得到的信息，即有些学生仅仅学习到浅层地分析文章的字面特征，没有理解本节课的深层学习目的，即语言的使用深受交际情景的影响，而因其使用的场景，学术语言的特征，恰恰能够有效地呈现其蕴含的学术思维。

三、案例使用反馈

(一) 学生反馈意见

在本节课结束后，共 279 名学生针对课程内容的难度以及自身在学习过程中的兴趣、投入与收获进行了评价。根据反馈信息，过半数学生对课程表现出兴趣，在学习过程中很投入。大部分学生(70%)认为本课所学内容对他们未来专业的学习与发展很有帮助。课程总体难度适中，讨论和课堂任务所用素材只有在阅读专业学术论文部分(即第三个母乳喂养相关的文本)学生反映难度较高，其他任务对学生而言难度较低。这主要是由于学生对文章背景知识、专业词汇的缺乏及对学术论文这一体裁的陌生造成的，也从侧面反映了本课程的必要性。

通过本节课的学习,学生普遍表示(79%)掌握了在不同学术语境下区分口语与书面语的特征的能力。有学生写道,"学会从语境、沟通方式、目的和读者等方面来分析学术语言的特点""对日常英语与学术英语的区别有更系统的认识,并学习到在不同场合使用不同程度的学术语言"。不少学生能够领会到学术语言与学术思维之间的关系,并在反馈中表示这有助于他们更好地阅读和理解学术文章。但同时也发现有部分学生在学习过程中更多地关注教学例文中的知识性信息,而忽略了对语言背后更深层的学术思维、逻辑的理解。比如,有学生提到,"本节课中,我了解了母乳喂养与婴儿智力发展的关系",这位学生明显抓错重点,误解此项教学任务的目的。这说明学术语言与思维的关系是本节课的理解难点,建议教师多花时间讲解两者的关系,避免将重点过多放在浅层解析文章的字面意思和特征上。

(二) 教师反馈意见

本节课的内容涉及理论较多,因此备课的一大难点是如何将抽象的概念通过生动有趣的方式让学生理解。首先,教师应该对这些理论有深入的、系统化的认识,进而理解整节课的教学思路,这样才能真正清楚每一项教学内容背后的目的,引导学生由理论进入实践,最终在实践中深化对理论的认识。其次,在解释抽象概念时,善于运用生动的例子帮助学生理解。比如 Dutro 及 Moran(2003)提出的砖块(bricks)与混凝土(mortar)的比喻,将具体学科的专业术语比做砖块,通用学术用语比做混凝土,形象地点出两者的特点与互相间的关系。另外,在课堂上可以通过提问、小组讨论的方式诱导学生去发现、总结不同语境下的语言特征,待学生讨论后再给出定义。

本节课的内容较多,故如何合理安排时间是备课的第二个难点。备课时应根据各项教学任务的目的及难易程度预估所需的时间。如介绍学术语言5个层次的能力要求(语音、词汇、语法语篇发展和认知能力)其实是为了引出后面关于学术思维(即认知能力)的练习,故讲解时不必逐一展开详细解释;而任务二,即详读第三个文本是本节课的重点及难点,这个环节应重点准备,多预留些时间让学生完成任务。

附录3.1 课堂讨论

(一) 讨论一

What are the contexts in which the following texts/discourses(Gibbons,1998)are used?

Text 1　Look,it's making them move.(Face-to-face interaction)

Text 2　We found out the pins stuck on the magnet and so did the iron filings. Then we tried the pencil but it didn't stick.(Oral retelling)

Text 3　Our experiment was to find out what a magnet attracted. We discovered that a magnet attracts some kinds of metal. It attracts the iron filings and pins,but not the pencil.(Written summary)

Text 4　The magnet is a piece of metal that is surrounded by an invisible field of force which affects any magnetic material within it. It is able to attract a piece of iron or steel because its magnetic field flows into the metal,turning it into a temporary magnet. Magnetic attraction occurs only ferrous materials.(Academic text)

(二) 讨论二

What are the communicative purposes,producers and contexts of usage for these texts?

Text 1 I was well until a few months ago. In the beginning, I just felt off-colour and a bit tired. But lately I've been feeling completely worn out at the end of the day. I'm not eating any more than usual but I've put on nine kilos in the last year. My motions are hard and my hair has started to fall out. (A patient talking to a doctor)

Text 2 A 50-year-old housewife, who had been well until four months previously, complained of tiredness and malaise. She had gained 9 kg in weight in the year before she presented to her GP although she denied eating more than usual. She was constipated and she noticed that her hair had started to fall out. (Case report)

附录3.2 学习任务

(一) 任务内容

Comparing the following texts and analyze their differences in terms of <u>communicative purposes, audience, contexts of usage, and mode of interaction</u>. Fill in the table to summarize the differences.

Text 1

Beth Ruyak: Since 1997, the American Academy of Pediatrics has recommended women breast-feeding their babies exclusively for six months. The World Health Organization recently did the same, but with some concern. They feared that in many places around the world mothers not receiving adequate nutrition might be putting their babies at risk for anemia and other nutritional deficiencies. So an international plea went out for physicians to do research on the topic, and the American results are in.

Host: The difference between breast-feeding your baby exclusively for four months and breast-feeding exclusively for six months may not sound like much, but a recent study finds that those eight weeks can make a world of difference.

Dr. Chantry: So we know that breast-feeding is dose responsive—the longer is better in general and the more is better. But we didn't know specifically if there's a point at which there are diminishing returns.

(Transcript from "Insight with Beth Ruyak" http://www.capradio.org/news/insight? page)

Text 2

A new study is adding more evidence to the connection between breast-feeding and intelligence. The study links intelligence in adults to how long they were fed their mother's milk as a baby. It found that babies who were breast-fed for nine months grew up to be more intelligent than those breast-fed for less than one month. Researchers at Copenhagen University Hospital in Denmark carried out the study. *The Journal of the American Medical Association* reported the finding.

Other studies have examined the link between mother's milk and intelligence in children. Organizers of the new study say theirs is the first to show a link between breast-feeding and adult intelligence. The organizers say their study also examined other considerations, such as a mother's education and economic situation.

In the 1970s and 1980s, researchers used two tests to measure the intelligence of those children. One test was given to almost 2,300 men when they entered Danish military. Their average age was nineteen. A different test was given to about 970 men and women. Their average age was 27. The Danish and American scientists found that babies who had been breast-fed for nine months did better on the intelligence test as adults. Breast-feeding longer than nine months had no additional effect on the test results.

It is not clearly why breast-fed babies may perform better in intelligence test as adults. However, the scientists note that mothers' milk contains substances not found in cow's milk products for babies. For example, breast milk contains two fatty acids that appear to support brain development. They are among hundreds of nutrients found in breast milk and not in other milk products.

The scientists say the physical and emotional relationship between a mother and child that develops during breast-feeding also might be important. They say women who breast-feed their babies may spend more time with them.

(Adapted from SCIENCE IN THE NEWS-May 28, 2002: Breast-Feeding and Intelligence Linked? https://learningenglish.voanews.com/a/a-23-a-2002-05-24-1-1-83111557/120161.htm.)

Text 3

For 100 years, the IQ has been at the heart of scientific and public debates about nature versus nurture [1-3]. Twin studies document that differences between individuals' IQs are under strong genetic influence, but twin studies also attest to the existence of nongenetic, environmental influences on IQ, particularly for young children [4,5]. In the past 5 years, the nature versus nurture debate has shifted toward interest in how both nature and nurture work together [6]. An integral part of this new focus is research that tests how genetic differences moderate the effects of environmental influences on individuals' health and behavior [7]. Here we report replicated evidence that a measured genotype can moderate response to an environmental influence on children's IQ. We began our investigation of gene-environment interaction in IQ by selecting for study an environmental factor thought to influence neurodevelopment and known to predict IQ. We selected being fed breast milk (hereafter breast-feeding) as the environmental exposure because the biological processes underlying its benefits for the developing brain are increasingly well understood [8]. A gene involved in these putative biological processes would be a good candidate for framing a gene-environment interaction hypothesis [9]. Thus, selecting breastfeeding as the environmental exposure allowed us to nominate a novel candidate gene for this study of IQ. (Caspi, et al., 2007)

(二) 学习任务

Task 1　Finish the table to summarize the differences.

	Text 1	Text 2	Text 3
Communicative Purposes			
Audience			
Contexts of Usage			
Mode of Interaction			

Task 2　Read text 3 and answer these questions.

1. What are the moves/steps in this paragraph?

2. How are thoughts kept ordered, logical and consistent by using academic vocabulary and grammar?

(三) 参考答案

Task 1

	Text 1	Text 2	Text 3
Communicative Purposes	To inform	To inform	To inform To evaluate
Audience	General public	General public	Peer researchers
Contexts of Usage	TV program	Radio program	Academic journal
Mode of Interaction	Conversation	Monologue	Written texts

Task 2

According to Swales' (1990) CARS model, there are four moves in this paragraph:

1. Introduce the topic——IQ and show its importance.

2. Review and summarize previous research pertinent to IQ research.

3. Identify the trend in recent IQ research and indicates the new focus.

4. Introduce the present research with the new focus "gene-environment interaction".

The paragraph introduces the development of IQ research concisely and clearly, using reporting verbs such as "document" and "attest to" to confirm the well evidenced finding that while individuals' IQs are under strong genetic influence, there is a role for nongenetic influences. "has shifted to" and "the new focus is" indicate the latest development. Other choice of words such as "under strong influence" "the existence of" "work together", and "moderate" gradually display how the influence of nongenetic factors have become the focus of study and its influence has become more specific.

参考文献

Anstrom K, DiCerbo P, Butler F, et al., 2010. A review of the literature on academic language: Implications for K-12 English language learners. Arlington: George Washington University Center for Equity and Excellence in Education.

Benesch S, 2009. Critical English for academic purposes. Journal of English for Academic Purposes, 8: 81-85.

Caspi A, Williams B, Kim-Cohen J, et al., 2007. Moderation of breastfeeding effects on the IQ by genetic variation in fatty acid metabolism. Proceedings of the National Academy of Sciences of the United States of America, 104(47): 18860-18865.

Castells M, Flecha R, Freire P, et al., 1999. Critical education in the new information age. Lanham: Rowman & Littlefield Publishers, Inc.

Cummins J, 1979. Cognitive academic language proficiency, linguistic interdependence, the optimum age question and some other matters. Working Papers on Bilingualism, 19: 121-129.

Daly B, 1997. Writing argumentative essays [2019-11-29]. http://www.doc88.com/p-0012453410385.html.

Dewey J, 1909. How we think. Boston: D. C. Heath and Co., Publishers.

Diaz-Rico L, Weed K, 2002. The cross-cultural, language, and academic development handbook: A complete K-12 reference guide. Boston: Allyn & Bacon.

Dutro S, Moran C, 2003. Rethinking English language instruction: An architectural approach. // García G. English learners: Reaching the highest level of English literacy. Newark: International Reading Association, 227-258.

Fisher A, Scriven M, 1997. Critical thinking: Its definition and assessment. Center for Research in Critical Thinking (UK)/Edgepress (US).

Gibbons P, 1998. Classroom talk and the learning of new registers in a second language. Language and Education, 12(2): 99-118.

Glaser E, 1941. An experiment in the development of critical thinking. Advanced School of Education at Teacher's College, Columbia University.

Halliday MAK, Hasan R, 1985. Language, context and text: Aspects of language in a social-semiotic perspective. Geelong: Deakin University Press.

Hyland K, 2006. English for academic purposes: An advanced resource book. London: Routledge.

Insight with Beth Ruyak [2019-11-29]. http://www.capradio.org/news/insight.

Norton B, Toohey K, 2004. Critical pedagogy and language learning. Cambridge: Cambridge University Press.

Scarcella R, 2003. Academic English: A conceptual framework. University of California Linguistic Minority Research Institute, technical report 2003-1.

Science in the news, 2002. Breast-feeding and intelligence linked? [2019-11-29]. https://learningenglish.voanews.com/a/a-23-a-2002-05-24-1-1-83111557/120161.html.

Scriven M, Paul R, 2003. Defining critical thinking. http://www.criticalthinking.org/University/univclass/Defining.html.

Swales J, 1990. Genre analysis: English in academic and research settings. Cambridge: Cambridge University Press.

Zwiers J, 2008. Building academic language: Essential practices for content classrooms. San Francisco: Jossey-Bass.

第四章 学术口头报告

蔡 珩 杨 苗

一、对教学主题和教学思路的解读

口头表达能力是个人学术能力的重要组成部分,是学生未来职业发展所需的基本能力。在很多学术活动中,参与者都需要拥有良好的口语表达能力,比如各种研讨会、小组讨论、口头报告、辩论和学位答辩等,尤其是各种国际学术会议中最常见的口头报告(oral presentation)与壁报(poster presentation)。学术口头报告从广义上来讲包括上文提到的小组讨论、大会发言、壁报介绍、学位答辩、会议发言等多种学术口头活动,但最基本的技能都是口头上就某一特定主题分享学术信息,并且往往借助多媒体进行。无论是日常教学还是专业领域内的学术交流,口头报告都是最常见的口语表达形式。本章从教学可操作性出发,仅限于这一基本技能。壁报报告因为涉及学术写作等技巧,在本书中放在综合技能案例部分阐述。

尽管对现在很多学生而言,做口头报告并不陌生,但他们在完成的过程中仍普遍感到焦虑,且完成效果也经常不尽如人意。抛开演讲焦虑和外语焦虑的影响,造成这一现状的原因,一方面是很多学生对口头报告的结构和要求没有明晰的认识,另一方面是缺乏具体的指导和训练。针对这些问题,我们将在这一章中明确学术口头报告的定义、结构和要求,梳理从准备到完成一个成功的学术口头报告的详细步骤,以及每一步所需要注意的细节和可以运用的技巧,给学生们提供一份实用的操作指导。

(一)教学主题

1. 学术口语的特点:在第三章介绍学术语言这一概念时,我们提到了基础人际沟通能力(basic interpersonal communicative skills,BICS)与认知学术语言能力(cognitive academic language proficiency,CALP)的区别(Cummins,1979)。学术口语就处在这两者的交集处,既是学术语言的一种,又属于口语范畴。根据Halliday(1989)的理论,口语有其区别于书面语的专属特征,这些特征包括:① 语速变化(快/慢);② 肢体语言(手势、表情、眼神交流等);③ 语调升降变化;④ 音量变化(大/小);⑤ 重音(重读/弱读);⑥ 韵律;⑦ 停顿;⑧(根据语义群)断句。每一种特征都包含了说话者传递的一部分信息,而当口语被转化为书面语的时候,这些特征也会随之消失。反之亦然,当我们将书面信息转化为口语时,应该充分利用这些特征来辅助传达原来文本的信息,使得口语中的文字性信息能够尽可能简化到让听者一听即懂。这一点对做好学术口头报告至关重要。

同时,为了使大脑可以更快、更易于处理听到的信息,口语的语法在很大程度上被简化了。比如口语中大量使用的各类代词、简单句和并列结构等,都是为了降低词汇密度,提高信息碎片化程度以适应口语的即时性。因此,纵然良好的学术书面语风格使人读来愉悦,却需经过一番基于口语特征的"改头换面"才能最终转化为同样令人愉悦的演讲。

2. 学术口头报告的定义与基本结构:口头报告在大学课堂中应用广泛,是一项能够有效训练学生口语表达能力的活动,同时亦有助于培养学生的学习自主性、信息检索能力和独立思考能力。学术口头报告是一种特定的、结构清晰的方式,意在介绍与讨论学术信息的行为和过程。它是学生融入高校学术环境的重要实践,是学生逐步成长为学术社群中的一员的必备技能。口头报告的本质是个体面向观众的公开演讲。其结构与一般文章类似:开头介绍背景,引入主题;主体部分阐述核心观点,展示相关论据和讨论细节;最后,结尾总结全篇,升华主题。具体到介绍某项具体研究的学术口头报告,其开头部分可以对应研究背景和研究目的,主体部分介绍研究方法和研究结果,结尾处总结研究结论以及结论中所反映出来的对该研究领域的贡献和启示。在报告结束后通常还有观众问答环节。

3. 口头报告的准备要领:口头报告的准备工作分为两部分。首先是内容上的准备,即收集材料,根据报告的主题、目的及目标受众确定演讲内容,然后列提纲,写讲义。很多学生将口头报告等同于演示文稿(如 Power Point,即 PPT 讲义),因此误以为只要写好讲义就已完成任务,结果在做报告的过程中完全依赖 PPT,干巴巴地照念上面的文字,没有加以适当的解释。事实上,口头报告本质是信息的传递,PPT 只是演讲过程中的辅助工具。我们会向学生介绍结合 PPT 进行口头表述的技巧,强调以报告人为主体、以 PPT 为辅的原则。其次,要对报告进行预演。很多研究表明(Carrell 及 Menzel,1994;Child,Kahl 及 Pearson, 2006),针对演讲过程的准备,例如准备演讲稿、制作备忘卡片、预演练习等,均能帮助演讲者在口头报告中有更好的表现。其中,预演对提高临场发挥水平的效果尤其明显(Frymier 及 Smith,2006)。预演时可以有不同的形式,如加入时间限制以增强对时间的把控;对着镜子练习以发现并纠正不自然的肢体语言;在同伴前预演能够模拟临场的紧张感以帮助适应,克服怯场。为兼顾可能出现的情况,也需要和学生讲一下在不使用 PPT 的情况下(比如会场没有多媒体设备)列提纲、准备演讲稿、制作备忘卡的重要性,这时候预演尤为重要。

4. 口头报告的评分标准:本课程所采用的针对口头报告的评分标准共有三大维度,即内容、语言和台上表现。在内容方面包含了四点要求:① 统一性(unity),指是否传递了一个统一完整的核心信息,开头与结论是否能相呼应。在学术口头报告中具体体现为科研信息的完整性,即是否包含研究方法/理论框架、结果/预期结果、结论/意义等关键信息。② 论据充分性(support),不仅指是否有足够的证据支持,更包含了对于论据如何支撑论点的详细解释。比如,在学术口头报告中,演讲者应提供开展此项研究的充分的依据。这包括介绍议题的重要性、目前的研究现状、当前研究存在的问题,以及此研究将如何解决这些问题,以此体现此项研究的必要性或贡献。③ 条理性(coherence),是指结构是否清晰,各部分是否排序合理、衔接自然,便于读者理解演讲内容。在学术报告中具体体现为信息推进的逻辑连贯性。例如,研究问题应从研究背景中提炼,研究方法应针对研究问题而设计,结论应由研究结果推导出来并最终回答研究问题,研究结果和结论应该与研究问题相呼应。④ 观众意识(audience awareness),指演讲内容和所用的语言是否适合目标观众的水平。在学术口头报告中应考虑听众的理解能力,用听众所能理解的方式解释复杂的专业内容,同时适当运用技巧保持观众的兴趣。在语言上,我们要求学生有清晰易懂的发音和相对准确流畅的语言表达。在台上表现上,我们则更多关注演讲过程中的细节,比如是否与观众保持眼神交流,肢体动作是否恰当自然,是否与观众互动良好,是否合理分配时间并在规定时长内完成演讲。如果学生使用了 PPT,其呈现效果也会纳入这部分的评分,要求图文比例恰当,内容简明易懂,设计风格统一,简洁美观。

(二) 教学思路

1. 以 Halliday(1989)对口语特点的总结和例子来介绍口语与书面语的差异,并设计相关练习。

2. 从具体学术场景中明确口头报告的定义和特点。按照时间顺序,从演讲前的准备到演讲过程中的技巧,再到演讲结束后如何与观众互动,帮助学生梳理一遍做好学术口语报告应该注意的每一个细节。

二、教学案例设计

(一) 教学目标

1. 学生能够描述学术口头报告的定义和基本结构。
2. 学生能够分辨学术口语的语言特点,并熟练掌握学术书面语与学术口语的相互转换。
3. 学生能够了解学术口头报告的准备流程及演讲过程中的各种技巧,并运用到实际任务中。

(二) 教学内容

1. 学术口语的特点

教学内容	注解
❖ **Spoken language has the following characteristics**(Halliday, 1989, p. 31) ✓ Variation in speed—but it is generally faster than writing ✓ Loudness or quietness ✓ Gestures—body language ✓ Intonation ✓ Stress ✓ Rhythm ✓ Pitch range ✓ Pausing and phrasing	先让学生完成任务一,讨论之后介绍 Michael Halliday 提出的口语特征,引导学生思考口语与书面语的差异,以及形成这些差异的原因。之后让学生完成任务二

2. 口头报告的基本结构及准备过程,以及演讲过程的具体建议

教学内容	注解

❖ **The structure**
✓ Presentation
  • Introduction
    — What do you intend to do?
    — How do you intend to do it?
  • Main Body
    — State your points
    — Provide information and argument
  • Conclusion
    — Restate the main points
    — Invite question
✓ Discussion/Questions
	这部分主要介绍口头报告的基本结构,以及每一部分的主要内容

(续表)

教学内容	注解
❖ **Preparing for a presentation** ✓ Knowing about your topic, purposes and audience. ✓ Preparing your PPT (font sizes, colours, visual tools etc.) ✓ Preparing your scripts and notes ✓ Practicing your presentation	这部分需提醒学生不要忽略对演讲过程的准备，重点介绍如何通过使用演讲稿和练习预演来克服怯场心理和提高临场发挥水平

❖ **Tips on how to give an academic presentation**
✓ How to begin
✓ How to engage the audience and create interest
✓ How to use visuals (key words, pictures, graphs & videos, etc.)
✓ How to explain graphs
  • Describe graphs
  • Describe data
  • Interpret data
✓ How to signpost
✓ How to end
	我们备课时精选了许多 TED 演讲片段，用于展示相应的技巧。每讲完一个要点，播放相应的 TED 演讲片段，让学生在真实例子中直观体会每一个建议的实际运用（任务三）。在这里要特别强调如何结合 PPT 进行有效讲解，因为背稿或照读 PPT 是许多学生的通病

3. 口头报告的评分标准

教学内容	注解

❖ **Criteria for oral presentation**
✓ Content
  • Unity
  • Support
  • Coherence
  • Audience awareness
✓ Language
  • Pronunciation
  • Accuracy
  • Fluency
✓ Delivery
  • Eye-contact
  • Body language
  • Interaction
  • Time-management
  • PPT design
	展示本课程所采用的口头报告评分标准，确保学生准确理解每一条规则的含义。内容（content）相关的四条标准相对抽象，需要更多解释，必要时加入示例说明

(三) 学习任务

任务一 对比口语与书面语的语法特征

任务内容 学生阅读三段分别在不同语境下（书面/口语）对同一场景的文字描述，对比三段文字的语言特征，进而总结出口语和书面语在语法上的差异。

任务完成形式/师生互动形式 学生独立完成任务，之后老师以提问的形式引导学生总结书面语与口语在语法上的区别。

任务二 学术论文书面语转换成学术口语

任务内容 学生阅读两段从正式发布的学术论文中摘录的文本，将其转述成自然的口语表达。

任务要点 学生依据口语的语法特征，将句法复杂、信息密度大的学术书面语转化为符合口语表达习惯的简单易懂的口头语。

任务完成形式/师生互动形式 学生独立完成任务，之后老师以提问的形式检查任务完成情况。

任务三 分析口头报告的视频实例

任务内容 学生观看真实的学术口头报告的视频片段（教师可根据学生的专业在 www.ted.com 选用合适的视频），观察并分析演讲者的表现。

任务要点 学生依据之前课上介绍演讲过程中的不同技巧去分析演讲者是如何开场、结尾，如何运用肢体语言，如何与观众互动等等。

任务完成形式/师生互动形式 此任务应与介绍演讲过程中的具体建议的部分相结合。可以每讲完一个方面，随即播放相应的视频片段加深认识；也可以在所有的建议讲完后，播放一个完整演讲视频，让学生根据所学内容点评分析。学生先就此进行小组讨论，然后请代表展示，老师点评。

(四) 课后作业

根据一篇他人正式发表的研究类学术论文做一个小组学术口头报告（Find a published research article and give a presentation [15min+5min Q&A] to introduce the research）。

作业要求和说明：这个作业是学生完成初级阶段课程后的主要考核项目。学生的最终表现不仅取决于个人做口头报告的能力，更需要完整、准确地理解该学术论文并进行有效概括。因难度较大，为给学生充分的准备时间，此作业在第一周介绍课程时就已布置，学生在最后一周以小组为单位做报告。在学术论文的选择上，我们要求学生选择结构最经典的研究型论文（即包括 introduction, methods, results 和 discussion/conclusion）。为避免有的学生选择了错误类型或者内容过于专业的文献，我们团队在医学人文的框架下确定了六大主题，每个主题由老师们筛选出难度适中的 10 篇文献（即第二章所介绍的课程团队自建的文献库），以此为范围让各组学生从中选择他们感兴趣的论文来准备口头报告。同时，为了帮助学生更好地理解所选文献的内容，在课程的模块设置上，我们将学术阅读的相关内容放在课程的前半段，让学生们学会通过语步分析（move analysis）梳理出文献的逻辑架构，进而准确概括论文中的核心信息。有了这个坚实的基础，学生在本章中学习学术书面语与口语的转化，以及关于如何准备口头报告的具体步骤和技巧时，才有更明确的目标和动力。同时，在学生们做学术口头报告的前一周，我们会轮流与每个小组见面（teacher-student conference），帮助他们解决在准备过程中遇到的问题。在此过程中，老师能够提出更有针对性的个性化的建议。因为做学术口头报告是一个较为正式的场景,为了加强仪式感和真实感,我们要求学生衣着正式、得体,不一定需要全套西装,但也不能过于随意,这也体现了对观众的尊重。

三、案例使用反馈

(一) 学生反馈意见

在课程开始之初,当学生们得知本阶段的考核任务为做一次学术口头报告时,很多人表现出焦虑或信心不足。而调查问卷显示,在完成课程以后,学生们的态度和自信程度均有明显的积极的转变。绝大多数学生(该次共有 302 位学生参与问卷调查)认为自己的学术口头报告技巧与能力得到了提高(73%),能够更好地区分学术书面语与学术口语的差异(80%),能够完成两者之间的转换(72%)。接近七成学生认同所学内容对其未来专业的学习与发展很有帮助。不少学生表示,在医学专业中,他们经常遇到将专业知识灵活转化为通俗易懂的科普性语言的情况,通过这节课,他们加强了"听众意识",也学到了增强演讲趣味性的技巧。在课程内容的设置和选材上,学生们反映难度适中,实用性强。尤其示例的演讲视频很有代表性。上课中学到的不同演讲技巧(如开场和结尾、图表运用、肢体语言等),学生们都能从各个视频中得到很好的示范。

(二) 教师反馈意见

授课老师的反馈意见集中在学术口语和学术口头报告两个主题,针对每个主题都提出教学重点、难点和可供改善教学的建议。

1. 学术口语

1) 重点:让学生掌握学术英语口语的特点,以及学术报告的基本框架。其中包括要使用规范恰当的学术语言和得体的肢体语言,在规定的时间内,向目标群体完成学术报告。

2) 难点:① 让学生区分学术英语口语和日常口语,以及书面语的不同。因为学生容易进入两个误区,一是认为学术英语口语与日常口语表达没区别,所以在做报告时表达过于随意和松散,使用很多不恰当的表达;二是过度正式,以为把论文里面的表达摘出来照读照背就可以,表达极其僵硬冗长。② 既要让学生掌握规范的学术表达,也要做到生动有趣,让目标群体对自己的演讲产生兴趣和共鸣。

3) 建议:① 示例,可以让学生观摩成功的学术演讲,教师最好提供专家学者的例子,以及优秀和失败的学生学术演讲范例,让学生在讨论中归纳成功与失败的学术演讲规律。② 实操,可以在课堂上给学生一些比较简短的任务,比如一个学术报告的开头,如何引入;或者学术报告的结尾,如何总结;或者是如何在最后问答环节答疑;还有如何举例、解释,等等。让学生在课堂上有更多机会展示自己的处理,再邀请学生点评,这样会比单纯的理论更让学生有所领悟。③ 教师点评和示范,教师的及时反馈以及自身的课堂示范非常重要。学生需要老师的及时反馈、点评。教师的课堂就是一次重要的示范。

2. 学术口头报告

1) 重点:① 规范考核标准。把对学生的要求,例如正确地使用学术语言和肢体语言,正式着装,在规定时间内完成报告,实现生动与趣味性、互动性等先放到要求里,让学生在准备时有明确目标。② 教师点评。教师点评既是重点,也是难点,因为既要及时反馈,又要击中要害,让学生有收获,所以可以参照考核标准,再次提醒学生。

2）难点：在口头报告的问答环节让学生针对同伴的学术报告提问，有时会出现问题不恰当，或者冷场的情况。

3）建议：让学生平时在课堂上多实践，教师也可示范，并且可以对优质的提问和点评进行鼓励，接触多了，学生就能够有锐眼发现问题，提出好问题。

附录 4.1 学习任务

（一）学习任务一

Compare the grammatical features of the following sentences.

1. A sentence from a written text The use of this method of control unquestionably leads to safer and faster train running in the most adverse weather conditions	Spoken language has： • more verb-based phrases • more predicative（表语）adjectives • more pronouns（*it*,*they*,*you*,*we*） • more first-person reference（*I*） • more active verbs than written language • fewer complex words and phrases • more lexical repetition Spoken texts are： • more fragmented ——more simple sentences and more use of coordination *and*,*but*,*so*,*because* rather than subordination（embedding） • lexically less dense • longer
2. A typical spoken variant If this method of control is used, trains will unquestionably（be able to）run more safely and faster（even）when the weather conditions are most adverse	
3. A more natural spoken version You can control the trains this way and if you do that you can be quite sure that they'll be able to run more safely and more quickly than they would otherwise, no matter how bad the weather gets	

（二）学习任务二

Change the texts into more natural spoken English.

1. Text appear in a published article

A. The role of trace elements in the development of tooth decay has been an area of study since the identification of fluoride's protective effects. Lead, which accumulates in bones and teeth, is of particular interest because of its wide distribution in the environment (Moss, et al., 1999).

B. Our study also highlights the potential for preventing heart failure through interventions that decrease the prevalence of obesity and high blood pressure (Bibbins-Domingo,et al. ,2009).

2. Text in an oral presentation on the same topic

A. After the protective effects of fluoride were identified, researchers began to study the influence of trace elements in tooth decay. Lead accumulates in bones and teeth. We are particularly interested in lead because it widely distributes in the environment.

B. From the study, we can see that if we do something to prevent obesity and high blood pressure, it is very possible that there will be much less heart failure.

附录 4.2　学术口头报告评分标准

Criteria for Oral Presentation

Presenter _____

Poster Title _____

Rater _____

Note: Please select a proper number to evaluate the oral presentation; the bigger the number, the higher your evaluation. Please circle first and then add up the total.		
Content　40%		
1. **Unity**: Unified with a central message	1 2 3 4 5 6 7 8 9 10	
2. **Support**: Point of view supported by sufficient evidences	1 2 3 4 5 6 7 8 9 10	
3. **Coherence**: Clearly structured and logically progressed	1 2 3 4 5 6 7 8 9 10	
4. **Audience awareness**: Content and language at appropriate level for intended audience	1 2 3 4 5 6 7 8 9 10	
Language　30%		
5. **Pronunciation**: Correct and easy to understand	1 2 3 4 5 6 7 8 9 10	
6. **Accuracy**: Grammatically accurate	1 2 3 4 5 6 7 8 9 10	
7. **Fluency**: Speaking fluently with little repetition and hesitation	1 2 3 4 5 6 7 8 9 10	
Delivery　30%		
8. **Eye-contact**: Maintaining eye-contact with audience	1　2　3　4　5	
9. **Body language**: Natural and relaxed with proper posture and gesture	1　2　3　4　5	
10. **Interaction**: Creating interest and involving audience	1　2　3　4　5	
11. **Enthusiasm**: Speaking with strong interest and feelings	1　2　3　4　5	
12. **Time-management**: Observing time limit and using time wisely	1　2　3　4　5	
13. **PPT design**: Clear, pleasant & easy to read and understand	1　2　3　4　5	
Total score		

参考文献

Bibbins-Domingo K, Pletcher MJ, Lin F, 2009. Racial differences in incident heart failure among young adults. The New England Journal of Medicine, 360: 1179-1190.

Carrell LJ, Menzel KE, 1994. The relationship between preparation and performance in public speaking. Communication Education, 43(1): 17-23.

Child TJ, Kahl Jr DH, Pearson JC, 2006. Preparation meeting opportunity: How do college students prepare for public speeches? Communication Quarterly, 54(3): 351-366.

Cummins J, 1979. Cognitive academic language proficiency, linguistic interdependence, the optimum age question and some other matters. Working Papers on Bilingualism, 19: 121-129.

Frymier AB, Smith TE, 2006. Get 'real': Does practicing speeches before an audience improve performance? Communication Quarterly, 54(1): 111-125.

Halliday MAK, 1989. Spoken and written language. 2nd edition. Oxford: Oxford University Press.

Moss ME, Lanphear BP, Auinger P, 1999. Association of dental caries and blood lead levels. JAMA, 281(24): 2294-2298.

第五章　学术听力基本技巧

余　凡　谢黎嘉

一、对教学主题和教学思路的解读

英语听力向来是学生语言学习的薄弱环节。学术英语听力不但具备了学术语言自身的特点,结构上要比普通英语更为复杂,词汇难度更大,在内容上也对专业知识素养有着较高的要求。本章向学生介绍了学术听力的基本技巧,重点强调略听和寻听(skimming and scanning),自下而上、自上而下和交互式三种听力模式(bottom-up, top-down, and interactive listening strategies),以及如何做笔记(有效地记录要点和重要信息)。最后通过课堂听力练习,结合课后作业,帮助学生练习如何运用听力的基本技巧。

(一) 教学主题——学术听力基本技巧

Lynch(2011)认为,学术英语听力的概念有狭义与广义之分。狭义的学术英语听力指的是听学术讲座以及做笔记。后者包括了各种需要运用听力的学术活动,有单向的听力活动,如授课、实验课、会议报告等;有双向的学术交流,如讲座或报告之后的答疑、小组讨论(panel discussion)、教师辅导和团队活动等各种需要用到听力的互动场景。

无论是广义或狭义,单向或双向,学术听力与普通听力相比,两者既有共性,也有区别。共同点在于,在听的过程中,听者并非被动地接受信息,而是积极主动地运用各种类型的知识来理解说话者表达的真实意图(Anderson 及 Lynch, 1988)。两者的区别在于,学术听力作为听力理解中的更高层次,对听者提出了较高的要求。听者不仅要理解长篇讲座的内容与结构,还要学会根据不同的听力目的选择不同的听力技巧,如略听和寻听,以便获取所需的专业信息。略听与寻听原本是阅读理解的概念:略读与寻读。有研究者认为,略读(skimming)与寻读(scanning)同样适用于学术听力(Glisan, 1988),可将相应技巧转化为略听与寻听。当听者需要了解听力内容的大意,应该选择略听;当听者需要获取特定信息,应该使用寻听。

要达到最佳听力效果,有必要帮助学生了解三种基本听力模式,然后结合不同的听力目的和情景,有意识地调整自己的听力模式。三种基本听力模式是:自下而上模式(bottom-up)、自上而下模式(top-down)和交互模式(interactive)。自下而上模式把听力理解过程视为从音节、单词开始直至完整文本的线性的信息解码过程(Nunan, 1998)。该模式强调的是语言本身的元素。自上而下模式的理论依据是图式理论,由英国心理学家 Bartlett(1932)首度使用,指的是人脑对于过去的反应或者经验产生的一种积极的构建。自上而下模式就是运用图式(背景知识与宏观理解)来解读信息(Duzer, 1997)。交互模式则认为自下而上与自上而下两种模式是不可分割的,成功的听力理解来自语言信息、情景线索以及知识经验储备的相互作用(Hedge, 2002)。虽然三种听力模式不可分割,但根据不同的听力目的与场合,对听力模式的选择和运用会有所侧重。

懂得如何做笔记也是学术听力的一个基本技巧。做笔记包括了解学术讲座使用的特定语言和基本结构;对相关学科的知识要有一定的储备,掌握相关的学科词汇;具备敏锐的思辨能力,准确推断暗含的信息与讲者的态度,评估信息的重要性,最终提取有效信息(Gillett,2019)。这里面既需要理解,也需要批判性思维,才能有所取舍。

以上就是本章的主要内容。这些基本听力技巧能帮助学生从学术听力环境中获取最需要、最有效的信息,为接下来学习批判性听力打好基础。

(二) 教学思路

本节课按照引入概念、技巧概览、练习巩固这一顺序来设计教学。首先,上课以提问开始,让学生讨论什么是学术听力,以及学术听力所包括的情景。接着请学生回顾听力理解中碰到的困难和阻碍,让学生明白听力理解并非仅仅关注语言本身,还需要背景知识以及思维能力,激发他们想提高学术听力的动机。之后引入正题:学术听力的基本技巧。在介绍每一种学术听力技巧的同时,提供相应的听力范例,有 TED 演讲、考试听力和讲座片段。所有这些范例均为学术听力的场景,目的在于让学生理解如何在不同的学术情境中运用各种听力技巧。

二、教学案例设计

(一) 教学目标

1. 学生能够了解学术听力的定义和使用场景,能够识别不同的学术听力技巧。

2. 学生能够结合不同的听力场景,运用不同的听力技巧(略听和寻听)和理解模式(自下而上、自上而下、交互式三种听力模式)。

3. 学生能够在学术听力场景中运用做笔记的技巧。

(二) 教学内容

1. Academic listening skills—overview

教学内容	注解
❖ **Discussion:What is academic listening?** ✓ Narrow interpretation 　• Listening to lectures and taking notes ✓ Broad interpretation 　• Participating in a variety of academic communicative events requiring the effective use of reciprocal listening skills ✓ One-way listening: 　• Lectures in university courses 　• Conference presentations ✓ Two-way listening(communicative events) 　• Small-group/panel discussion, tutorials, seminars, meetings with supervisor/advisor, etc.	首先给出 Lynch(2011)对学术听力的广义和狭义的阐释,让学生对学术听力有一个全面的了解

(续表)

教学内容	注解
❖ **Common problems in listening** √ New vocabulary √ Fast Speech √ Unfamiliar accents √ Uninteresting content √ Difficult material √ Listening for details, not central ideas √ Decoding words (such as word-by-word translation)	通过讨论听力中常见的障碍,让学生思考如何克服这些困难
❖ **How can we overcome these problems?** √ Tip 1: Practice makes perfect √ Tip 2: Before you start listening, do some preparation √ Tip 3: Listen with a purpose	介绍提高听力常见的技巧
❖ **More skills...** √ Recognizing lecture structure (main points and subsidiary points) √ Utilizing various ways of making sense of the words you hear √ Deducing the meaning of words √ Recognizing implications √ Identifying the speaker's attitude √ Evaluating the importance of information √ Understanding intonation	概览在学术听力阶段,学生还需要掌握哪些技巧
❖ **Skills for successful academic listening** √ Skimming (listening to obtain gist) and scanning (listening to obtain specific information) √ Listening modes: top-down, bottom-up, and interactive mode of listening √ Practicing your note-taking skills	指出本单元的学习重点:学术听力的基本技巧

2. Skimming and Scanning

教学内容	注解
❖ **Skimming in academic listening** √ Listening to obtain gist ❖ **Scanning in academic listening** √ Listening to obtain specific information ❖ **In a test-taking task** √ Step 1. Skimming: read fast through the choices before listening to get the main idea	从阅读的略读和寻读的概念引入学术听力中的略听和寻听,并解释二者的区别

(续表)

教学内容	注解
✓ Step 2. Predicting: with the general idea, you can predict what questions might be asked about your listening task ✓ Step 3. Listening: listen with your predicted questions in mind ❖ **In your autonomous study** ✓ The 1st time: listening for gist (skimming) ✓ The 2nd time: listening for details (scanning)	提醒学生要学会根据不同的听力目的和场景采用不同的听力技巧

3. Three Listening Modes

教学内容	注解
❖ **The process of listening** ✓ Bottom-up listening: making as much use as you can of the low-level clues ✓ Top-down listening: making as much use as you can of your knowledge and the situation ✓ Interactive listening: Making use of the interaction between both types of listening; listening in both directions	区分自下而上、自上而下、交互式三种听力模式,然后完成学习任务一

4. Note-taking Skills

教学内容	注解
❖ **Why do we take notes?** ❖ **What is note taking?** It is the action of writing down the main ideas, important points, outline, or summary of information presented in speaking or writing	介绍做笔记的重要性以及定义
❖ **How can we take effective notes?** 1. Listen carefully for main ideas and jot them down 2. If possible, listen again for subsidiary points and necessary details 3. Third, make your notes as concise as possible during listening 4. Organize your notes when you finish listening	讲述学术听力中做笔记的技巧,同时简单介绍如何使用一些常见的符号做速记,如何系统地、有层次地记录听到的内容,其中包括著名的康奈尔笔记法,即由康奈尔大学首创的笔记法,将记笔记的空间划分为"主题""细节"和"总结"三大部分
❖ **Note-taking can be used in various academic listening settings** • Self-study • Test-taking listening • Listening to talks, lectures or seminars	介绍如何在不同的学术听力场景中做笔记,记录听力要点,然后完成学习任务二

(三) 课堂学习任务

任务一

任务内容　学生听一个关于肺结核的讲座片段(郝长江 等,2008),然后简述听力内容。

任务要点　学生使用三种听力模式,首先运用常识和相关的知识背景对将要听到的内容进行预测,并收集与肺结核相关的专业词汇。

任务完成形式/师生互动形式　学生听讲座之前口头交流与肺结核相关的背景知识和专业词汇,互相补充信息。听后先让学生与同伴简述所获取的信息,然后教师邀请个别学生在课堂上简述,给予反馈。

任务二

任务内容　听一个 Ted 演讲"Programming Bacteria to Detect Cancer"(Danino,2015)

任务要点　学生听前先了解相关背景知识和词汇,预测听力内容与结构,然后补充完成思维导图。让学生在练习中体验如何综合运用略听、寻听和交互模式。

具体步骤

步骤一:教师告诉学生演讲的标题(Programming Bacteria to Detect Cancer),让学生在 10 分钟内在互联网检索英文背景信息,并在课堂口头汇报。教师可以示范如何查找与演讲题目和演讲人相关信息。例如,在发布演讲的官网上查找关于演讲人和题目的介绍,或根据官网上的关键词 synthetic biologist,quorum sensing 等进一步检索信息。

步骤二:教师通过一个词汇匹配练习(图 5.1),让学生掌握相关生词。这里可以跟学生强调,在真实场景中,我们无法预测所有出现的生词,所以平时应该通过专业学习和文献阅读等方式积累词汇。

1.	urine	A. exploding star
2.	generate	B. helping to treat
3.	molecule	C. to shine with soft light
4.	synchronize	D. infectious, lethal
5.	trigger	E. produce
6.	coordinated	F. liquid waste from a person's or animal's body
7.	virulent	G. the smallest unit
8.	glow	H. to set something off
9.	supernova	I. to work together
10.	therapeutic	J. united

图 5.1　本学习任务相关词汇匹配练习

步骤三:让学生根据背景知识和词汇预测听力内容。

步骤四:略听,先让学生听第一遍,掌握内容大意。

步骤五:寻听,教师给学生一个思维导图(图 5.2),其中关键内容空缺,让学生听第二遍的时候填入。如果需要且时间允许,学生可以多听几遍。

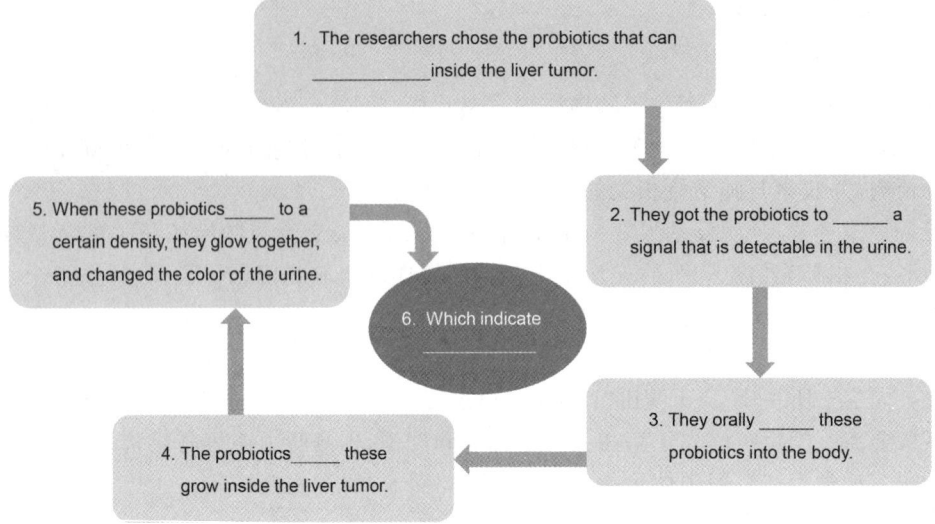

图 5.2 本学习任务思维导图

(四) 课后作业

Watch a TED talk *Programming Bacteria to Detect Cancer*（Danino，2015），take notes and finish two tasks：

1. draw a thinking map to display the main ideas in the talk.

2. write a summary (100-150 words) for the talk.

(五) 学生作业点评

作业范例与点评 1

A mind map to indicate the content of the talk：

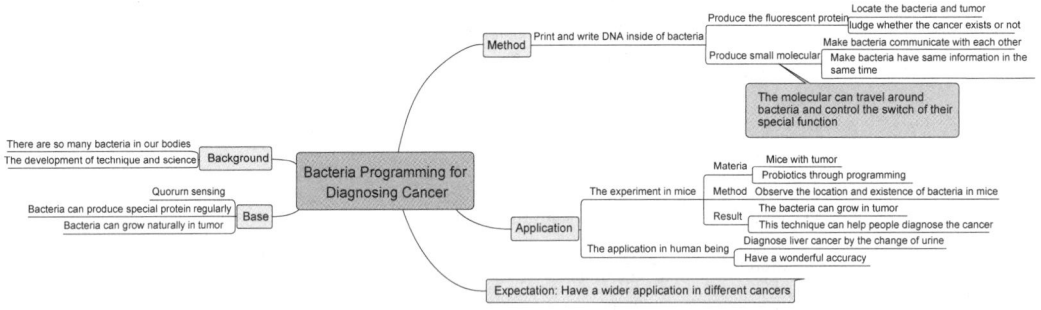

点评：该思维导图基本上把"bacteria programming"实施的前提条件、方法、应用梳理出来。美中不足之处在于没有具体呈现"how the programmed bacteria were used for cancer diagnosis"。

作业范例与点评 2

A summary of the talk：

Sample 1：The speaker aims to illustrate the quorum sensing of bacteria and show the possibility to apply this peculiarity to liver cancer treating. Quorum sensing is a situation that a group of bacteria can act as a whole when its density grows up to a critical density. And one of another characteristics of bacteria is that they can grow naturally in tumor.

With advanced technology, scientists can rewrite the DNA of some eatable and harmless bacteria, which can release some indicators to change the color of urine when it reaches to certain density. In that case, liver cancer, which was hard to be detected, can be found timely and precisely. Moreover, this technique can not only be used in cancer detecting but also in cancer treating by releasing some molecules to shrink the tumor. There are bright prospects lying ahead.

点评：该学生能利用本次课程中所教的 skimming 和 scanning 的技巧，既抓住了大意，又把握住了重要信息。

Sample 2：With technology involving today, people are able to program bacteria by writing DNA into bacteria. Programmed bacteria may be able to help detect and treat diseases like cancer. *We can make it happen because our immune system has no access to the tumors which makes it possible for bacteria to grow and thrive in the tumors.* These bacteria are programmed to produce signals to show if there is tumor in the body. And also, programmed therapeutic bacteria can be used to treat diseases like cancer.

点评：这份作业中对于讲座的大意基本概括正确，但是在具体细节的理解上出现偏差，如斜黑体部分属于强行建立因果关系。

A summary provided by the teacher:

Liver tumor is one of the hardest tumors to detect. When the immune system within tumors has been greatly diminished, bacteria can find tumors and use them as a natural habitat. When bacteria reach a critical density, quorum sensing or the behavior of functioning together will occur. Synthetic biologist Tal Danino exploited these characteristics to detect even treat liver cancer by genetically instructing probiotic, edible bacteria to glow together when they find and accumulate to a certain density within tumors, which can be revealed in the urine. Likewise, the researchers have been working to program bacteria to generate therapeutic molecules as well.

三、案例使用反馈

（一）学生反馈意见

在课程反馈问卷中（有效人数为 277 人），67.87％ 的学生表示学习学术听力技巧对于今后的学习很有帮助；超过一半以上的学生表示，通过本单元的学习，"（能够）通过查资料和了解背景知识提出问题，根据问题有目的地听讲""学会速记技巧及判断记录的重点信息""学会了运用关键词进行学术听力：先提取听力里面的关键词并记录，然后形成逻辑顺序"。

对教学内容的难度调查发现，78.1％ 的学生认为任务一的难度适中，54.5％ 的学生认为任务二难度大，原因包括专业词汇多、演讲节奏跟不上、学术听力模式不熟练等。这些阻碍因素也让他们进一步意识到学生听力的难度和听前预备工作的重要性。

（二）教师反馈意见

本章对听力基本技巧的讲解可以非常简略，重点应该放在对这些技巧的综合运用上，尤其是通过学习任务营造一个接近现实学术听力活动的氛围，引导学生一步步完成听前准备、边听边写和听后总结。学习任务一难度较低，二年级的医学生已经具备肺结核的专业背景知识，所以听前活动主要是进行信息交流，这样做可以帮助学生熟悉相关信息，尤其是专业英语词汇。学习任务二是更接近真实场景的学术讲座，虽然没有涉及特别艰深难懂的专业术语和内容，但对学生和教师来说"quorum sensing of bacteria"是全新的概念。教师需要在备课的时候先"补课",了解与此相关的背景知识,并找到可向学生推荐的可靠的文献来源。这样学生在进行信息检索时可以得到有价值的建议。播放视频时,可以根据学生的听力程度,选择是否播两遍,是否播放带英文字幕的视频。

参考文献

Anderson A,Lynch T,1988. Listening. Oxford:Oxford University.

Bartlett FC,1932. Remembering:A study in experimental and social psychology. Cambridge:Cambridge University Press.

Duzer CV,1997. Improving ESL learners' listening skills:At the workplace and beyond [2018-11-10]. http://www.cal.org/caela/esl_resources/digests/LISTENQA.html.

Gillett A,Listening comprehension & note-taking [2019-11-29]. http://www.uefap.com/index.htm

Glisan E,1988. A plan for teaching listening comprehension:Adaptation of an instructional reading model. Foreign Language Annals,21(1):9-16.

Lynch T,2011. Academic listening in the 21st century:reviewing a decade of research. Journal of Academic English for Academic Purposes,10(2):79-88.

Nunan D,1998. Approaches to teaching listening in the language classroom. In Proceedings of the 1997 Korea TESOL Conference.

Hedge T,2002. Teaching and learning in the language classrooms. 上海:上海外语教育出版社.

Tal D,2015. Programming bacteria to detect cancer and maybe treat it [2019-11-29]. https://www.ted.com/talks/tal_danino_programming_bacteria_to_detect_cancer_and_maybe_treat_it.

郝长江,国林详,2008. 医学英语视听说. 青岛:中国海洋大学出版社.

第六章 批判性学术听力

谢黎嘉 蔡 珩

一、对教学主题和教学思路的解读

本章是第五章"学术听力基本技巧"的提高篇。进行学术听力活动的首要目的是听懂对方所讲的专业内容,但更为重要的是批判性地听取他人的学术观点,并做出自己的思考和判断。

(一)教学主题——批判性学术听力

批判性学术听力与批判性思维密不可分,涉及对所得信息进行评估和判断(Fisher及Scriven,1997)。在学术听力中,学生首先需要理解接收到的学术观点,分析其依据的可靠性,综合其他信息(比如演讲者的身份和其他研究者的发现)进行评估判断,并给出反馈。在这一过程中,批判性思维与学术听力交织在一起,互相影响:批判性思维的发展影响着批判性学术听力能力,而批判性学术听力的训练有助于提升批判性思维能力。

SIER(Steil, Watson及Barker, 1983)是常用的批判性学术听力模型,通过"理解(sensing)—解读(interpreting)—评估(evaluating)—回应(responding)"这四个由下而上的环节,培养听者全面运用语言与非语言因素解构信息、重构意义,并给予讲者回应。"理解"指的是利用所有感官去接收、理解言语的和非言语的信息,抓住大意和主要细节;在学术听力中则是了解主要学术观点和学术理据,这是批判性学术听力的基础。"解读"指的是对信息进行解码、重构、编码,并以此做推理、下结论、做预测。"理解"和"解读"这两个环节通常是听力考试考查的重点。"评估"是基于对信息的准确理解,听者能够区分观点和事实,进而评估信息的准确性、可靠性和权威性。"回应"则是在评估的基础上提出自己的看法和反馈意见。

在"解读"和"评估"过程中,听者需要把讲者的经历、知识、态度等因素考虑进去,需要辨别讲者所采用的理据的有效性、逻辑性和合理性,也即亚里士多德在《修辞学》(Aristotle,1989)中提到的"劝说三式":Ethos、Pathos和Logos。"Ethos"指的是通过讲者的权威性和可信性来说服听者。也就是说,讲者利用自己的身份(如专家、名人)向听者显示他所说的内容是可信的。作为一名听者,我们应该了解讲者的身份、学识和专业领域等背景信息,从而评估他所讲内容与其专业资历是否一致。"Pathos"指的是讲者通过情感来感染听者,引起共鸣,产生行动共识。在听的过程中,一定要谨慎对待讲者所用的语言、语气和例子,不要被其情绪带动。"Logos"是指讲者摆事实、举例子、列数据、引经据典,并通过类比、因果分析等方式引导听者顺着讲者的思路进行思考,从而达到说服的目的。

综上所述,作为听者,一定要在听的过程中运用批判性思维,检验、评估讲者的学术身份、学术观点和所用理据的有效性及可信度,进而表达自己的学术看法。在这一过程中,批判性思维和批判性学术听力是相互促进、共同发展的。本章节的教学活动也是围绕着这两者进行设计,旨在训练学生的批判性学术听力技巧、提高批判性思维能力。

（二）教学思路

我们结合SIER模型以及亚里士多德的劝说三式，采用理论与实操相结合的方式，步步递进，层层提高，训练学生的批判性学术听力，强化他们的批判性思维意识。本节课大致可以分为两部分。第一部分，由介绍批判性听力的概念入手，进而引导学生思考怎么样才能做到批判性地听。接着，引入SIER模型。在介绍SIER模型每个环节时，先理论后实践，让学生在了解每个环节的重点之后，进行训练。第二部分主要介绍亚里士多德的劝说三式以及其他具体的批判性听力技巧。这一部分建构在SIER中interpreting和evaluating环节的基础上，通过学习活动让学生分析听到的内容，辨别讲者采用的"劝说"策略。本节课的最后一个学习活动为综合应用，由于涉及学生学术观点的表达，这一部分作为课后作业。

二、教学案例设计

（一）教学目标

1. 学生能够理解何谓批判性听力，并了解其在学术活动中的重要性。
2. 学生能够解释SIER模型及其各环节的重点，并在学术听力场景中有意识地应用。
3. 学生能够列举各种批判性听力的技巧，并在学术听力场景中有意识地应用。
4. 学生能够判断、辨别演讲者采用的技巧（Pathos, Logos, Ethos），并对所讲内容做出相应的判断。

（二）教学内容

1. Critical listening

教学内容	注解
❖ **What is critical listening?** √ A rational process of evaluating arguments put forward by others' speaking ❖ **What would happen if you are not listening critically?** ❖ **Basics of critical listening** √ Listening critically ≠ Claiming that the information you are listening to is somehow faulty or flawed	这部分解释批判性听力的内涵，澄清学生的误解，旨在加深学生对批判性听力的认识

2. SIER

教学内容	注解
❖ **What is SIER?** √ Sensing √ Interpreting √ Evaluating √ Responding	
❖ **What is SIER?** ❖ **Sensing & interpreting** √ Required in most cases of listening comprehension, e.g. in exams	整体介绍SIER的构成，以自下而上的形式展现每个环节及其重点 通过学习任务一加深学生对sensing和interpreting的认知。听力活动分为两个步骤。步骤

(续表)

教学内容	注解
	一,听录音、记笔记。步骤二,利用笔记内容完成相应的听力理解练习,并引导学生对所进行的听力活动类型进行反思

3. **Critical listening techniques**

教学内容	注解
❖ Focus of criticism ✓ Ethos 　• Understanding the speaker and the context ✓ Logos 　• Evaluating the strength of the speaker's main ideas and the quality of supporting evidences ✓ Pathos 　• Recognizing the use of loaded language, stereotypes, and/or emotional appeals ❖ Other techniques ✓ Recognizing the difference between fact and opinion ✓ Distinguishing between referencing and giving personal opinions ✓ Recognizing the general tone, the speaker's degree of certainty	此部分重点介绍亚里士多德的劝说三式,让学生先从讲者的角度出发,思考演讲策略;强调应该从听者的角度来分辨这些策略,并运用其他批判性听力技巧对听到的内容进行评判。 　　学习任务二训练学生对"Logos"策略的分析;学习任务三训练学生对"Pathos"策略的分析;学习任务四训练学生对其他批判性听力技巧的运用,如判断观点和事实、辨别不同的立场与看法

(三) 学习任务

任务一

任务内容　学生听两个听力片段,一则为讲座,另一则为学生间关于某学科的对话,边听边记笔记。听力片段播放完毕之后,让学生根据笔记完成相应的听力理解练习,并反思两则听力的类型。此处的听力材料可以选取大学英语四六级考试听力材料或雅思、托福的听力材料,因可供选择的素材很多,本章不提供此任务讲义。

任务要点　加深学生对 SIER 模型中 sensing 和 interpreting 的认知。

任务完成形式/师生互动形式　学生独立完成任务,之后老师以提问的形式检查任务完成情况。

任务二

任务内容　学生观看视频片段"Steve Jobs liver transplantation"(方卫 等,2013)并回答问题。

任务要点　训练学生在听力过程中找出不同讲者的观点及其依据。

任务完成形式/师生互动形式　学生独立完成任务,之后老师以提问的形式检查任务完成情况。

任务三

任务内容　学生观看视频片段"The best gift I've ever survived"(Kramar,2010),分析

讲者采用的策略。

　　任务要点　训练学生在听力过程中，找出讲者的观点及其依据，辨别讲者采用的情感策略。

　　任务完成形式/师生互动形式　学生独立完成任务，之后老师提问、点评。

任务四

　　任务内容　学生观看视频片段"Assisted death or murder"（方卫 等，2013），回答问题。

　　任务要点　训练学生在听力过程中判断观点和事实、辨别不同人的立场与看法。

　　任务完成形式/师生互动形式　学生独立完成任务，之后老师提问、点评。

　　任务拓展　老师邀请学生就自己关于视频片段涉及的事件发表看法。

（四）课后作业

Directions：Watch the talk "Don't suffer from your depression in silence"（Allen，2017），using the critical listening skills（SIER）that you have learnt，then

　　（1）Draw a mind map to show the speaker's argument(s) as well as the evidences she used.

　　（2）Analyze the strength of her argument(s) by examining how she developed her idea，i. e. Does the speaker give logical argument for her attitude? Is the speaker combining Logos with Pathos?

（五）学生作业点评

作业范例与点评 1

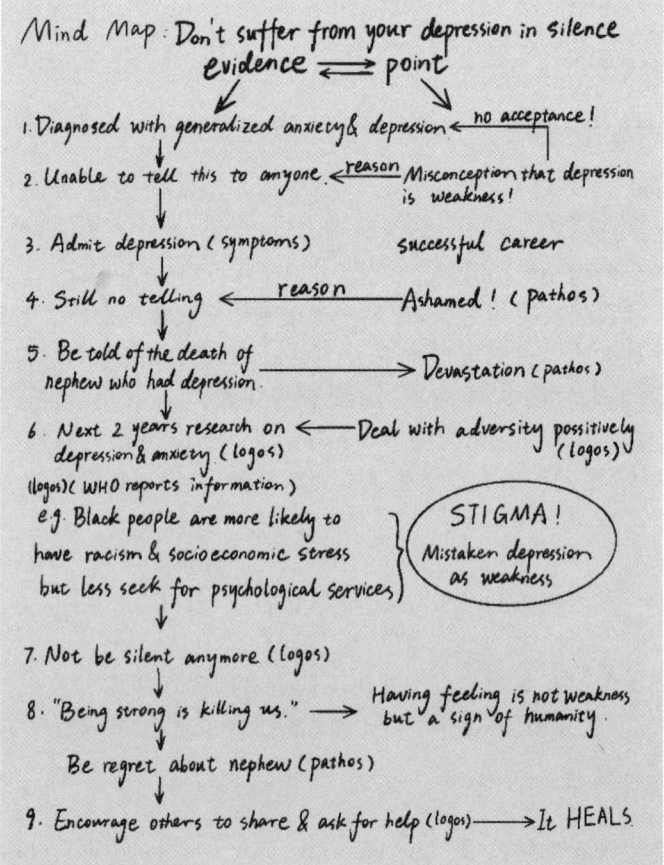

Analysis: The speaker had experienced a tough period with depression, and the silence caused by shame and stigma. But the death of her nephew, who was also killed by depression, triggered her to search more information about depression. The speaker shared her story as well as analyzed the causes, results and solutions of depression. Her main points were as follow. The leading cause of depression is the heavy burden of life. Shame and stigma worsen the mental condition. Sharing stories with others is helpful to cope with pressure and relaxation. She sincerely hopes that her speech can help others who also suffer from depression.

The speaker developed a relatively logical argument. The causality of most evidences and points are clear and reasonable. However, I don't think the point that sharing stories is helpful to improve depression can be well supported by, or closely related to the evidence that depression can be improved by therapy, medication and treatment. The speaker perfectly combined pathos with logos. She combined real events with professional research. She analyzed human's behaviors and feelings with precise data.

点评：在思维导图中，这位学生列出了演讲人的主要论点和相关论据，并标出了各个部分是采用了逻辑说理（Logos）还是情感共鸣策略（Pathos）。这样的思路整理有效帮助他在第二部分对演讲者的论述进行评估和回应。不足之处是，该思维导图基本沿袭了原演讲的顺序，论点间呈简单并列关系，没有突出主次或呈现任何内在联系，信息的整合不够充分。

在第二部分的评估中，这位学生在对演讲的主要论点论据及所采用的情感策略进行分析后，给予了有理有据的回应。这位学生指出演讲人提到"分享自己的故事有助于改善抑郁症"这一论点缺乏相关证据支持，这其实属于误解，与演讲人的真正观点有偏差。总而言之，虽然学生的回应并非滴水不漏，但已经充分使用批判性听力技巧完成这份作业，应该给予鼓励。

作业范例与点评 2

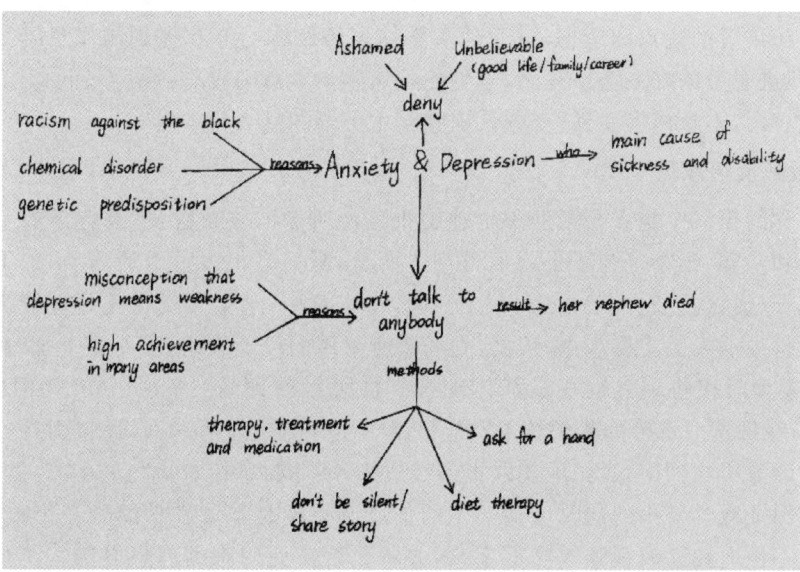

Analysis: The speaker gave a logical argument for her attitude; she also combined logos with pathos. She firstly talked about the success she had had to show her attitude on the diagnoses results at the beginning which is couldn't believe she got diseases. And then she changed her thought and admitted she was ill but she felt guilty because she thought she didn't have the right to be depression for her life was good and couldn't let others down. After that she explained what changed her attitude to facing the anxiety and depression directly which was knowing her nephew's death who suffered from anxiety and depression for many years. After sadness, she began to get to know about those diseases, and found out depression was horrible and people couldn't get rid of it completely. Especially for black people in America, stress from discrimination and economy force them to have mental diseases and many thought that depression was kind of weakness. However, she also found that under treatments and medication many people can make progress. So she wanted to share her stories to spark a national conversation. At last she shared some tips about dealing with her anxiety and depression and encouraged people to get help when they felt stressed.

  点评：这位学生的思维导图展示了演讲的主要内容和各部分之间的联系，但未能清楚体现主要论点与论据的对应关系，亦未标出各部分分别采用了何种逻辑或情感策略。这样的思维导图对于分析演讲的论点论据与情感策略帮助不大。

  在第二部分的评估中，这位学生虽然给出了结论——"演讲人在论述过程结合运用了逻辑说理和情感策略"，却没有给出相关依据，而仅仅只是复述演讲的主要内容，没有体现批判性思维。另外，语言表述方面瑕疵较多，句子过长，缺乏有效切分。

三、案例使用反馈

（一）学生反馈意见

  课程反馈问卷显示，近七成学生（问卷有效回答人数为277人）表示本章所学的批判性听力技巧对他们很有帮助，大部分学生认为自己的批判性思维能力（74%）和学术听力技能（63%）有所提高。超过半数学生表示自己对本章内容感兴趣，能够很投入地学习，收获颇丰。同时，我们也注意到学生对内容的难度评价不一，这也许是因为学生群体中存在听力水平的差异。自认为"听力是短板"的学生表示："学术听力中的生词以及演讲的节奏仍是很大困难，在听力中要同时进行推断和逻辑分析，感觉有点吃力。"值得注意的是，很多学生在反馈中提到了他们学会了如何在听力中"抓重点"，包括心中带着问题去听、提取关键词、有意识地寻找演讲者的论点和论据，进而理清整体逻辑结构。亦有提到制作思维导图是帮助整理思路、促进思考的好办法。总之，学生们虽然感觉本章内容有挑战性，但总体反馈良好，甚至有学生表示，本章内容使其"充分认识到学术英语的魅力与本质"。

（二）教师反馈意见

  本章教学的第一个重点是帮助学生理解批判性听力的真正含义，其背后有一整套严谨的思维方法和步骤，绝不是为了批评而批判。而且，听力是很多学生的弱项，加上学术听力普遍时长较长、语言复杂、内容枯燥、专业性强，在本章中，学生需要在充分理解听力内容的基础上去分析说话人的主要观点、依据、立场及所采用的说理策略，更是难上加难。因此，在讲解SIER模型时应将重点放在最能体现批判性思维的评估（evaluating）和回应（responding）环节。在做这两部分的相关练习时应该给学生充分的思考时间，通过引导与讨论让他们完成自己的分析与回应，真正地实践批判性思维，而非简单核对答案。

  如何在保证教学效果的同时增加学生的信心和兴趣是本章教学的另一个重点和难点。因怕学生听不懂而在播放视频时加上字幕，并不是解决此困难的理想方法。在观看带字幕的视频时，学生自然而然更多地依靠字幕获取信息，这样他们锻炼的是阅读能力，而不是听力。要解决这个难点，首先在听力选材上要考虑学生的能力水平，避免选择难度过大或专业性过强的材料，比如让低年级的学生听专业的医学学术报告就不现实。因此，选择一些医学人文相关的话题或者日常科普类的内容也许更符合低年级学生的能力，也更能引起他们的兴趣。其次，可以多次播放材料让学生反复听，也可通过设置播放器放慢语速，务必给学生更多时间揣摩和消化。同时，做好听前准备，如提供背景资料或生词释义，必要时可将本章内容安排成两次课。

附录6.1 学习任务

(一) 学习任务二

Listening for logical argument: watch a clip about Steve Jobs' liver transplantation (方卫 等,2013)and answer the questions:

1. Does the guest speaker, Art Caplan, believe that Jobs is able to get a liver more quickly than other people because of his money?

2. What are Caplan's arguments for this opinion?

(二) 学习任务三

Listening to feel the psychological/emotional appeals: watch the talk "The best gift I've ever survived"(Kramer,2010) and answer these questions:

1. Does the speaker give logical argument for her attitude?
2. Is the speaker combining logos with pathos?
3. Are you responding merely to the pathos?

(三) 学习任务四

Listening to identify facts from opinions: Watch a news report "Assisted death or murder"(方卫 等,2013) and answer these questions:

1. What facts have been reported here?
2. Whose opinions have been discussed here?

(四) 参考答案

学习任务二参考答案

1. Yes.
2. Caplan's arguements come from three aspects:
   A. Jobs has insurance.
   B. Jobs is able to pay and show to be a good candidate for a transplant.
   C. Jobs can get multi-listed on the waiting list.

学习任务三参考答案

1. No.
2. No, she uses pathos mainly in her talk. Examples of loaded language or emotional appeals include "feel loved and appreciated"."Adoration and admiration will overwhelm you. It will recalibrate what's most important in your life." "Your life will have new meaning. Peace, health, serenity, happiness, nirvana."
3. 这个问题是开放性的,可以引导学生讨论对演讲者"以情动人"的演讲方式的回应,并适当进行理性质疑。

学习任务四参考答案

1. The 54-year old man killed his wife who had been suffering from cancer with a gun while she was asleep.
2. **Defense attorney**: This is a very sad and unique circumstance.

Prosecutor：It is a murder.

Neighbor：He is not a monster/not a bad guy.

参考文献

Allen NK，Don't suffer from your depression in silence［Video file TED.（2017，June）］［2020-03-30］. https://www.ted.com/talks/nikki_webber_allen_don_t_suffer_from_your_depression_in_silence.

Aristotle，1989. The art of rhetoric. Harvard：Harvard University Press.

Fisher A，Scriven M，1997. Critical Thinking. Its Definition and Assessment. Book Reviews Perspectives in Public Health，130(5)：239-239.

Steil L，Barker L，Watson K，1983. Effective listening：Key to your success. New York：Addison Wesley Publishing Company.

Kramer S，2010. The best gift I ever survived［Video file TED.（2010，Feb）］［2020-03-30］. https://www.ted.com/talks/stacey_kramer_the_best_gift_i_ever_survived.

方卫，王燕，承雨，2013. 医学人文英语视听说教程. 上海：上海交通大学出版社.

第二篇

学术读写模块

第七章 学术书面语特点

谢黎嘉　李晓玲

一、对教学主题和教学思路的解读

"Different styles of language should be applied in different registers",意为在不同语域使用不同语体。这也是人际交往中的一条黄金法则:"见什么人说什么话"。学术场景中使用的语言不同于日常表达,有着自己的特点,这在第三章"学术思维语言"里已经提到。本章节从词汇、句法等角度着重介绍学术书面语的特点,以帮助学生更好地进行学术阅读与写作。

(一) 教学主题:学术语言特点

Halliday及Hasan(1985)认为"语域"是按照使用情况划分的不同语言变体,它由一系列相关联的语言特征构成。语域包括语场(field)、语旨(tenor)和语式(mode)三个要素。语场决定了交际的内容,语旨展示了交际双方的关系,语式则是语言在交际中的使用(Thompson,2000)。这三者相互作用,使得语言行为形成了适应于某一特定活动类型、具有某种具体用途的功能变体。张德禄等(2005,p.49)认为,"学生可以通过语篇来学习语言,也可以通过语篇来学习其他学科的知识"。

学术书面语是学术写作场景下表达学术观点、介绍学术发现所使用的特殊语言变体,本章参照Gillett等(2009)的归纳,从正式性、客观性、复杂性、明晰性、谨慎性、责任性和简练性七方面阐述学术书面语的特点。学生通过对这些语言特征的学习、分析,一方面了解学术内容、学术思维是如何通过学术语言呈现出来的,另一面又掌握相关学科知识,尤其是特定学科领域里的专业词汇和表述结构。

(二) 教学思路

为帮助学生具体感知学术书面语的特点,本节课先以口语文本例子分析入手,简单回顾口语的语言特点(有关学术口语特点的论述详见第四章)。紧接着,以"例子引入—练习巩固"的形式介绍常见的学术书面语特征。

学术书面语对正式性的要求主要体现在正式的词汇和句法表达;客观性主要体现在避免使用带主观、感情色彩的词汇,常用被动语态;复杂性主要体现在名词化现象和复杂句式;明晰性则主要体现在语篇标示词(signpost)的使用。这四方面的特征比较直观,学生比较容易理解。我们以学术论文的句子或语段为例分别介绍这些特征,并辅以练习巩固。

学术书面语特征还包括谨慎性,特别体现在模糊语(hedging)的使用。模糊语这一概念对学生来讲比较陌生,需要通过例子对比,向学生展示如何使用模糊语来表现作者提出的主张的强度、作者对主题的确定性或信心程度。责任性也是学术书面语的一大重要特征,这也是学生平时比较容易忽视的地方。引用的标记、参考文献的罗列、转述和概述的使用突显了作者对学术观点的尊重和负责。这两方面的语言特征涉及比较深层的认知能力,需要学生具备一定的学术思维能力,因此是本章节的学习难点。

不管是期刊论文或者其他学术文体,比如开题报告、壁报、汇报幻灯片等,对字数都有一定的要求和限制,因此文字简练而内容完整是对学术书面表达不可或缺的要求。Wallwork(2011)指出,表达的简练性可以减少语言表达的错误,使得学术内容的表述更清晰,进而增加可读性和文章的影响力。针对这一部分内容,我们主要介绍让表达更简练的各种方法,并辅以练习强化,最后以课程作业学术壁报的写作进行综合应用训练。

本次课内容比较多,授课时可以酌情考虑分成两个学时段完成。

二、教学案例设计

(一) 教学目标

1. 学生能够识别学术书面语的重要语言特征并举例说明。
2. 学生能够借助语言特征提升文献阅读与理解能力。
3. 学生能够在学术书面表达中有意识地采用这些语言特征,增强表述的学术性。

(二) 教学内容

教学内容	注解
❖ **What is academic writing?** ✓ Either an exam question to answer or a research project to report on with an obvious audience and a clear purpose	本部分为开放性讨论,目的在于让学生对学术书面语所用场景有所认识
❖ **Formality** ✓ Avoid colloquialisms and idioms ✓ Use formal vocabulary ✓ Avoid using multi-word verbs ✓ Avoid the "not ＋ verb" negative form and contraction	以文本对比让学生自己体会、发现学术书面语的特征。此处安排课堂讨论一、二,详见附录7.1;学习任务一、二,详见附录7.2 本部分教学采用"解释—举例—练习"的形式。例子与练习多取自 Andy Gillett 的教学网站：http://www.uefap.com/ writing/ writfram.htm
❖ **Objectivity** ✓ Avoid subjective language and emotive language ✓ Use passive voice	
❖ **Complexity** ✓ Longer and more formal words ✓ More complex sentence structures ✓ Denser lexicons ✓ Noun-based phrases or nominalization	以学术口头表达与书面表达作对比,突出书面语的"复杂性"。此处安排课堂讨论3,详见附录7.1;学习任务三、四,详见附录7.2
❖ **Explicitness** ✓ Use signaling words to indicate the organization of ideas ✓ Common signaling words, or signpost: because, however, in addition, moreover, etc	这一特征再一次证明了学术语言与学术思维之间的关系 通过例子展现学术语言对于思维的呈现,然后再通过学术文献选段分析加深学生对 explicitness 的认识。此处安排课堂讨论4,详见附录7.1

(续表)

教学内容	注解
❖ **Hedging** ✓ Cautious or vague language ✓ Indicating your stance on a particular subject, or the strength of the claims you are making ✓ Common hedging: introductory/modal verbs, adverts of frequency, modal adverbs/adjective/nouns, that/to clause, etc	Hedging（模糊语）的使用是学术书面语的一大特征，它体现了作者对于所表达的观点、所描述的事实、事实与观点之间的关系等的态度、立场。因此，这部分练习从句子分析入手，再提高至文段分析。此处安排课堂讨论5，详见附录7.1；学习任务五，详见附录7.2
❖ **Responsibility** ✓ Be responsible for your claims ✓ Be responsible for demonstrating an understanding of the source text (citation and references)	Responsibility这一特征要着重强调"文者有责"，为以后学术写作中的"概述""转述"作先行介绍
❖ **Conciseness** ✓ Cut redundant words ✓ Avoid tautologies ✓ Choose the shortest expressions ✓ Conciseness in academic writing	在实际教学中，本部分内容可作为一次独立课，其教学目的、教学活动设置主要用于帮助学生完成大作业学术壁报。介绍实现conciseness的不同方法，让学生综合运用到学术壁报写作中。此处安排学习任务六，详见附录7.2

（三）学习任务

任务一

任务内容　学生阅读句子，判断哪些地方没有体现书面语的正式性特征并进行同义改写。

任务要点　通过改写句子，让学生注意学术书面表达词汇、语法的正式性。

任务完成形式/师生互动形式　学生独立完成任务，之后学生交换评判。老师提问检查。

任务二

任务内容　学生阅读并改写句子，使句子更具书面语的客观性特征。

任务要点　通过改写句子，引起学生对学术书面表达客观性的重视。

任务完成形式/师生互动形式　学生独立完成任务，老师以提问的形式检查任务完成情况。

任务三

任务内容　学生根据书面语的名词化现象对句子进行改写。

任务要点　名词化表达使得内容表述更加凝练，但同时增加学术阅读的困难度。在改写句子时，需要引导学生注意名词和动词互相转化后句子结构发生的改变。

任务完成形式/师生互动形式　学生独立完成任务，老师以提问的形式检查任务完成情况。

任务四

任务内容　学生从书面语复杂性特征的角度对比分析两段同主题文段。

任务要点　这一任务设计在书面语与口语对比、名词化现象介绍之后，属于综合性练习，目的在于让学生在学术文献阅读中能主动意识到文段中出现的各种复杂性形式。

任务完成形式/师生互动形式　学生独立完成任务，老师以提问的形式检查任务完成情况。

任务五

任务内容　学生辨别出句子、文段中模糊语的使用情况。

任务要点　这一任务由易到难，让学生从句子到文段体会模糊语的使用及其表达传递的信息。

任务完成形式/师生互动形式　学生分组讨论完成任务，老师以提问的形式检查任务完成情况。

任务六

任务内容　学生改写句子，让句子表达更简练。

任务要点　强化学生书面表达的"简练"意识。

任务完成形式/师生互动形式　学生独立完成任务，老师以提问的形式检查任务完成情况。

（四）课后作业

1. Read and compare two excerpts in terms of the different features of academic written language.

（1）Can you identify the context each one may be found in?

（2）Can you recognize the differences between them? Find examples of the following features in the excerpts and write them in the appropriate column. (Some squares will remain blank.)

	Excerpt 1	Excerpt 2
Formal vocabulary		
Passive voice		
Cautious language		
Objective language		
Subjective language		
Emotive language		
Use of questions		
Contracted forms		
Reference		

Excerpt 1：A clear problem in academic writing is that of the assessor or "assignment setter", as described by Ivanic and Simpson (1992: 146). This person is posing a challenge and a threat to the student, and positioning him as a writer, and exercising control over him. However stimulating the assignment may be... it is also face-threatening because it will be judged. "Students" knowledge that the work they have written will be assessed may oblige them to consider their writing from different perspectives, namely, what they deem acceptable and what their tutors deem acceptable. This is often difficult for students to achieve.

Excerpt 2：I don't think there is a case for this argument at all. How could anyone imagine putting such a proposal forward when it's so clearly ludicrous? I believe that the more people are aware of this issue, the better off we would all be. (Gillett et al., 2009, p. 88-89)

2. Select a formally published academic article, read the article and look for examples of academic written language in terms of "formal, concise, and responsible".（注：此项可以根据学生的英语水平作为拓展练习使用。）

三、案例使用反馈

（一）学生反馈意见

本章节的课程反馈调查涉及 279 位本科二年级学生，超过半数的学生明确表示对这部分内容感兴趣(52.64%)，在学习过程中很投入(57.29%)；大部分学生认为所学内容对他们未来专业的学习与发展很有帮助(70.2%)，收获很大(56.96%)。大部分学生认为学习学术语言特点，可以帮助他们分析学术文章中的语言特点，更好地理解文献，并有助于学术写作。对此章节的总体评价是内容很充实、实用性强。

对于本章节内容，部分学生认为难度较大(37.08%)。有的学生反映由于专业词汇量不够，文献阅读量有限，以及对句式特点、文章结构等不熟悉等原因，他们无法根据想要表达的意思选择最合适的书面语，或在日常用语和符合学术语言特点的词语的转换上遇到困难。有的同学则觉得虽然掌握了学术书面语的特点，但要运用到学术写作上还是有一定难度。

在教学内容安排和教师指导方面，学生也给出了不少中肯的建议。有的同学觉得课时较短，对学术语言特点的理解还不够透彻，如要熟练掌握，需要老师多举例子并增加练习。他们还建议提供更多的文献阅读材料以便更深入理解学术文献的词汇、句法和结构特点。这些建议体现了学生对学术书面语特征的重要性有较强的意识，希望能真正运用到学术阅读和写作中。

（二）教师反馈意见

本章节的内容涉及的学术英语术语和概念较多，比如 formality、tautology 等，因此备课的一大难点是如何将这些术语和概念解释清楚。首先，教师应该对这些术语和概念有深入和清楚的理解。其次，在解释术语和概念时结合具体的例子和练习帮助学生理解。比如 be formal 的备课难点是如何让学生理解 being formal 和 being informal 的区别。这两个概念比较抽象，学生虽然大概知道，但在落笔时还是常常有 informal 的表达。所以我们将 informal 归纳为口语化、主观性、情绪化、设问以及缩略形式等方面。Formal 与之相反，是书面化、客观性、表述性以及较为完整、复杂的用词方式。这些特征形成鲜明的对比，需要通过针对性举例和练习，强化学生的概念。

本章节的内容较多，备课时要考虑每个课堂练习和活动的目的和所需时间，也要预测学习难点，设计相关的提示和点评。比如学习任务六是把冗长的表达变成简洁的学术语言，有些学生不知如何入手，教师可以给予适当的提示，比如主动和被动语态的转换，省略形式化表达（如形式主语）等。本章节选取的语料素材，有的来自科普书籍，有的来自专业性较强的学术论文，教师可根据学生的语言水平，模仿本章的任务设计方式，自行选取其他来源的素材。

附录 7.1 课堂讨论

1. Read and figure out the reasons why the text is not a written one.

I don't think there is a case for this argument at all. How could anyone imagine putting such a proposal forward when it's so clearly ludicrous? I believe that the more people are aware of this issue, the better off we would all be. (Gillett, et al., 2009, p. 88)

Possible answers:

(1) Colloquialisms

(2) Subjective language

(3) Emotive language

(4) Use of questions

(5) Contracted forms

2. Read and underline all the subjective language.

Everybody knows about the threat of global warming to our earth. We all pollute the atmosphere with gases and we all throw away rubbish that could be recycled. As far as I am concerned, these are two aspects that can be improved. I believe that everyone should use more public transport and leave their car at home. I also think that we can all learn to recycle more of our plastic and glass bottles. Even our left-over food can be used as compost. (Gillett et al., 2009, p. 95)

3. Compare the following sentences (Halliday, 1989, p. 79-81) in spoken and written contexts and analyze what makes the written language more complex than the spoken one.

Spoken	Written
You can control the trains this way and if you do that you can be quite sure that they'll be able to run more safely and more quickly than they would otherwise, no matter how bad the weather gets.	The use of this method of control unquestionably leads to safer and faster train running in the most adverse weather conditions.
The cities in Switzerland had once been peaceful, but they changed when people became violent.	Violence changed the face of once peaceful Swiss cities.
The government banned smoking in public places in 2007. Since then, fewer people have been admitted to hospital for smoking-related diseases.	The ban on smoking in public places in 2007 has led to a fall in hospital admissions for smoking-related diseases.

4. Read through the extract below and underline the words or expressions used as signpost.

The aim of this paper is to demonstrate the relevance of possible-world frameworks to the study of poetic text worlds. My argument will proceed as follows. In the first part of the paper, I will briefly discuss the development of the notion of possible worlds from logic to the semantics of functionality, and consider the way in which a possible-world approach can be used to describe and classify fictional worlds; I will focus particularly on the framework developed by Ryan (1991a, 1991b). In the second part of the paper, I will show how possible-world models, and specifically Ryan's approach, can be applied to poetry. In particular, I will adopt a possible-world perspective in order to consider:

i. The internal structure of the world projected by a particular poem;

ii. The projection of deviant situations of address;

iii. The description of different types of poetic worlds.

I will conclude with a discussion of the main weaknesses of possible-world frameworks, and with some suggestions for future developments in the study of text worlds. (Semino, 1996, p. 190)

5. Read and compare the sets of sentences.

(1) The virus starts in an animal.

　　The virus may start in an animal.

(2) The virus was probably spread in cough droplets.

　　The virus could have been spread in cough droplets.

附录7.2　学习任务

（一）学习任务一

Rewrite the following sentences, replacing the informal expressions with a more formal equivalent.

1. A primary education system was set up throughout Ireland as early as 1831.

2. This will cut down the amount of drug required and so the cost of treatment.

3. Dieters often feel that they should totally get rid of high-fat and high-sugar foods.

4. Discussion of the outcome of experiments that have used this method will be put off until Chapter 7.

5. This was before he had read the guidelines on how to carry out the research.

6. The new study doesn't support many of the initial findings.

7. There isn't much research on this topic.

8. The future of Federal funding is up in the air.

9. It is widely accepted that election campaigns go the extra mile in their final weeks.

10. The company, in an attempt to cut costs, fired 5% of the workforce in 2004.

(Gillett, A. Features of academic writing. Retrieved from http：//www. uefap. com/writing/exercise/feature/styleex3. htm)

（二）学习任务二

Rewrite the sentences by using passive voice.

1. The researchers transcribed many genes and synthesized many proteins.

2. They replicated these findings.

3. Somebody claims that the drug produced no undesirable side effects.

4. Researchers believe that the only problem with daytime sleep is that it is too short.

5. Although the government expects the patient to pay for his treatment, he will be reimbursed via the state medical insurance scheme.

(Gillett, A. Features of academic writing. Retrieved from http：//www. uefap. com/writing/writfram. htm)

（三）学习任务三

Rewrite the sentences using the words in brackets.

1. His theory emphasized the fact that it is important to read extensively in language acquisition. (emphasis, importance)

(key：His theory places emphasis on the importance of extensive reading in language acquisition.)

2. The model explains how the figure fluctuates in this period. (explanations, fluctuation)

(key: The model provides an explanation for the figure fluctuation in this period.)
(蔡基刚,2014,p. 142)

(四) 学习任务四

Read the following two texts. How do you compare them in terms of the complexity of the language?

1. All organisms reproduce and sometimes when they reproduce, the children vary. This is an important characteristic of life. If organisms did not reproduce, life would quickly come to an end. How did the earliest single-celled organisms reproduce? They duplicated their genetic material and then they divided in two. Two daughter cells resulted from this process; they were identical to each other and to the parent cell. But sometimes as the genes duplicated, they changed or mutated. These errors are not very common but they provide the basic material for life to evolve. So when the genetic material duplicates, they reproduce and they make errors. As a result, there is a change in what the genes are composed of. When these processes combine, life evolve.

2. Reproduction with variation is a major characteristic of life. Without reproduction, life would quickly come to an end. The earliest single-celled organisms reproduced by duplicating their genetic material and then dividing in two. The two resulting daughter cells were identical to each other and to the parent cell, except for mutations that occurred during the process of gene duplication. Such errors, although rare, provided the raw material for biological evolution. The combination of reproduction and errors in the duplication of genetic material results in biological evolution, a change in the genetic composition of a population of organisms over time.

(Purves, et al., 2004, p. 3)

(五) 学习任务五

Hedging

1. Identify the hedging expressions in the following sentences.

(1) There is no difficulty in explaining how a structure such as an eye or a feather contributes to survival and reproduction; the difficulty is in thinking of a series of steps by which it could have arisen.

(2) For example, it is possible to see that in January this person weighed 60.8 kg for eight days.

(3) For example, it may be necessary for the spider to leave the branch on which it is standing, climb up the stem, and walk out along another branch.

(4) There is experimental work to show that a week or ten days may not be long enough and a fortnight to three weeks is probably the best theoretical period.

(5) Conceivably, different forms, changing at different rates and showing contrasting

combinations of characteristics, were present in different areas.

(6) One possibility is that generalized latent inhibition is likely to be weaker than that produced by pre-exposure to the CS itself and thus is more likely to be susceptible to the effect of the long interval.

(7) For our present purpose, it is useful to distinguish two kinds of chemical reaction, according to whether the reaction releases energy or requires it.

(8) It appears to establish three categories: the first contains wordings generally agreed to be acceptable, the second wordings which appear to have been at some time problematic but are now acceptable, and the third wordings which remain inadmissible.

(Gillett, A. Features of academic writing. Retrieved from http: //www. uefap. com/writing/exercise/feature/hedgeex. htm)

2. Analyze the following text and identify the places where language of hedging is used.

Our study also highlights the potential for preventing heart failure through interventions that decrease the prevalence of obesity and high blood pressure. Obesity was common among black participants in the CARDIA study, particularly black women,[37,38] and it is possible that preventing obesity in this population may reduce the subsequent incidence of heart failure. Recent national data suggest that young adults with hypertension are much less likely than their middle-aged counterparts to be aware of this diagnosis or to be receiving treatment.[39,40] The reasons for low rates of treatment for hypertension among young adults may include barriers in access to medical care.[41,42] It has been suggested that blood-pressure control may be more difficult to achieve among black patients, although a consensus statement on treating hypertension in blacks concluded that the failure of health professionals to initiate therapy early in accordance with established guidelines was the major obstacle to achieving effective blood-pressure control.[43,44] When they receive treatment according to the guidelines, blacks and whites appear to have similar rates of control.[45]

(Bibbins-Domingo, et al., 2009, p. 1186. 1188)

(六) 学习任务六

Rewrite the sentences to make them more concise, either by removing redundant words or using shortest expressions.

1. As we have already noted in Section 4. 3. 1, the presence of X can influence Y.

2. Rows and cells are highlighted in different colors in order to give a more effective view.

3. Chemical reactions between organic materials and pigments lead to discoloration phenomena.

4. Our research activity consists of X and Y.

5. The solution adopted was to carry out a test of all the software on the market.

6. This has made it possible for us to do...

7. From now on these will be referred to as X and Y.

8. As shown in Figs. 13 and 14, the calculation makes a prediction that X will...

9. An increase in X of 30% was achieved.

10. Particular care has been taken in the design of X.

(Wallwork,2013,p. 128,143,148,150)

参考文献

Bibbins-Domingo K,Pletcher MJ,Lin F,et al.,2009. Racial differences in incident heart failure among young adults. The New England of Medicine,360:1179-1190.

Gillett A,Hammond A,Martala M,2009. Successful academic writing. Harlow:Pearson Education Limited.

Gillett A,Features of academic writing [2020-03-25]. http://www.uefap.net/writing/writing-features/writing-features-introduction.

Halliday MAK,Hasan R,1985. Language,context and text:Aspects of language in a social-semiotic perspective. Geelong:Deakin University Press.

Purves WK,Sadava DE,Orians GH,2004. Life:The science of biology. New York:W. H. Freeman & Company.

Semino E,1996. Possible Worlds in Poetry. Journal of Literary Semantics,25(3):189-224.

Thompson G,2000. 功能语法入门. 北京:外语教学与研究出版社.

Wallwork A,2011. English for writing research papers. New York:Springer Science.

Wallwork A,2013. English for academic research:Writing exercises. New York:Springer Science.

蔡基刚,2014. 综合学术英语教程4. 上海:上海交通大学出版社.

张德禄,苗兴伟,李学宁,2005. 功能语言学与外语教学. 北京:外语教学与研究出版社.

第八章 研究论文结构分析

谢黎嘉 余 凡

一、对教学主题和教学思路的解读

"套路"是一个近年流行起来的网络用语,指的是使用某种特定不变的方式来处理问题。语言表达同样也存在着"套路"。比方说,我们的语言表达总有"起—承—转—合",叙述某件事情总会谈及事情的"起因—经过—结果",论证一定需要"论点—论据—论证"。学术研究论文也不例外。本章的目的在于通过展示在国际学术期刊发表的研究论文结构上的"套路",帮助学生更好地阅读理解,加深他们关于"学术语言与学术思维"关系的认识,也为他们以后的学术写作打基础。需要说明的是,本课程在校内实施时面向理工科学生,因此主要以理工科研究论文的结构为主,社科类研究论文的结构略有不同,比如会为文献综述专辟一节,或根据论述需要将"结果"(Results)与"讨论"(Discussion)两部分合二为一,想使用本章的教师可以根据学生的专业领域略作调整。

(一) 教学主题——研究论文结构

谈及研究论文结构,就必须提及在学术英语教学中广泛使用的"体裁教学法"。关于体裁的概念和体裁教学法,我们在第二章有详细介绍,这里不再赘述。但我们在本章会应用到许多研究者在研究论文体裁分析方面的研究成果,如 Swales 及 Feak(2012),Ruiying 及 Allison(2003)和 Lim(2006)。

了解和掌握论文的体裁、文本特点,对于初阶学生来讲,可以帮助他们更好地把握论文的结构,理清作者的思路,提炼文章的要点,加深他们对"学术语言是学术思维的载体"的认识;对于高阶学生来讲,可以帮助他们更有逻辑地表达自己的学术观点,更好地运用学术语言呈现自己的学术思维。因此,本章节既是研究论文阅读的基础,也是研究论文写作的基础。之所以把它放在"学术阅读"模块,主要是因为根据 Krashen 的语言习得理论(1982),在语言学习过程中必须是先有"输入",才有"输出";而阅读属于信息输入,写作属于信息输出。另外,按照学习技能的发展习惯,通常我们是先学习如何阅读,再练习如何写作;通过阅读加深对文本体裁的认识;通过写作巩固对文本体裁的应用。

(二) 教学思路

本章借用 Swales(1990)的 CARS 模型理论以及其他学者(Lim,2006;Ruiying 及 Allison,2003)对于论文各部分的体裁、文本特征的研究成果,向学生逐一展示论文各部分的语步和文本特征。

在对各部分的体裁、文本特征进行介绍时,我们采用系统功能语言学派的教学模式,以"解构范文""共同建构文本"和"独立建构文本"为三大教学步骤(Martin,1999)。在"解构范文"时,或通过提问引发学生思考可能出现的特征,或带领学生一起对范文进行分析,并引导学生思考原因。最后,学生以小组形式分析既选论文的语步与文本特征,以加深、强化他们的认识。

由于此部分内容比较多,学生在独立分析的过程中需要更多的时间进行操练,因此建议此部分可分为两个专题进行教授:第一个专题主要介绍论文的"引入""方法"部分;第二专题介绍"结果""讨论""结论"这三个部分。

二、教学案例设计

(一) 教学目标

1. 学生能够描述研究论文的结构以及各部分的写作目的。
2. 学生能够分析论文各部分的语步特征和文本特征。
3. 学生能够综合运用论文的语步与文本特征,分析论文,提炼论文中心内容。

(二) 教学内容

1. Structure of Research Articles

教学内容	注解
❖ **The purpose of research articles** √ To inform the readers of what has been found and how it contributes to the current body of knowledge ❖ **Structure of research articles** √ A linear structure: Preliminaries—main text—end matter ❖ **IMRD** √ Introduction: to provide the rationale for the paper, and to identify the research gap in the existing literature √ Methods: to describe methodology, materials, and procedures √ Results: to describe findings √ Discussions/conclusion: to offer an account of what has been learned in the study	此部分从 Gillett(2019)对论文的线性结构分析入手,逐一介绍论文各部分的功能

2. Rhetorical Moves and Stylistic Features in Each Section

教学内容	注解
❖ **Introduction section** √ Functions √ John Swale's Create-A-Research-Space(CARS)Model 　√ Move 1: establish a territory 　√ Move 2: establish a niche 　√ Move 3: occupy the niche	本部分具体介绍 John Swale 的 CARS 模型(Swales,1990),并引导学生对范文进行语步分析。值得注意的是我们在这里采用的是比较广为人知的 CARS 模型的"三步骤"版本,事实上在 Swales 早期的论著里还有"四步骤"版本(Swales,1981; Swales 及 Najjar,1987) 此部分完成学习任务一

(续表)

教学内容	注解
❖ **Methods section** ✓ Functions ✓ Rhetorical moves of *Methods* section • Move 1：describe data collection procedures • Move 2：delineate procedures for measuring variables • Move 3：elucidate data analysis procedures	带领学生略读定量研究和定性研究论文的"方法"部分，让他们总结采用不同研究方法的研究论文在该部分中的共同点。接着，参考 Lim（2006）的研究成果，向学生展示"方法"部分的语步和文本特征 　　此部分完成学习任务二
❖ **Rhetorical moves of Results section** ✓ Move 1：provide background about theory/research aims/methods ✓ Move 2：reporting and present findings	"结果"部分的内容呈现主要与研究方法的介绍相对应，语步分化不明显，所以分析的重点放在此部分如何与"方法"部分一一对应。此部分完成学习任务三
❖ **Rhetorical moves of Discussion/Conclusion section** ✓ Move 1：comment on results ✓ Move 2：evaluate the study ✓ Move 3：make deductions from the study	此部分完成学习任务四
❖ **Linguistic Features in RA Sections** ✓ The linguistic features in each section are closely related to its writing purposes and rhetorical functions. ✓ Writing purposes 　A. to introduce 　B. to evaluate 　C. to argue 　D. to conclude ✓ Rhetorical functions 　A. Critical 　B. Informative 　C. Descriptive ✓ Linguistic features 　A. Tenses（present vs. past） 　B. Voices（active vs. passive） 　C. Hedging 　D. Responsibility（citation）	对论文各部分的文本特征的总结借鉴了 Lim（2006）和 Swale 及 Feak（2012）的研究成果，并联系每部分的写作目的和修辞功能进行分析 　　此部分完成学习任务五

（三）学习任务

任务一

　　任务内容　　学生阅读研究论文前言部分选段，分析该部分所包含的语步。

　　任务要点　　让学生熟悉 Swale 的 CARS 模型理论，并运用该理论分析论文引入部分的语步。

　　任务完成形式/师生互动形式　　教师设置问题，引导学生进行探索性阅读。之后教师以提问的形式检查任务完成情况。最后，教师总结并向学生展示前言部分的语步。

任务二

任务内容 学生阅读研究论文的方法部分,指出该部分所包含的语步。

任务要点 让学生认识到不管是采用哪种方法进行的研究,其论文的"方法"部分内容都有共同的构成要素。

任务完成形式/师生互动形式 学生浏览、比较、小结,之后老师以提问的形式检查任务完成情况。

任务三

任务内容 阅读研究论文的"结果"部分选段,分析选段中的语步。

任务要点 让学生在分析"结果"部分的写作顺序时不断回顾"方法"部分对不同研究方法或策略的介绍,分析两部分如何一一对应,以及文本特征方面的相似之处。

任务完成形式/师生互动形式 个人独立分析,小组讨论,之后老师以提问的形式检查任务完成情况。

任务四

任务内容 阅读研究论文的"讨论"和"结论"部分选段,分析选段中的语步。

任务要点 "讨论"部分对批判性阅读要求最高,要引导学生分清哪些是对研究结果的总结,哪些是对研究结果的分析、评价或推论。与此相应的是该部分某些突显的文本特征,如过去时态和现在时态的交替使用、模糊限制语的大量使用等,都需要老师多引导。

任务完成形式/师生互动形式 由于此任务难度较高,也可以由教师带领学生分析该选段的某些段落,然后再由学生独立分析,最后,老师以提问的形式检查任务完成情况。

任务五

任务内容 快速浏览整篇研究论文,总结各部分的文本特征,并完成表格。

任务要点 此项任务旨在帮助学生归纳总结研究各部分内容的文本特点,并强化他们的认知。

任务完成形式/师生互动形式 学生独立完成,邀请学生进行讲解。

(四) 课后作业

为强化学生对研究论文的语篇结构和体裁特点的认识,我们布置了和课堂任务相似的语步分析任务,但由学生根据自己的研究兴趣自主选择进行分析的研究论文。为培养学生的批判性思维,我们鼓励学生寻找与课堂上所用范例有差异的研究论文进行分析,并写出自己的看法。因这份作业比较冗长,在此不进行点评,但在以下教师反馈部分我们会提到学生进行语步分析时遇到的难点,是我们批改课后作业的心得,可供授课教师参考。

三、案例使用反馈

(一) 学生反馈意见

参与课程评价的 277 名学生中,大部分对于课程的内容持肯定态度。他们表示,本单元的学习帮助他们更好地把握研究论文的结构(91%),增强了他们对文本体裁的分析能力(86%),能更好理清作者的思路(86%),提炼文章的要点(84%)。对研究论文结构的分析加深了他们对研究论文的写作模式的认识,例如如何开篇,如何写结论(73%),如何有逻辑地表达自己的学术观点(64%)。

他们同时也提出了一些中肯的建议,比如为较难区分的语步提供更多范例,以加深印象;再如提供一些不按"套路"的范文,帮助他们了解可以如何灵活或"有个性"地写研究论文。

(二) 教师反馈意见

本单元的重点是通过语步分析了解论文结构和内容。教学的难点是有些语步比较难以界定,比如"讨论"部分的语步往往交织在一起,会比较难于分辨。例如,commenting on the results 和 evaluating the study,或者 evaluating the study 和 making deductions from the study,都是比较容易混淆的语步。还有一些文本同时兼容几个语步的功能,如讨论部分有些文本既是解读研究结果,又是总结。上课时要解释清楚各种语步的组织如何呈现学术写作的思路和逻辑,避免照本宣科。同时也要向学生强调:语步分析是对大多数研究论文的归纳总结,但不代表每一篇论文都会呈现所有的语步,不需要每一步都生搬硬套。

同样道理,引导学生对研究论文的文本特征进行分析时,也要强调共性与特性的呈现。他们需要认识到每一篇研究论文,除了具备和其他论文在结构和语言特征上的共性外,也有自身的特性。例如对时态的运用,有些论文在"引入"部分大量使用过去时态,有些却多使用现在时态,这和作者对前期研究结果的认同度有关。再如"方法"部分的引用频率(citation)一般不高,但一些研究可能在这一部分引用很多他人的研究,以论证该研究方法以及数据分析程序的合理性,说明研究结果的信效度。这种写法体现了作者对研究方法在论文中的重要性的强调。总而言之,需要向学生传递一个重要的信息:一篇好的研究论文,它的语步和文本特征都是为写作目的服务的,都体现了作者的学术态度与观点。

附录 8.1 学习任务

(一) 任务内容

Read each section of the selected article (Kouwenhoven et al., 2015) and fill in the results of move analysis. The basic moves in each section has been listed in the table, but you are encouraged to identify "new" moves and discuss possible varieties. (授课老师课可根据学生的具体专业自行选择其他合适的研究论文作为语步分析的案例。)

(二) 学习任务一

Rhetorical moves in Introduction section

Moves	Texts in RA
Move 1: establishing a territory	
Move 2: establishing a niche	
Move 3: occupying the niche	

(三) 学习任务二

Rhetorical moves in Methods section

Moves	Texts in RA
Move 1: describing data collection procedures	
Move 2: delineating procedures for measuring variables	
Move 3: elucidating data analysis procedures	

(四)学习任务三

Rhetorical moves in Results section

Moves	Texts in RA
Move 1: providing background about theory/research aims/methods	
Move 2: reporting and present findings	

(五)学习任务四

Rhetorical moves in Discussion/Conclusion section

Moves	Texts in RA
Move 1: summarizing the results	
Move 2: commenting on results	
Move 3: evaluating the study	
Move 4: making deductions from the study	

(六)学习任务五

Stylistic features of each section

Textual element	Introduction	Methods	Results	Discussion/conclusion
Tense				
Voice				
Citation				
Hedging				

参考文献

Gillett AJ, 2019. Use of a writing web-site by pre-masters students on an English for academic purposes course. http://www.uefap.com/writing/writfram.htm.

Hammoond J, Derewianka B, 2001. Genre. // Carter R, Nunan D. The Cambridge guide to teaching English to speakers of other languages. Cambridge: Cambridge University Press, 186-193.

Johns AM, 2003. Genre and ESL/EFL composition instruction. In Kroll B (ed.), Exploring the dynamics of second language writing. Cambridge: Cambridge University Press: 195-217.

Kouwenhoven et al., 2015. Opinions about euthanasia and advanced dementia: a qualitative study among Dutch physicians and members of the general public. BMC Medical Ethics, 16: 7. https://bmcmedethics.biomedcentral.com/articles/10.1186/1472-6939-16-7.

Krashen SD, 1982. Principles and practice in second language acquisition. Oxford: Pergamon Press.

Lim JL, 2006. Methods sections of management research articles: A pedagogically motivated qualitative study. English For Specific Purposes, 25: 282-309.

Martin JR, 1999. Mentoring semogenesis: "genre-based" literacy pedagogy. In Christie F (ed.), Pedagogy and the shaping of consciousness: Linguistic and social process. London: Continuum, 123-155.

Ruiying, Allison, 2003. Research articles in applied linguistics: Moving from results to conclusions. English For Specific Purposes, 22: 365-385.

Swales JM, 1990. Genre analysis. Cambridge: Cambridge University Press.

Swales JM, 1981. Aspects of article introductions. Birmingham, England: University of Aston.

Swales JM, Feak C, 2012. Academic writing for graduate students: Essential tasks and skills. 3rd ed., Michigan series in English for academic & professional purposes. Ann Arbor: University of Michigan Press.

Swales J, Najjar H, 1987. The writing of research article introduction. Written Communication, 4(2): 175-191.

第九章 多文本阅读技巧

杨 苗

一、对教学主题和教学思路的解读

很多学生对英语阅读并不陌生,但都比较习惯单文本阅读。即使在中文阅读中,他们也很少阅读一系列文章并进行分析、比较和总结。但是,学术阅读最重要的目的是从不同来源的文献中寻找与研究主题相关的信息并形成自己的结论,因此多文本阅读技巧是学术阅读的重要教学内容。本章上承学术论文结构与学术语言分析,下接学术写作各项技巧和任务,是由学术阅读过渡到学术写作的关键一步,因为如果没有多文本阅读技巧,将缺失学术写作最至关重要的基础——对现有文献进行综述。本章要突出的教学主题包括文本之异同点及理性质疑、评价性阅读和整合性阅读。但在讲这些教学主题之前,有必要先简单介绍"互文性"这个概念,以便学术英语教师理解多文本阅读技巧的理论基础。

文本性(textuality)指的是基于独立文本产生的理解。然而,我们对一个文本的理解很多时候是受其他文本信息影响的,由此产生的深度理解,是基于多文本之间的关联性(interrelationship),因此出现互文性(intertextuality)的概念(在中文文献中也称"文本间性")。追源溯本,此理念最初来自瑞士语言学家索绪尔(F. Saussure)的语言观和苏联著名文艺理论家及批评家巴赫金(М. М. Бахтин)的对话理论,后由法国符号学家克里斯蒂娃(J. Kristeva)正式提出"互文性"的概念,并形成较为完整的理论,由此持续影响了文化界,尤其是文学界,长达40年之久。本章在此借用爱尔兰文学理论家艾伦(G. Allen)浅显易懂的语言,对互文性进行解释。

Texts, whether they be literary or non-literary, are viewed by modern theorists as lacking in any kind of independent meaning. They are what theorists now call intertextual. The act of reading, theorists claim, plunges us into a network of textual relations. To interpret a text, to discover its meaning, or meanings, is to trace those relations. Reading thus becomes a process of moving between texts. Meaning becomes something which exists between a text and all the other texts to which it refers and relates, moving out from the independent text into a network of textual relations. (Allen, 2000, p. 1)

我们进行文献阅读时,即使只涉及一个研究主题,也必须同时涉猎许多不同来源的文献,以便形成对该研究主题的历时和共时的、全面的理解和认识。他人的文献是对不同研究的解读,是对不同研究文本的联系进行意义建构的成果,而我们进行多文本阅读的目的,是通过了解这些文献的互文性,建立起自己的意义认同,形成自己和其他研究者之间的学术对话。

(一) 教学主题

1. 文本之异同点及理性质疑:对两个或两个以上的文本进行对比,总结其异同点,并质疑产生这些异同点的原因,是进行多文本阅读的第一步,也是批判性阅读的起点(Rosen 及 Behrens,2003)。我们需要引导学生意识到,同一主题的多个来源的文本必定对相关事实、对事实的解读和判断有相似或不同之处,对其异同点提出疑问,并寻求答案,正是学生作为读者与文献进行交流的开端。质疑将引发更深层次的思考,并引导读者做更加深入的调研。

2. 评价性阅读:在理解文本的含义之后,学生需要对文本进行评价(read to evaluate)。针对专业文献的文本评价一般有四个目的:区分作者阐述的事实和作者本人的观点;区分作者的假定与读者的假定;评判解释性文本的有效性;评判评论性文本的有效性(Rosen 及 Behrens,2003)。虽然学生的评价可能仅仅基于独立文本,但在独立评价每个文本之后所产生的理解将是多文本阅读的基础,在第十二章综述写作里,我们将通过注释文献的任务,把学生对独立文本的理解及评价和所研究的主题联系起来,开始建立文本间的关联。在这一主题里讲到的对解释性和评论性文本的评判,恰好能够帮助学生针对研究论文里的"方法"和"讨论"两大部分进行评价,也为学生在综述写作中需要完成的注释文献进行铺垫。

3. 整合性阅读:整合性阅读,也即 read to synthesize。整合并非简单地总结每个文本的要点并堆放在一起,也非仅仅对比异同点,而是深入分析多个文本所侧重之主题、研究之优劣、各方观点之联系,从而形成对该主题全面的理解并提出自己的见解(Karimi,2017)。如果把每篇文献比喻为拼图的碎片,整合性阅读之后形成的拼图必定形状各异,因为由文献产生的拼图碎片经由不同人的思考,所萃取的成分各不相同,其最终拼图也不会一样。有效的整合性阅读必须达致四个目的:对同一主题的多个文本进行理解和评价;对该主题形成自己的观点;依据自己的观点在多文本间建立联系;以自身观点为主线,援引多个文献来源形成学术对话(Rosen 及 Behrens,2003)。学生需要掌握三大整合性阅读的技巧:交叉引用、建立文本间联系、绘制思维导图。

(二)教学思路

多文本阅读涉及许多复杂、高阶的思维(Segev-Miller,2007),必须依赖学生对文献内容的深度理解,很难在课堂上进行深入练习,所以课堂的教学要点在于以比较浅显易懂的实例教授阅读的技巧,课后的任务则可以涉及较为专业的文献阅读,并预留多一点时间让学生完成。我们在实际教学中,把这一章与第十二章和第十三章的综述写作结合在一起,以便学生将多文本阅读的成果用到综述写作中。但是在本书中,考虑到章节内容的连贯性,我们还是把多文本阅读放在概述和转写技巧之前。在简单解释互文性的概念后,教学重点在于后三个主题:文本之异同点及理性质疑、评价性阅读和整合性阅读。我们以两个洗发水广告引入对不同文本的异同点的分析和质疑,之后使用部分美国学术能力评估测试(Scholastic Assessment Test,SAT)的批判性阅读考题,让学生当堂练习。SAT 的批判性阅读考题大部分是两个文本(短的每篇 100 字左右,长的可达 1000 多字)的对比阅读,短篇的对比阅读非常适合在课堂使用。评价性和整合性阅读部分都是先介绍阅读目的和技巧,然后使用以前学生的注释文献作业作为实例,介绍运用这些阅读技巧之后做的阅读笔记。关于文献阅读笔记,在综述写作的章节里我们会更详细、系统地指导学生。

二、教学案例设计

(一)教学目标

1. 学生能了解多文本阅读需要掌握的技巧,并能熟练运用到文献阅读中。

2. 学生能熟练运用各种思维导图呈现文本之间的联系。

(二) 教学内容

1. Searching for and questioning similarities and differences.

教学内容	注解
❖ Compare two ads and answer these questions? ✓ What are the similarities? ✓ What are the differences? ✓ Why are these similarities and differences?	此部分先以学生耳熟能详的洗发水广告(视频网址见本章参考文献)引入教学主题,引导学生对洗发水广告背后体现的性别定型、文化价值观和社会背景等方面的差异进行思考。鼓励学生运用维恩图(Venn diagram)(注:英国哲学家和数学家维恩发明的图表,用于展示不同事物群组之间的逻辑联系)或表格总结分析结果,完成任务一
❖ Compare two passages and answer these questions? ✓ What are the similarities? ✓ What are the differences? ✓ Why are these similarities and differences?	学生对两篇有关生态旅游的短文(SAT Critical Reading,2011,详见附录9.1)和两篇有关烟草广告的短文进行对比分析,同样用维恩图或表格总结分析结果,完成任务二

2. Reading to evaluate.

教学内容	注解
❖ Goals for reading to evaluate ✓ Distinguish between an author's use of facts and use of opinion ✓ Distinguish between an author's assumptions and your own ✓ Judge the effectiveness of an explanation ✓ Judge the effectiveness of an argument	
❖ Facts vs. Opinions ✓ A fact is any statement that can be verified. ✓ An opinion is a statement of interpretation and judgment.	为帮助学生区分事实与观点,可以当堂给几个陈述(statements)让学生判断
❖ The author's assumption vs. Your own assumption ✓ Assumption is a fundamental belief that shapes people's views. ✓ You need to identify and determine to what extent you agree or disagree with the author and why. ❖ Judging the effectiveness of an explanation ✓ who are the intended readers——general public / experts / observers / evaluators / supervisors	此处同样可以举例帮助学生理解

(续表)

教学内容	注解
✓ What is defined and explained? Is it successful? ✓ Is the information trustworthy and current? ✓ If a procedure is explained, what is the purpose? Who would carry out the procedure? When? For what reasons? Does the author present the stages?	此处以研究论文里的"研究方法"部分为例,分析如何判断这部分解释的有效性
❖ **Judging the effectiveness of an argument** ✓ What is the author's conclusion? ✓ What reasons/evidences are presented? Are they logical? Has the author acknowledged or responded to other points of view? ✓ Is the writing appealing to your logic, your emotions, or your respect for authorities?	此处以研究论文里的"讨论"部分为例,分析如何判断这部分论证的有效性
❖ **Example of reading to evaluate**	以学生对一个研究的评价为例(例子和点评详见附录9.3),介绍如何进行评价阅读并写笔记

3. Reading to synthesize

教学内容	注解
❖ **Goals for reading to synthesize** ✓ Read to understand, respond to and evaluate multiple texts on a topic, problem, or issue. ✓ Understand your own view or purpose on the topic, problem, or issue. ✓ Forge relationships among text materials, according to your purpose. ✓ Create a conversation among sources.	学生进行整合性阅读时往往没有形成自己的观点,因此在这里有必要强调:必须通过整合阅读形成自己的观点,并以此观点为主线统整所有文献
❖ **Techniques for synthesis** ✓ Cross-reference each part and summarize ✓ Forge relationships among the texts ✓ Organize your ideas by thinking maps	
❖ **Cross-reference** ✓ Read materials from different journals and books ✓ Evaluate materials and think about their relevance to your topic of study ✓ Divide the topic into subtopics ✓ List specific page references to each subtopic ✓ Create an index (or matrix) to your reading selection	

(续表)

教学内容	注解
❖ **Forging relationship** ✓ Comparison; Contrast; Definition; Example; Cause-effect; Personal response	讲完整合阅读的技巧之后,安排学生完成课堂任务三
❖ **Organizing by thinking maps** ✓ Several commonly used thinking maps to display eight logical relationships: circle diagram, tree diagram, star diagram, horizontal tree diagram, circle diagram & network diagram (Kress & van Leeuwen, 1996; Martinec & van Leeuwen, 2008)	
❖ **Examples of reading to synthesize**	以学生对若干文献进行整合阅读后画的思维导图为例(例子和点评详见附录9.4),呈现整合性阅读的成果

(三) 学习任务

任务一

任务内容　学生观看完两个洗发水广告后对比分析其异同点。

任务要点　学生以维恩图或表格的形式将异同点记录下来,并列举产生这些异同点的原因。

任务完成形式/师生互动形式　学生独立完成任务,之后老师以提问的形式检查任务完成情况,并引导学生思考造成广告异同点的深层原因,包括广告的故事内容、人物特点、社会氛围、性别定位、文化价值观等。

任务二

任务内容　学生阅读四篇短文并两两对比,分析其异同点(相关讲义见附录9.1)。

任务要点　学生以维恩图或表格的形式将异同点记录下来,并列举产生这些异同点的原因。

任务完成形式/师生互动形式　可以安排班级讨论分析前两篇短文,后两篇短文的对比分析则由每个学生独立完成,之后老师以提问的形式检查任务完成情况,并引导学生思考造成异同点的深层原因,包括作者的立场和写作目的。

任务三

任务内容　学生阅读几个关于烟草广告与青少年吸烟行为的文本,以思维导图的形式呈现对这些文本的整合理解(相关讲义见附录9.2)。

任务要点　学生练习交叉引用的技巧,包括对文本话题进行分类总结,建立文本间联系,并画出思维导图。

任务完成形式/师生互动形式　学生独立完成任务,之后老师邀请若干学生介绍自己的思维导图,并给予点评。

三、课后作业

(一) 作业内容及要求

Select several research articles on a same research topic and finish these tasks:

A. Analyze the similarities and differences in between these articles and use different visuals (thinking maps) to help organize your thoughts.

B. Develop your thoughts into two paragraphs, one describing the similarities, the other the differences.

(二) 学生作业点评

1. Analyze the similarities and differences in between these articles and use different visuals (thinking maps) to help organize your thoughts.

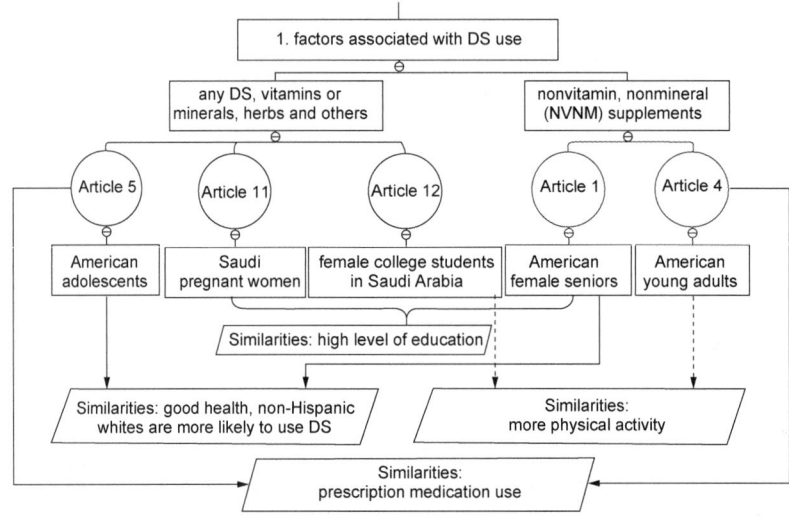

2. Develop your thoughts into two paragraphs, one describing the similarities, the other the differences.

Similarities:

The five articles are similar in study purpose and study design. First, they aimed to investigate the prevalence of dietary supplement (DS) use and analyze the factors associated with this use. Second, all the five articles used questionnaire to collect the relevant information and used descriptive statistics as one of the data analytical methods.

Article 1, article 4 and article 5 conducted their surveys in the United States and used logistic regression in statistics analysis besides descriptive statistics. Article 4 and article 5 come from the same research team (Nancy P Gordon, et al, 2007). Both of them used multivariable logistic regression performed in SAS software to assess factors associated with DS use. Article 11 and article 12 also come from the same research team (Hanan A Alfawaz, et al, 2017). They both conducted a cross-sectional survey in Saudi Arabia. In addition, in these two articles, Pearson Chi-square test performed in SPSS software were used to examine differences between use of dietary supplements and some factors.

Some of them drew the similar results on the factors associated with DS use. Article 1, article 11 and article 12 all supported that higher education was associated with use of DS. High physical activity level was found as one of the factors in article 4 and article 12, while prescription medication use was found in article 4 and article 5. Besides, article 1 and 5 revealed that good health increased likelihood of DS use and non-Hispanic whites were more likely to use DS than other race.

Differences:

There were many differences in these five articles. Firstly, they studied different groups and conducted the survey in different years. Article 1 did the survey among women aged 65-84, while article 4 studied the

DS use of young adults aged 18-30. Article 5 analyzed the data from the 1999-2002 National Health and Nutrition Examination Surveys (NHANES) for adolescents age 11 to 19, whereas article 12 invited 137 pregnant women attending prenatal care from King Salman Hospital to complete the questionnaires in 2016. Secondly, article 1 and article 4 only analyzed the factors associated with nonvitamin, nonmineral (NVNM) supplements, which was different with three other articles. Thirdly, each study had its own distinct findings on the factors associated with DS use. For example, article 4 found that alcohol and smoke may increase the use of DS, which was not mentioned in other articles. Fourthly, the focus of the discussion was also different in five articles.

点评：该学生对所读文献进行仔细分析和对比，基本达到作业要求。思维导图对相似点描绘得较全面，对不同点的分析显得略为单薄。但是段落里对异同点的解释很全面，表述异同点的词句也非常清晰恰当。不足之处在于在分析异同点时尚未形成自己的研究焦点，感觉是为了找异同点而找异同点。当然，学生在刚开始阅读、整合文献时往往未能确定自己的聚焦点，这是普遍存在的现象。

四、课程使用反馈

（一）学生反馈意见

课程反馈（共302名学生参与）信息显示，64%的学生认为本课所学内容对他们未来的专业学习与发展很有帮助，但是仅有45%左右的学生自评自己对此部分的教学内容很有兴趣、学习投入很多、学习收获很大，47%的学生认为多文本阅读技巧难度很大，由此可见多文本阅读与其他学习内容相比难度比较大。

（二）教师反馈意见

课堂学习任务一以洗发水广告为素材，学生反应很热烈，能畅所欲言，原因在于他们觉得对常见的广告进行重新解读非常有意思。任务二共涉及四篇文本，后两篇比较长，要多给学生阅读的时间。在这个任务中，"question the similarities and differences"是一大难点，需要老师多花时间启发。评价性阅读的难点在于如何分清事实与观点，如何在涉及作者的观点或假设时进行评价和质疑。另外，整合性阅读需要安排更多的课堂时间进行口头汇报和讨论，让学生展示他们如何理解所阅读的文献，之后老师需要做出中肯的点评，点评的重点在于引导学生从自己研究的兴趣出发，以及该文献的自身特点，例如相关话题的发展趋势、研究方法来找异同点，而不要盲目地比较异同点。

这一章对授课老师而言是比较大的挑战。学生进行多文本阅读时选题不一，要求老师对每一个选题都有深入了解几乎是不可能的。我们要求学生在指定六大主题的文献库里选择文献进行阅读（有关文献库的建设见第二章），在一定程度上减少了教师的备课压力。同时，我们把选择同一主题的学生分到同一组进行讨论交流，有利于互相启发思路，加深对文献的理解。老师在参加课堂讨论和口头汇报时因势利导，多进行启发性提问。上完本单元后我们感觉和学生一样收获颇丰，尤其是看到学生对同一主题的文献做出各有千秋的解读时，深感教学相长的道理。

附录9.1 学习任务二

（一）任务内容

Read the passages and finish the tasks：

1. Search for similarities and differences between Passage 1 and Passage 2, Passage 3

and Passage 4.

2. Display the similarities and differences in Venn diagram or table chart.

3. Discuss what has caused the similarities and differences.

Passage 1

Ecotourism has been broadly defined as recreational travel that is focused on the natural environment and that seeks to minimize its impact on that environment.

However, there is little doubt that increasing numbers of ecotourists also pose a threat to the quality and sustainability of natural ecosystems. Numerous accounts of tourists' "loving nature to death" have been reported, and concern is growing that ecotourism is becoming nothing more than a "green" label that dresses up exploitative and destructive human behavior. Despite widespread advocacy for education as a solution to minimizing ecotourists' impacts on the natural environment, few tests of the effectiveness of educational programs in controlling tourists' behavior have been conducted.

Passage 2

Although a substantial part of tourism is the "sun, surf, and sand" variety, the fastest-growing segment is ecotourism. There is, however, substantial concern about the potential negative impacts of ecotourism on the environment and about the necessity to plan and regulate ecotourism to prevent them. There clearly have been abuses and mismanaged activities. Better planning and regulation are essential. Yet ecotourism brings many people into environments in which they can learn about the locale and learn environmental principles that can heighten their awareness of and commitment to environmental protection in general. Increased emphasis on environmental learning as part of ecotourism could help prevent or reduce ecotourism's negative impacts.

(From SAT Critical Reading, January, 2011, http: //ishare. iask. sina. com. cn/f/33698966. html)

Passage 3

Even if a teenager has no intention to start smoking, tobacco advertising and promotional items can lead one-third of them to try, according to an article in the February 18 issue of *The Journal of the American Medical Association* (*JAMA*).

John P. Pierce, Ph. D., from the University of California, San Diego, in La Jolla, and colleagues conducted the first longitudinal study on the effect of cigarette promotion on teenagers. In 1993, they interviewed 1,752 California adolescents (age 12 to 17 years old) who had never smoked and who had said they had no plans to start smoking, even if a friend offers them a cigarette. The adolescents were reinterviewed in 1996.

They write: "From these data, we estimate that 34 percent of all experimentation in California between 1993 and 1996 can be attributed to tobacco promotional activities."

The researchers found that those who had a favorite cigarette advertisement in 1993 were twice as likely as those who did not, to either have started smoking by 1996 or were willing to start smoking.

Those who owned a cigarette promotional item or who were willing to use one in 1993 were nearly three times as likely to progress to smoking by 1996 than those unwilling to use a cigarette promotional item.

The researchers write: "This longitudinal study provides clear evidence that tobacco industry advertising and promotional activities can influence nonsusceptible never smokers to start the process or becoming addicted to cigarettes... Our data establish that the influence of tobacco promotional activities was present before adolescents showed any susceptibility to become smokers."

They also write: "Exposure to other smokers in this analysis does not appear to significantly influence which adolescents begin the smoking uptake process, which is somewhat contradictory to previous studies."

(From Tobacco ads, promotional items linked with teen smoking, Science News Update, American Medical Association)

Passage 4

Several studies have found that teenagers who smoke (or who say they might) are more apt to recall cigarette advertising and to view it favorably. Such findings do not necessarily mean that advertising makes adolescents more likely to smoke. It is just as plausible to suppose that teenagers pay more attention to cigarette ads after they start smoking, or that teenagers who inclined to smoke for other reasons are also more likely to have a positive view of cigarette ads.

In reporting on research in this area, the mainstream press tends to ignore such alternative interpretations, consider the coverage of 1995 study published in the Journal of the National Cancer Institute. The study, co-authored by John Pierce, found that teenagers who scored high on a "receptivity" index—which included "recognition of advertising messages, having a favorite advertisement, naming a brand [they] might buy, owning a tobacco-related promotional item, an willingness to use a tobacco-related promotional item" ——were more likely to say they could not rule out smoking in the near future. Such "receptivity" was more strongly associated with an inclination to smoke than was smoking among parents and peers.

According to the New York Times, these results meant that "[t]obacco advertising is a stronger factor than peer pressure in encouraging children under 18 to smoke." In reality, the study showed only that teenagers who like smoking-related messages and merchandise are more receptive to the idea of smoking—not exactly a startling finding.

(From Cowboys, cameels, and kids, Jacob Sullum.)

(二) 参考答案

Passage 1 vs. Passage 2

The similarities and differences between Passage 1 and Passage 2 are displayed in the venn diagram below.

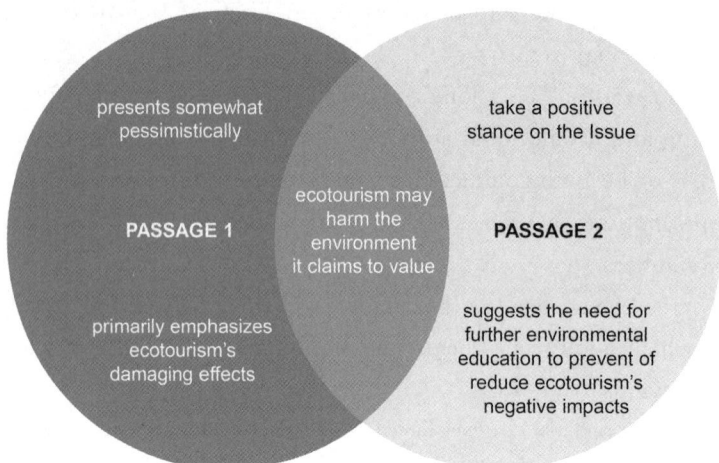

The authors of both passages realize the harmful effects of ecotourism on environment, but they view this issue from different stances, hence the focus on the damaging effects in Passage 1 and the emphasis of environmental education to support ecotourism in Passage 2.

Passage 3 vs. Passage 4

The similarities and differences between Passage 3 and Passage 4 are displayed in the table below.

		Passage 3	Passage 4
Similarity	Citation	Both cite data reported by John Pierce and his colleagues.	
Differences	The author's stances	Endorses the findings, points to cause-and-effect relationship without critical comments	Acknowledges a correlation but not causation relationship
	The evidences	Report quotes extensively	Quotes only briefly
	The writing purposes	To neutrally summarize the article for general readers	To criticize

Even though both passages are reporting on two separate studies, the findings of each of these studies are so close that they are virtually identical. So, both passages focus on similar information about advertising and teenager smoking.

Obviously the two passages draw very different conclusions from the findings of Pierce and his colleagues. Passage 3 essentially states that tobacco advertising has a strong influence in terms of making adolescents open to smoking. Passage 4, on the other hand, suggests that as young people become more receptive to the idea of smoking, they respond more positively to cigarette advertising and promotion.

附录9.2 学习任务三

(一) 任务内容

Read the excerpts on the topic of teenage smoking, divide the excerpts into different subtopics and use a tree map to make connections across the excerpts.

1. You have to give advertising some credit: It has helped to transform what might otherwise seem a strange and nasty habit-the deliberate inhalation of noxious fumes, followed by a bit of littering-into something with a certain glamorous allure. This little bit of glamour-heightened by the cigarette's bad-boy (and bad-girl) image in popular culture, may be enough of a lure to get a certain number of new smokers hooked every year. But ads aren't the only reason young people light up, and restrictions on ads often prove ineffective. In Canada, the percentage of smokers has actually *increased* slightly in the eight years since the country instituted a cigarette ad ban.

——DAVID FUTRELLE, "Smoke and Mirrors" (1997)

2. Eighty-six percent of youth (12-17) smokers prefer Marlboro, Camel and Newport-the three most heavily advertised brands. Marlboro, the most heavily advertised brand, constitutes almost 55 percent of the youth market but only 35 percent of smokers over age 25.

——CAMPAIGN FOR TOBACCO-FREE KIDS, Tobacco Use among Youth" (2000)

3. Research indicates that the most important factors influencing whether a teenager will smoke are the behavior of his peers, his perceptions of the risks and benefits of smoking, and the presence of smokers in his home. Exposure to advertising does not independently predict the decision to smoke, and smokers themselves rarely cite advertising as an important influence on their behavior.

Critics of the industry have been quick to seize upon studies indicating that teenage smokers disproportionately prefer the most advertised cigarette brands. But such research suggests only that advertising has an impact on brand preferences, which the tobacco companies have conceded all along.

——JACOB SULLUM, "Cowboys, Camels, and Kids" (1998)

4. A long-term decline in trends of both per capita cigarette consumption and in the proportion of adolescents initiating smoking started in 1973, shortly after the advertising ban on the broadcast media... Recently released confidential tobacco industry documents clearly indicate the concern of senior members of the tobacco industry shortly after this decline became manifest and reveal their solution to focus on the youth market.

The major innovative campaign, predicted by these confidential industry documents, was the Joe Camel campaign, which was launched in 1987... This cartoon character was very attractive to young children as well as to young adolescents, and it was noted that increases in market share had occurred mainly in younger smokers. The unprecedented decline in adolescent smoking over a 12-year period was halted, and the incidence of initiation of smoking in the 14- to 17-year old age group began to increase again.

——JOHN PIERCE,"*Advertising and Promotion*"(1998)

5. The tobacco industry starts early in aiming its six-billion-dollar-a-year advertising and promotional programs at your children. Until recently they have used cartoon characters for the young ones and awarded prizes (gym bags,hats,t-shirts and other gear) that appeal to teen smokers. Young children are the target of their business minds as they attempt to replace smokers who die or quit with new and younger ones. *Advertisers know that nearly all first use of tobacco occurs before high-school graduation and that children are the chief source of new customers.*

——ROBERT SCHWEBEL,"*Preventing Tobacco Problems*",

Saying No Is Not Enough (1998)

(These excerpts are adopted from Rosen & Behrens,2003,pp. 32-33.)

(二) 参考答案

These excerpts can be divided into 3 subtopics:① Connections between advertising and smoking;② Evidence that tobacco advertisers target teenagers; and ③ Evidence that advertising does/does not influence young people to smoke. Their connection can be displayed in the following tree map.

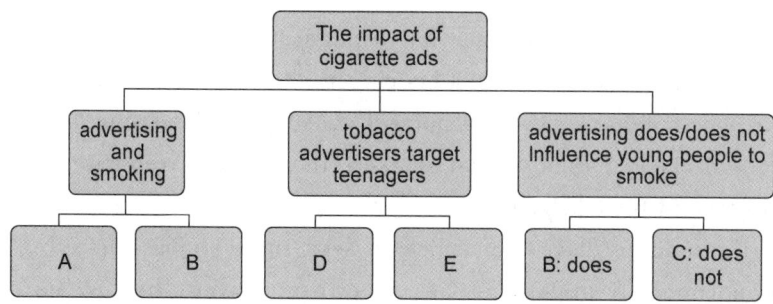

附录9.3 评价性阅读笔记实例点评

The use of Dietary Supplements (DS) during the previous 12 months was ascertained through 2 questions from the general survey:"have you used the following 19 different complementary and alternative medicine (CAM) modalities to help treat or prevent health problem" and "did you use any nutritional supplements in the past 12 months". As DS is a subset of CAM and the second question provided a comprehensive checklist including common DS and a space to write in other supplements,the results may reflect the actual pattern of DS use in female seniors. However,since this study was conducted in nearly 15 years ago,the self-reported data it utilized was even more ancient,and the study population was restricted to one specific area,its results should be interpreted with caution. (Reading notes from a SUMC student,used here with permission.)

点评：这段文字是学生是针对某篇文献的研究方法部分进行的评价。阅读笔记的第二句对研究所使用的问卷的信度进行评价;第三句对研究的时效性进行评价;第四句对研究的可推广性做了评价。这些点评体现了该研究对其研究主题的参考价值,在后期文献综述的作业里,该学生对此文献只是点到即止,没有过多引用。

附录9.4 整合性阅读思维导图实例点评

例1

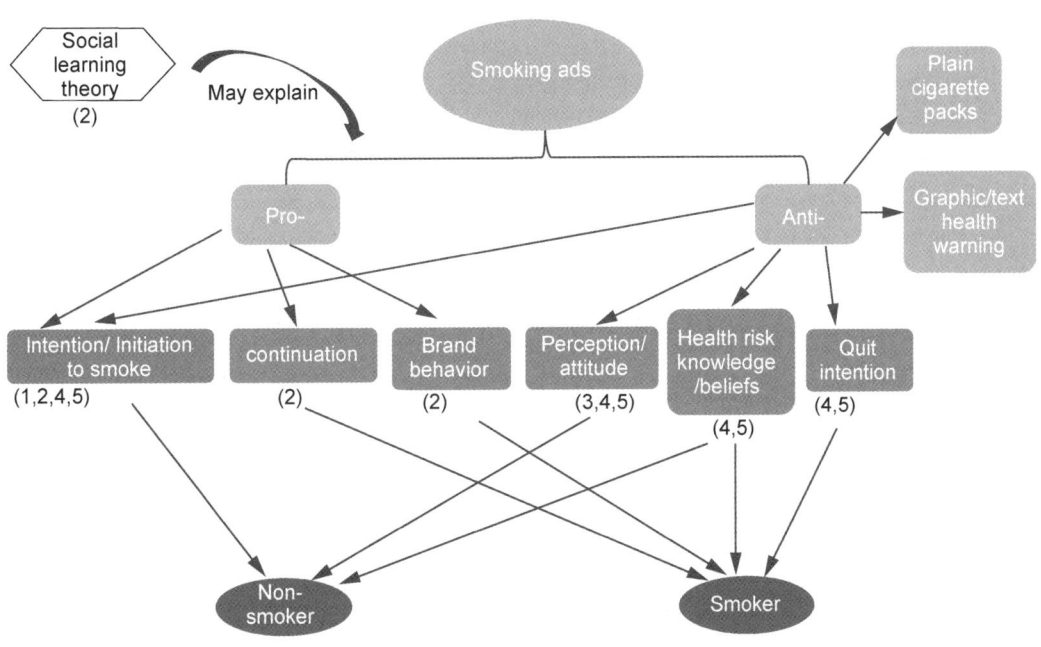

点评:学生对烟草广告的大主题进行更细的主题切割,先分出促进吸烟和反对吸烟两大类,之后进一步区分这两大类研究所涉及的具体主题。该学生还注明可以用 social learning theory 来解释烟草广告对吸烟行为的影响,说明他在看文献的过程中开始形成自己的分析框架。但是,美中不足的是他尚未形成自己对研究主题的观点,因此未能从导图看到更成熟的思路。

例2

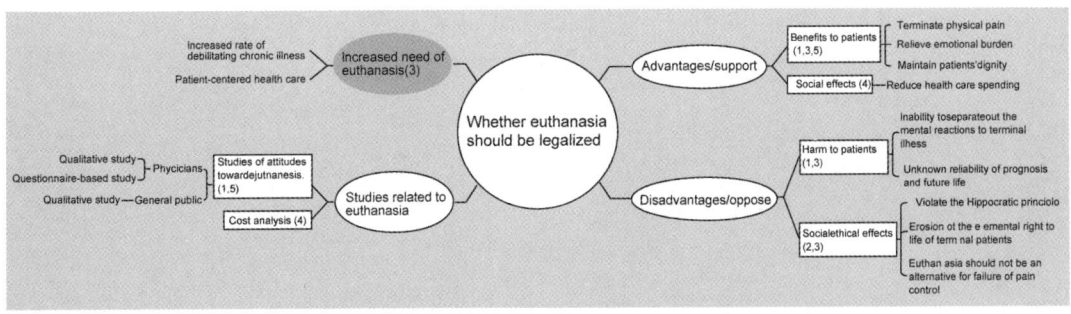

点评:学生在写这个思维导图时已经形成研究问题的思路,即思维导图的中心:Whether euthanasia should be legalized。围绕这个问题,她将文献整理到四大板块,然后再细分。这是一份完成得比较好的整合性阅读笔记,不仅体现出对文献的分析和整合,还以研究问题为主线统整所有文献。

参考文献

Allen G, 2000. Intertextuality. New York: Routledge.

Karimi MN, 2017. The mediated/unmediated contributions of language proficiency and prior knowledge to L2 multiple-texts comprehension: A structural equation modelling analysis. Applied Linguistics: 1-22.

Kress G, van Leeuwen T, 1996. Reading Images: The Grammar of Visual Design. London: Routledge.

Martinec R, van Leeuwen T, 2008. The Language of New Media Design. London: Routledge.

Rosen LJ, Behrens L, 2003. The Allyn and Bacon Handbook. 5th ed. New York: Longman.

Segev-Miller R, 2007. Cognitive processes in discourse synthesis: The case of intertextual processing strategies. // Torrance M, van Waes L, Galbraith D. Writing and cognition: Research and applications. Amsterdam: Elsevier, 231-250.

Sullum J, 1998. Cowboys, camels, and kids. Reason, April. Extract from Science News Update: Tobacco ads, promotional items linked with teen smoking. Journal of the American Medical Association, 279: 32-39.

第十章 同义转化技巧

余 凡 赖佩芳

一、教学主题和教学思路的解读

本章和第十一章都聚焦学术写作中的引用策略(citation strategies)，本章先概述引用策略，然后重点讲述同义转化技巧。

（一）教学主题

1. 引用策略概述：多数学生对引用的意义认识较为片面，局限地认为它只是避免抄袭和认可其他研究的手段。事实上，引用有着更丰富和深刻的意涵。学术写作中的引用不只提供参考来源，还可建立并呈现其他研究之间，以及我们的研究与其他研究之间的关联。它有助于作者将自己的研究置于广泛的学术图景中，在某一领域内创建一种深入、生动对话的关系网格(Lingard,2018)。引用可以让作者更深思熟虑地探究问题、建立文本间的联系和对话、认可前人和其他研究者的观点和贡献、深化推进研究（Hyland,2004；Swales 及 Feak, 2004）。引用可以为我们的论述提供论据支撑，让我们的论点更为有力，让我们自己的观点与其他观点互相争鸣，在与其他观点的沟通、辩论或交锋中推动理论发展。学术写作的引用充分体现了学术文本的社会性和交互功能（Hyland,2004）。

这部分的教学目的是让学生对引用策略有一个全面的认识，理解为什么学术写作中需要引用策略，以及辨别各种基础概念，如引用格式和引用策略的区别，何为直接引用、同义转化、概述和综述。我们需要向学生解释各种引用策略如何服务于不同的写作目的：需要体现原文的重要细节的时候，就用同义转化；只需提供原文大意时，更适合概述；原文表达生动，精练，直接引用更佳；需要多个来源来论证观点，则用综述。

2. 同义转化：同义转化指的是改写，或"翻译"他人的观点，将其转化成引用者自己的文字，字数与原文大致相同(Swales 及 Feak,2004)。本章的教学主题是帮助学生了解同义转化的意义，在何种语境需使用同义转化，以及使用当中要避开哪些误区，从而掌握正确使用同义转化的技巧与步骤。

在同义转化中，有些学生对原文没有真正理解，只是机械地把原文的一些词语换成同义词，这其实是一种变相的抄袭，称为"plagiphrasing"，因为其结构与原文结构过于近似(Wilson,1997)。在表达上做到与原文不同，一来可以避免抄袭，更重要的是，这才是同义转化的本质——保留与原文同样的含义，但转化为与原文不同的结构形式，同时还要注意使用规范的学术语言。

（二）教学思路

要恰当、有效地进行同义转化，学生需要具备较强的语言能力。教学时理论部分尽量做到重点突出，简明扼要，给学生更多的机会练习，让他们在做中学，以理论指导实践，经实践促进认知。本章在学生每学习一个重点概念或者原则的时候,都提供了相应的范例、练习、课堂互评和教师反馈。每一次举例也作为训练,让学生讨论或者提出自己的意见,推动学生积极思考。例子与练习由易到难,从普通学术英语到医学论文中摘录的语句,让学生得到不同维度的锻炼。

二、教学案例设计

(一)教学目标

1. 学生对引用策略有一个全面基础的认识,包括理解引用策略的意义、认识文内引用和文后引用、区分引用格式和引用策略、辨别各种引用策略。
2. 学生能够掌握同义转化的概念、区分同义转化与其他引用策略的使用目的。
3. 学生能够了解同义转化的基本原则与步骤。
4. 学生能够评判他人的同义转化,也能够写出符合要求的同义转化。

(二)教学内容

1. Citation Strategies—Overview

教学内容	注解
❖ **Why do we cite**? ✓ To give credit where it's due/to avoid plagiarism ✓ To define and establish intellectual contexts ✓ To response to previous research statements ✓ To embed arguments and recreate a sense of lively debate ✓ To lead us to further research	
❖ **What is citation**? ✓ A citation is a reference to the source of information used in your research. ✓ Any time you directly quote, paraphrase or summarize the essential elements of someone else's idea in your work, an in-text citation should follow. ✓ In-text citation: a brief notation within the text of your paper or presentation ✓ End-of-paper citation: a fuller notation that provides all necessary details about that source of information	
❖ **Text citation strategies ≠ Citation Styles/format** ✓ Text citation strategies: paraphrasing, summarizing, quoting, synthesizing ✓ Citation Styles/format: eg. AMA—American Medical Association Manual of Style, APA—American Psychological Association (APA), MLA—Modern Language Association	

(续表)

教学内容	注解
❖ **Defining each strategy** √ Paraphrasing：rewriting, or "translating", someone else's ideas into your own words in approximately the same number of words as the original text √ Summarizing：summing up the main ideas of an author or the essence of their arguments, always substantially shorter than the length of original text √ Quoting：copying short sentences or passages from the original text word-for-word √ Synthesizing：summarizing and including multiple sources to support your arguments	
❖ **Selecting different citation strategies for different writing purposes** √ Paraphrasing：to elaborate the main argument with details √ Summarizing：to give the main argument √ Direct quotation：to use the originally expressive language and to add weight to your argument √ Synthesizing：to combine multiple sources to emphasize one point	本部分解释引用策略的重要性,介绍引用策略定义,区分引用策略与引用格式,并简介四种引用策略。这里除了参考 Hyland（2004）、Swales（1987,1990）、Swales 及 Feak（2004）,还参考了一些大学的网络学习资源,如耶鲁大学的 Poorvu 教学中心、纽约州立大学帝国州立学院的网络图书馆、墨尔本大学学术技能中心等,详见参考文献
❖ **Discussion：Which citation strategy will you use?**	讨论环节：教师举例,让学生讨论哪个例子适合何种引用策略,促进理解。此处完成学习任务一

2. **What is paraphrasing?**

教学内容	注解
❖ **The definition of paraphrasing** √ A paraphrase is a restatement (in your own words) of the ideas in the original (Swales & Feak, 2004, p. 158)	引入概念
❖ **The importance of learning paraphrasing** √ It is an important and frequently used citation strategy √ We must know how to paraphrase correctly ——when to paraphrase ——how to paraphrase √ To report findings, support our arguments and join the debate on related academic topics	阐明学习同义转化的重要性

3. Paraphrasing—principles

教学内容	注解
❖ **What do we need to avoid in paraphrasing?** ✓ Avoid replacing words in the original text with synonyms ✓ Avoid using computer or online thesauruses for word choice without understanding the contexts	
❖ **What should we follow in paraphrasing?** ✓ Alter the wording of the passage without changing its meaning ✓ Retain the basic logic of the argument ✓ Keep the basic sequence of ideas ✓ Retain the basic examples used in the passage ✓ Accurately convey the author's meaning and opinion	本部分强调同义转化的原则，提醒学生应该避开哪些误区，并介绍正确的同义转化技巧
❖ **Discussion：Is it properly paraphrased?**	讨论环节：教师举例，让学生对比原文和同义转化的例子，判断该转化是否正确。此处完成学习任务二和任务三

4. Paraphrasing—steps

教学内容	注解
❖ **What steps should we take in paraphrasing?** ✓ Step 1：Read — read important parts of the source material until you fully understand its meaning and the relationship between parts ✓ Step 2：Note — take down the key terms of source material ✓ Step 3：Write — write your own version without looking at the source material, only referring to the key terms ✓ Step 4：Check — if your version captures important parts and intent of the source material; if you have changed the structure and expressions; if you have reference indicating where your paraphrasing starts and ends using in-text citation ✓ Step 5：Edit — edit your paraphrasing until you are satisfied	举例说明同义转化是一个从理解、动笔、修改至完善的过程
❖ **Example & Practice**	每一步举例都先让学生思考练习；所有步骤讲完再做练习巩固技巧。此处完成学习任务四

(三) 学习任务

任务一：选择适用的引用策略

任务内容　Which citation strategy will you use?

例1：The history of all hitherto existing society is the history of class struggles. (Karl Marx,1948)

例2：Scientists today called for tighter controls on the use of nanotechnology, but said it had the potential to greatly benefit many areas of science and industry. (Tavender,2004)

任务要点　学生阅读两个例子，讨论各自适用的引用策略，同时必须提供恰当的引用。

任务完成形式/师生互动形式　① 学生讨论完成后在堂上回答，教师给予反馈：第一个是马克思的历史观，原文语言简洁精辟，更适合使用直接引用；第二个例子可以根据引用的目的，如果希望保留细节，就使用同义转化，如果只要传达大意，就用概述。② 教师请学生提供正确的引用表达，并给出参考答案：

√ Direct quotation for e. g. 1：As Karl Marx(1948) wrote,"The history of all hitherto existing society is the history of class struggles."

√ Paraphrasing for e. g. 2：While suggesting stricter monitoring on the use of nanotechnology, scientists still believed that it will possibly bring about big improvement in many area of science and industry (Tavender,2004).

√ Summarizing for e. g. 2：Scientists observed both the potential benefits and the necessity for control in the use of nanotechnology (Tavender,2004).

任务二：避开同义转化的误区——plagiphrasing

任务内容　Is it properly paraphrased?

原句　The meetings tourism market has been vigorously pursued by many former industrial cities in Europe and the U. S. as part of their strategies of post-industrial urban regeneration.

同义转化句　The meetings tourism industry has been energetically sought by several historically industrial cities in Europe and the U. S. as one element of their plan of post-industrial metropolitan rebuilding.

(Swales 及 Feak,2004,p. 158)

任务要点　学生阅读原句和同义转化句，讨论该转化是否正确，如正确，请说明理由，如错误，请写出正确的转化句。

任务完成形式/师生互动形式　学生讨论后在堂上回答，教师反馈，该转化句是错误的。因为句子结构基本上没改变，只是把一些词语换成同义词，这正是同义转化应该避免的做法。正确的转化应该是：Many cities in the U. S. and Europe that once relied on heavy industry are now trying to revitalize themselves by developing a meetings tourism industry.

任务三：避开同义转化的误区——口语化表述

任务内容　Is it properly paraphrased?

原句　Employers must ensure staff have healthy options through the day. (Smith,2009,p. 12).

同义转化句 1　Bosses have to make sure staff eat good food all the time.

同义转化句 2　Employees should be supplied with healthy choices by their management. (Smith, 2009)

任务要点　学生阅读原句以及两个同义转化句,讨论两句转化是否正确。如果正确,请说明原因,如果都错误,请给出正确的转化句。

任务完成形式/师生互动形式　学生讨论后在堂上回答,教师反馈:同义转化句1是错误的,因为该句是口语化表达,并非学术英语,而且缺乏文内引用。同义转化句2正确,因为该句转换了结构,用词也不同,既没有改变原文的含义,又能正确使用文内引用,而且表达是规范的学术语言。

(注:任务二与三都有共同的目标,即如何避开同义转化的误区,并给出正确的同义转化范例。)

任务四:同义转化的步骤

任务内容　Read—Note—Write—Check—Edit

Original: To the extent that a woman's self-image is challenged or threatened by an unattainable ideal of an impossibly thin female physique, she may well become susceptible to disruption of her self-regard, and may be more likely to develop an eating disorder (Polivy & Herman, 2004, p. 2).

任务要点　让学生体验同义转化的分解步骤。第一步为Read,让学生正确理解原文内容和内在逻辑。第二步为Note,掌握关键细节。第三步为Write,抛开原文,写同义转化句。第四步为Check,让学生自我检查所写句子有没有具备该有的元素。第四步为Edit,根据检查结果,以及相关准则,把句子修改至满意。

任务完成形式/师生互动形式

第一步:Read。学生阅读原文,理解大意后,使用自己语言(中英文均可)口头表达原文意思。教师反馈,并提示学生应当注意原文段的内在逻辑,如因果、转折、举例、列举等。这有助于学生结构性地理解文本。在本文段中,内在的逻辑关系为因果关系:cause, the self-image of a woman being threatened or challenged by an unachievable concept of getting an impossibly thin female physique; effect, the possibility that she might turn out to become susceptible towards disruption of her self-respect, and end up developing an eating disorder。

第二步:Note。学生做笔记,记下关键词。关键词代表了文本的重要细节。教师提问学生后反馈:参考关键词为self-image, threatened or challenged, impossibly thin female physique, disruption of self-respect, eating disorder。

此步骤主要目的在于使学生在进行下一步转写时不看原文,只看笔记里的关键词。这样可以避免受到原文的影响。教师提醒学生在不过度依赖原文的同时,不忽略重要细节。如果学生具备了这个意识,该步骤中可以简化成在原文上做标记。

第三步:Write。学生在理解的基础上,根据核心词汇进行同义转化。

第四步:Check。学生在教师指引下自我检查。教师给学生提供一个检查的框架:

A. Content: Does your version capture the intent and important parts of the source material?

B. Structure: Have you changed the structure and expressions?

C. Reference: Have you used in-text citation to indicate where your paraphrasing starts and ends and acknowledged the contribution of the original?

此时教师可以邀请学生分享所写的转化句并邀请其他同学点评。点评完后教师提供修改建议。如果学生觉得困难,教师也可以举例,让学生分析这些转化是否恰当。如:

Paraphrasing sample 1:The self-perception of a woman is decreased by an unachievable goal of getting an impossibly slim feminine figure. As a result, she may turn out to become sensitive towards disruption of her self-respect, and may end up having an bad eating disorder.

Paraphrasing sample 2:If a woman realizes the ideal thinness of the female figure far beyond reach in reality, she might become fragile.

Sample 1 只是简单转化一些词语为同义词,原句式基本没变。Sample 2 有改变句子结构,且有把大部分表达同义转化,但内容不完整。而且两个转化句子都没有文内引用,所以都不正确。指出错误后教师可以和学生探讨该如何修改。

第五步:Edit。学生独立修改自己的句子。教师可以再邀请学生分享其修改后的转化句。然后给出参考版本:If a woman realizes the ideal thinness of the female figure far beyond reach in reality, she might become fragile, with her self-esteem melting down and developing disruptive eating behavior (Herman 及 Polivy, 2007, p. 3).

(四) 课后作业

同义转化练习

1. Less widely known is that proven methods of prevention and early detection could further reduce the incidence of adult cancers in the U.S. by at least a third to a half and reduce cancer deaths by ≥50%. (Golemis et al., 2018, p. 868)

2. Exposure to a carcinogen can precede the development of cancer by decades or even a generation and may be influential only at a specific developmental stage (Golemis et al., 2018, p. 870)

3. A group of cancer risk factors that includes obesity, diet, and physical inactivity was first identified in affluent industrialized countries and is seen increasingly in populations around the world. (Golemis et al., 2018, p. 877)

4. Despite such success, it is probably fair to say that only by the broader use of proven methods of prevention and early detection, together with treatment, can one guarantee major reductions in current U.S. cancer death rates in the coming two decades. (Golemis et al., 2018, p. 893)

参考答案

1. 30%~50% of adult cancers and half of cancer fatalities could be avoided, with proper prevention and timely detection in America, but fewer people realize that. (Golemis et al., 2018, p. 868)

2. The impact of carcinogen exposure varies from occurring many years later or even across a generation to happening only at a certain developmental stage. (Golemis et al., 2018, p. 870)

3. Factors like obesity, poor diet and insufficient exercise, are now becoming the cause of cancer globally, though the first connection was found in developed countries. (Golemis

et al.,2018,p. 877)

4. The only way to minimize U. S. cancer deaths in the next twenty years is to promote proper prevention, timely identification and medical care, instead of being complacent about previous achievement. (Golemis et al.,2018,p. 893)

(五)课后作业范例与点评

1. Fewer people in America are aware that proper prevention and timely detection could reduce 30%—50% of adult cancers and half of cancer fatalities. (Golemis et al.,2018,p. 868)

点评:该句对原文的结构有所改变,如被动语态转化为主动语态;细节上对核心词汇,如名词、动词以及数词皆有恰当的同义转述;且有文内引用。不过,整体结构的变动不够大,建议有更大的结构性转变。其中 reduce 可以换成 avoid,或 prevent,避免与原文雷同。

2. People who are exposed to carcinogens or even their next generation can be influenced by carcinogens years later when cancer develops to a certain stage. (Golemis et al.,2018,p. 870)

点评:该句的"when cancer develops to a certain stage"成为整句的条件句,这与原文不符。原文的 when 引导的从句内容,与之前的内容是一个递进的关系。建议改为 People might have cancer many years or even one generation after their contact with carcinogens, and they can be affected only at a certain developmental stage. (Golemis et al.,2018,p. 870)

3. Obesity, unhealthy diet and insufficient exercise, the first-found risk factors contributing to cancer, are worldwide risk nowadays.

点评:首先,句子没有文内引用;同时也缺失一些原句的信息,如"affluent industrialized countries" "seen increasingly";加之还有语法和逻辑问题,如前面的"risk factors"搭配后面 worldwide risk。建议改为 Problems like obesity, unhealthy diet and insufficient exercise are becoming global caner risk factors nowadays, though they originated in developed countries. (*Golemis et al.*,2018,*p.* 877)

4. In the following 20 years, right prevention measures, early detection and medical care is the only way to reduce US cancer death rather than being satisfied with previous achievement.

点评:该句在结构上有所调整。但是,该句缺少了文内引用;语言上有语法错误,如系动词 is,还有 death 都应该是复数形式。另外,right 建议改为 correct 或者 proper,detection 最好换成 diagnosis 或 identification。整体修改可看该句参考答案(见"(四)"部分的参考答案)。

三、案例使用反馈

(一)学生反馈意见

完成本节课后,绝大部分学生表示学习引用策略对他们的学术英语写作很有帮助。学生表示,paraphrasing 最大的好处就是在写文章的时候用得特别多,学习时觉得课程可能有些枯燥,但是用的时候觉得很有用。大部分同学认为老师们提供的练习难度适中,部分同学表示有些难度,但可以克服。在同义转化过程中,他们碰到的问题有:① 词汇量不足;② 分析句子结构有难度;③ 不确定多大程度地使用同义转述以及保留原文;④ 不确定何时需要原文表述,何时需要同义转述;⑤ 有些专业内容难以理解。

(二)教师反馈意见

本章的重点是再现原句的核心内容,难点是在不曲解原文的基础上用自己的语言表达。在理论部分,要强调转述与其他引用策略的区别;以及如何避开转化的误区,正确地实现同义转化。但是理论部分需要简洁明了,给学生更多的机会练习,学会自评、互评、自我修改和改善表述。在练习环节,一定要调动学生的积极性,让他们自己动手写,然后通过小组讨论、同伴互评、班上点评、教师反馈等方式进行优化，并鼓励写得好的同学分享经验，让学生感觉到同义转化有技巧和原则可循，只要掌握了正确的方法，有足够的练习和经验，就能越写越好。另外，正确的理解需要和阅读相结合，实际上，每一篇学术论文里都有很多同义转化的表达，要鼓励学生在课外多阅读，多体会。

参考文献

Germain D, Hons B, Wakefield MA, et al., 2010. Adolescents' Perceptions of Cigarette Brand Image: Does Plain Packaging Make a Difference? Journal of Adolescent Health, 46: 385-392.

Golemis EA, Paul S, Beck TN, et al., 2018. Molecular mechanisms of the preventable causes of cancer in the United States. Genes & Development, 32: 868-893.

Herman CP, Polivy J, 2007. Norm-violation, norm-adherence, and overeating. Collegium antropologicum, 31(1): 55-62.

Hyland K, 2004. Disciplinary discourses: Social interaction in academic writing. Ann Arbor: University of Michigan Press.

Lingard L, 2018. Writing an effective literature review. Perspectives on Medical Education, 7, 133-135.

Polivy J, Herman CP, 2004. Sociocultural idealization of thin female body shapes: An introduction to the special issue on body image and eating disorders. Journal of Social and Clinical Psychology, 23(1): 1-6.

Research Skills Tutorial, esc. edu [2019-11]. https://subjectguides.esc.edu/researchskillstutorial/citation-parts.

Swales JM, 1987. Citation analysis and discourse analysis. Applied linguistics, 7 (1): 40-56.

Swales JM, 1990. Genre analysis: English in academic and research settings. Cambridge: Cambridge University Press.

Swales JM, Feak CB, 2004. Academic writing for graduate students: Essential tasks and skills. 2nd ed. Ann Arbor: University of Michigan Press.

Tavender R, 2004. Big future for nanotechnology. The Guardian. https://www.theguardian.com/education/2004/jul/29/highereducation.uk2.

Voice in Academic Writing, unimelb. edu. au [2019-11]. https://services.unimelb.edu.au/__data/assets/pdf_file/0004/471298/Voice_in_Academic_Writing_Update_051112.pdf.

Wilson K, 1997. Can note-taking solve the plagiphrasing problem? EA Journal, 15(1): 43-49.

Why Cite Sources in Your Academic Writing? poorvucenter. yale. edu [2019-11]. https://poorvucenter.yale.edu/writing/using-sources/principles-citing-sources/why-cite.

第十一章 文献概述技巧

赖佩芳 余 凡

一、对教学主题和教学思路的解读

文献概述既是一种引用策略,也是一种写作策略,广义上讲,也是一种学习方法。该方法既可用于较为私人的学习目的,比如为备考、参加小组讨论或撰写论文所写的资料总结,也可用于公开的学术交流场景,比如,在课程作业和文献综述中,文献概述是必不可少的一部分(Swales 及 Feak,2004)。为完成研究论文而搜集和提炼信息时就更需要文献概述,特别是当原文作为整体与我们自己的研究密切相关,却又因篇幅太长而不适合同义转述或直接引用时,文献概述就大有用武之地。概述写作是学术写作训练的重要内容,因此我们专门在本章中加以介绍。

(一) 教学主题

文献概述就是用自己的语言高度凝练地概括、重述原文的要旨和关键脉络(Swales 及 Feak,2004)。写成后的文献概述篇幅可长可短,完全取决于使用的目的和场景。在实际应用中,文献概述对原文篇幅浓缩的力度应结合具体的写作目的、写作任务要求、投稿刊物指引等因素综合考虑。本章的主要教学内容是文献概述的基本概念、应用目的和场景、写作标准和适当的步骤和技巧,以期学生写出准确、简洁、完整、符合规范的文献概述。

(二) 教学思路

Swales 及 Feak(2004)在专著中专辟一章讲述如何写文献概述,并设计了非常好的概述写作练习。本章主要从教学的角度出发,旨在由简入繁,帮助授课教师理清教学思路,在有限的授课时间内对概述的写作目的、要求、步骤和技巧做全面介绍,并结合适量练习,帮助学生初步掌握概述技巧,以便在课程的其他学习阶段加以有效运用。

我们在教学中先从一句话概述(one-sentence summary)入手,这其中又包括在句子层面的一句话概述和对较长原文的一句话概述;再进阶到一段话概述(one-paragraph summary),而后推进到到较长文本的概述,继而深入扩展到对学术论文各个部分的概述。

本章的选材和练习尤为重要。在语言处理的层面上,从短到长,由浅入深;练习的类型从有教师指引的练习逐渐过渡到学生自主完成的练习;任务的设置既有个人任务,又有小组任务,个人自主学习和小组合作学习相结合;写作步骤贯穿从写前规划到写后修改、反思、讨论分享的全过程;反馈方式包括同伴互评、组间互评、教师反馈、师生协商等。通过这样的教学设计思路,使文献概述成为一个植根现实学术场景、动态互动、自我协商、不断反思的开放式写作和学习过程。

我们在教学中注重该章与整个课程主线的横向联系,向学生清楚展示其上承同义转化,下接综述写作的重要位置。课后的扩展作业是对研究论文的不同部分进行概述,要求学生将其与之前所学的语步分析结合起来,确保在文献概述中涵盖研究论文各个部分的主要语步、忠实体现研究论文各部分的修辞功能。在语言表达方面,要求学生在文献概述的写作中继续体现在之前阶段所学的学术语言特点,以巩固所学,温故知新。

二、文献概述技巧教学案例

(一) 教学目标

1. 学生能够了解文献概述的标准和应用场景并在相关的学术场景中有意识地应用这一策略。

2. 学生能够透彻理解文献概述与其他引用策略(如同义转述、直接引用、文献综述)的异同。

3. 学生能够根据写作场景和目的运用适当的策略和步骤将篇章提炼成各种长度的文献概述,包括一句话、一段话或较长篇章的文献概述。

4. 能够在熟知研究论文的 IMRD(introduction, nethods, results, discussion)结构和分析论文各部分语步(move)的基础上,运用绘制思维导图等策略,将原文提炼写成一篇文献概述。

(二) 教学内容

1. Basic concepts of summaries.

教学内容	注解
❖ **Basic purposes and uses of summaries**: ✓ Collecting and condensing information for research papers ✓ Using the work of others to support your own view ✓ Integrating sources into your writing ✓ Explaining the content of the reading to someone who has not read it ✓ Taking notes on your readings / lectures ✓ Reviewing texts for exam	文献概述的应用场景丰富多样,应向学生强调概述技巧既可自成一体成为一项单独的小作业,也可作为一篇较长论文的一部分

2. Criteria of summaries

教学内容	注解
❖ **What makes a good summary**? ✓ Accuracy 　• Did you report the author's ideas accurately? ✓ Completeness 　• Did you include all the key points or main ideas? ✓ Emphasis 　• Did you replicate the importance the author placed on certain ideas? ✓ Readability 　• Did you write it in an easy-to-understand paragraph form?	准确性:要注意忠实再现原作者的观点,不要混淆自己的立场和原作者的立场 完整性:先理出原文的主干脉络,以大纲要点(bullet points)或思维导图(thinking maps)的形式切分、梳理要点,确保不漏点 详略得当:透过中心主题句、段落主题句、上下文反复出现的关键词,以及文章内部的结构和推理路径聚焦原文的核心信息,避免只见树叶,不见森林

（续表）

教学内容	注解
✓ Your Own Words • Did you mostly use your own words and put all of the author's words in quotation marks?	可读性：加强读者意识，可让学生在概述后朗读标出拗口的字句，或借由同伴互评互改来审视自己的概述中不易为读者理解的部分 用自己的语言表述方面：提醒学生只要连用原文多个单词就属于直接引用，务必加上引号，否则会构成剽窃，如医学学术领域规定是连用 6 个单词以上（WAME，2004）

3. Writing a one-sentence summary

教学内容	注解
❖ **Writing a one-sentence summary—Purposes and uses** ✓ To support our opinion in an article ✓ To answer short-answer test questions ✓ To increase our understanding when taking notes	文献概述成文的长度不拘，取决于原文的长度和写作目的，短至一个句子或一个段落，长至几个段落
❖ **Writing a one-sentence summary—steps** 1. Identifying the author's full name and the title of the source 2. Synthesizing the key ideas of the original work and rewriting them into a concise and coherent sentence 3. Integrating the identification and the synthesis information to formulate a unified one-sentence summary e. g. In "*I know English*": *Self-assessment of foreign language reading and writing abilities among young Chinese learners of English*, Huan Liu & Cindy Brantmeier (2019) explains... According to Huan Liu & Cindy Brantmeier (2019) in "*I know English*": *Self-assessment of foreign language reading and writing abilities among young Chinese learners of English*... As Huan Liu & Cindy Brantmeier (2019) vividly elucidates in "*I know English*": *Self-assessment of foreign language reading and writing abilities among young Chinese learners of English*...	无论原文篇幅长短，写一句话概述时总是先开门见山地介绍原作者全名和原文来源标题。教师可以提供较为丰富的句式结构供学生参考，同时引导学生在刊物中揣摩这类概述性的话语表达。左栏显示了一些引导性语句实例
❖ **Writing a one-sentence summary—skills** 1. Underlining the key words about the main point of the sentence and deleting unimportant or repeated words 2. Choosing a general term to replace a group of items or details of an action	

(续表)

教学内容	注解
3. Rearranging and simplifying the sentence patterns. (e. g. reduce complex sentences to simple sentences, simple sentences to phrases, phrases to single words; change a noun into a verb, an adj. into an adv.)	这些技巧有助于构建一份简短、信息丰富、符合语法规则的一句话概述。第一是信息取舍，即通过划线标记关键词、保留与核心信息紧密相关的动词或名词来确定重点；第二是信息转换，即把一系列具体的项目、动作或事件合并为广义、宽泛的表达；第三是重组句型，即从繁入简，包括将复合句转换为简单句、将短句转换为短语、将短语转换为单词 此处完成任务一

4. Writing a one-paragraph summary

教学内容	注解
❖ **Writing a one-paragraph summary—skills** 1. Reading, note-taking, mind mapping and outlining for the source, key points and main arguments. 2. Restating the main ideas in one or two sentences immediately after the identification of the source in the introductory sentence 3. Providing major supports and explanation concisely and neutrally and eliminating repetitious or minor details 4. Adding a concluding sentence to give a sense of completion 5. Providing transitions for a smooth and logical flow of ideas	一份写得好的一段话概述可以简洁、连贯地再现原文的重点、结构和关系。与一句话的概述相比，这种概述要兼顾原文重点和重要的论据，因此动笔之前的阅读、做笔记、写思路尤为重要。因行文较长，表述的连贯性和逻辑性就很重要，对语言表达能力也有更高要求 此处完成任务二

5. Summarizing longer passages -integration of the source information

教学内容	注解
❖ **Summary writing—referring to the author in a longer summary** ✓ Use author tags • When referring to the author for the first time, use their full name • When referring to the author after that, use "author tags", which are either the author's last name or a pronoun (he or she) e. g. 1) According to Peter Johnson (2018) in the article entitled,... 2) Johnson goes on to state /maintain /argue/ argue... 3) Johnson concludes that...	概述较长文本时，除了上述提到的概述技巧，还需要时不时提及文献来源，以提醒读者概述者仍然在陈述原作者的观点，而非表达自己想法 可以运用两种方法来显示文献来源：使用作者标记（author tag）和提示语"该文章"（the article）或"该文本"（the text） 在文献概述中首次提到原文作者时，一般使用作者的全名，其后只使用作者的姓氏或代词（他或她）。左栏的例句1)展示在文献概述中首次提及文献来源应如何介绍原作者信息，例句2)和3)展示了在已经介绍来源信息后应如何在其后的行文中引用原作者信息

(续表)

教学内容	注解
✓ Use reminder phrases such as "the article" or "the text". e. g. 4) The article further points out that... 5) Moreover, the article elaborates about...	
❖ **Summarizing longer passages—two ways of in-text citation** ✓ Integral citation—highlighting researcher • The cited author is part of the citing sentence • May indicate opinions or attitudes to the cited research ✓ Non-integral citation—highlighting research • The cited author stands outside the citing sentence, either in parentheses or as represented by a number • Accepting the cited research without evaluation • Allowing the citation of multiple sources	在对较长篇章的概述中，我们需要使用文内引用，它可以分为两种类型：integral citation（整合式引用）和 non-integral citation（非整合式引用），可以产生不同的修辞效果（Swales,1990, 2014；Swales 及 Feak,2004）
❖ **Summarizing longer passages—using reporting verbs** ✓ High frequency reporting verbs • describe, find, report, show, suggest, observe, study, point out, note, publish, demonstrate • develop, propose, expand, argue, claim, hold, think, say, discuss, explain, analyze, give, use (Adopted from Hyland,1999)	汇报动词（reporting verbs）是使用整合式引用进行文献概述时必用的，不仅能起到介绍文献的作用，更为重要的是能够微妙地表达概述者对所引用文献的评价。本单元对汇报动词仅作简单介绍，但在第十三章介绍如何在综述写作中表述己见时会重点讲述

6. Summarizing the different sections of a research article

教学内容	注解
❖ Write a summary of the Introduction, Methods, Results, Discussion sections of a research article based on move analysis, and then weave together the different summarized sections of the RA	本部分可安排为课堂略讲，然后布置为课后拓展作业。主要目的是加强学术阅读和写作的联系，鼓励学生运用第八章研究论文结构与语步分析的方法理清原文的主干脉络，然后才概述全文 对研究论文各部分的文献概述，需综合考虑各部分的主要修辞功能，包括描述性的修辞功能和批判性的修辞功能。此外还要仔细斟酌时态、模糊限制语等语言特点在各部分的体现。这样的学习任务能整合多方面的学术英语能力训练

（三）学习任务

任务一

任务内容 学生完成基于句子的一句话概述，即为一个长句写一句话概述。（此处选用医学研究论文的文本,授课教师可以根据学生的专业在相关领域的研究论文里选择其他类似的文本做为练习素材,但可参照此任务所分析的要点和完成形式。)

任务要点 原文的句子较为冗长,包含一些枝节信息,适合浓缩为一句话概述。学生需运用所学的一句话概述的技巧,遵循标记重点信息(如与主题密切相关的关键词)、删减冗余(如原文括号里的附加说明信息)、语言转换(如将冗长的、复杂的定语从句变成更简短的名词短语)等步骤,将原文转换为简洁的一句话概述。通过实例让学生意识到,罗列的项目可以合并为概括化的表达(从具体到一般);次要的、与主题关系不大的例子可以果断删减,这样学生在确立重点信息、删减次要信息、转换语言表达时会更有目的性。

任务完成形式/师生互动形式 学生独立完成任务,之后在组内交流探讨各自的一句话概述,互相给出建议后,每位学生结合同伴建议当场修订改善各自的版本,然后各组选出最好的一个版本,在课堂上与全班分享交流,老师给予口头点评,引导学生根据一句话概述的标准比对各个版本,在开放式讨论中共同总结其中涉及的技巧策略。

任务二

任务内容 学生完成基于一段文本的一句话概述,并进行互评。

任务要点 学生先进行写前活动,通过在原文标记重点信息、在页边做标记或记框架式笔记列出要点的形式积极阅读,然后独立撰写文献概述。引导他们从关键词和主题句等线索把握主要信息,之后组内交互阅读各自的概述并互相给出建议,共同达成一个综合组内意见的版本,再在班上进行分享。教师给予针对性点评,强调应先简略写明原文作者、出版年份、文章标题等信息。

任务完成形式/师生互动形式 学生独立完成任务,之后组内分享、互评;在班上选择三份不同层次的文献概述进行集体点评,老师给予反馈,师生在开放式讨论中共同总结其中涉及的技巧策略。

(四) 课后作业

Summarizing practice:

Write a summary of the source text excerpted from an article (Golemis et al. ,2018,p. 885-887). (因原文太长,此处略去。同样,授课教师可根据学生的专业领域选择相应的文本布置作业,但可以参照以下的作业点评。)

1. Read and take notes for the main idea and evidences.
2. Exchange notes with a partner to give each other advice.
3. Write a summary of less than 500 words based on your notes, applying the summarizing skills that you have just learnt.

(五) 学生作业点评

作业范例与点评1

An excerpt of student summary for analysis—a weak example

One idea is that the risk of cancer comes from one's own behavior, environment or specific risk-related factors, while another idea is that it roots in the inevitable biological program, which found cancer is associated with age. Tomasetti and Vogelstein reckoned the risk of many cancers depends largely on replication rate, which made it meaningless to prevent, by doing experimentation. However, for some certain tumor types, whose environmental or hereditary risk factors could be inferred, prevention is useful. Another experimentation by using high-throughput sequencing techniques proved that there was no significant correlation between age and number of mutations. Meanwhile, the contribution of replicative effects is also low, while that most of the risk of cancer is related to either hereditary or environmental effects. And although founding the most important carcinogenic factors for each cancer type, there are some similar environmental or behavioral factors could cause cancer.

(……)

点评：这是一份有待改善的学生概述习作。首先，它在段落起首没有用介绍原文作者和来源的句子来引入。其次，它也没有在概述中使用作者标记或报告动词来表示对原作者的尊重认可并传达适当的态度。此外，概述结尾没有提供参考资料。在内容上，它不能有效地提炼和再现原文的主要思想、主要论点或支撑点。

作业范例与点评 2

An excerpt of student summary for analysis—a good example

In an article published by Cold Spring Harbor Laboratory Press entitled Molecular mechanisms of the preventable causes of cancer in the United States, the authors Erica A. Golemis et al. (2018) discuss the topic of intrinsic and extrinsic causes of human cancers and the role of aging in cancer. They note that cancer can be avoided when it derives from some other causes like environment or behavior change in contrast to biological programming which is called "bad luck".

The authors first show a statistic analysis (Tomasetti and Vogelstein, 2015, cited in Golemis et al., 2018) which estimates the possible stem cell divisions in 31 different tissue types and then present the results according to age of cancer morbidity related to every tissue type, with the conclusion that it may not be possible to prevent those replication-related cancer types. Then the authors argue that some cancer types like smokers' lung cancer whose risk factors include environmental or hereditary risks can be intervened by introducing a follow-up study (Tomasetti et al. 2017) in which the relative contribution of these factors were separated. Furthermore,...

Otherwise, drawing on two phases of a study, the authors believe that aging-related changes may contribute to cancer through systematic changes (Campisi, 2003, 2013, cited in Golemis et al., 2018) including distinct processes such as weakened immune response, faulted DNA repair, and varied hormonal environment which make it possible to prevent aging-related cancer. Besides, the authors also indicate the medicine prospect to control cancer by delaying aging rate and eliminating aged cells.

Ultimately, what the authors are trying to convey through their article is that some cancer types associated with environment change, behavior change or aging other than biological programming are controllable, and they offer several reasons why this is so.

(Excerpted from Golemis EA, Scheet P, Beck TN, Scolnick EM, Hunter DJ, Hawk E, Hopkins N. 2018. Molecular mechanisms of the preventable causes of cancer in the United States. Genes & Development 32: 868-902.)

点评：这是一份摘自学生习作的较好的概述范例。它以一个介绍性的句子起首，简略介绍原文作者、来源和出版年份，并在第一次提及作者信息时使用作者的全名。在概述的其余部分中，它使用作者标记持续标地识原文信息，并通过使用 note、show、argue、believe、indicate、convey 等不同的报告动词恰如其分地传达原文作者的态度，避免用词的单调重复。此外，句子之间使用 first、then、furthermore、however、meanwhile、otherwise、besides、ultimately 等适当的转折用语或连接词，增强了各要点间的衔接。最后，这篇概述在正文之后附上原文的来源出处，符合学术规范。

纵观整篇概述，可见它准确地抓住了原文的要点、主要论据和解释，并以自己的语言重新表述。篇末以一个正式的结尾句子收尾，有始有终，不会虎头蛇尾。

诚然，这份概述也有一些尚待改善之处，在表达的简洁性和连贯性上面还可以再锤炼，在文末注释应补上概述中引用的其他文献。然而,总体而言,瑕不掩瑜,不失为一篇较为符合规范的文献概述。

三、案例使用反馈

(一) 学生反馈意见

在完成本单元学习后,学生针对课程内容的难度以及他们在学习过程中的收获与体会进行了评价。他们在进行文献概述时主要面临的问题和挑战包括:① 内容取舍方面分不清主次;② 不确定如何运用"Summarizing"来服务自己的写作目的;③ 语言表达方面不够简洁凝练;④ 在文献概述时未能使用恰当的"reporting verbs";⑤ 不确定自己是否准确传达了原文的内容。其中,③④⑤方面的困难尤为突出。

学生普遍表示学习包括文献概述之内的引用策略对学术英语写作和专业发展有帮助。有些学生在总结文献概述学习心得时写道,"感觉学术英语还是挺好的一个课程,获益挺多的""我觉得这一部分的学习使得我对某一话题能有更深入更详细的了解,同时也能够锻炼自己总结多篇文章,提炼主要思想的能力"。文献概述的学习和背景知识的积累相辅相成,学生表示获取与原文相关的背景知识对他们完成文献概述有帮助。有些学生特别提及课程中的一系列具体活动安排对他们的助益,有学生表示,"peer review 是一个很好的互相学习方法,可以帮同伴找出问题,同时也可以意识到自己哪里错了"。学生在课程中乐意采用合作学习的方法,并表示揣摩同伴写作中的有效引用策略有助于改善自己的引用策略。也有部分学生提到了绘制思维导图对他们完成文献概述的帮助。

(二) 教师反馈意见

本章的内容较为充实,涉及的概念、标准、步骤及技巧繁多,无论是所处理的语言单位还是所产出的语言单位跨度都比较大。其中,所输入的原文篇幅从一句话到整篇论文,所输出的文献概述成品长度也从一句话到一个段落乃至一个篇章,对阅读理解和书面表述都提出很大挑战,因此,对教师来说,把握信息处理和语言表达这条主线非常重要。

在内容取舍、分清主次方面,要提醒学生充分利用文内线索,从文章的中心主题句(thesis statement)、段落主题句(topic sentence)和合题句(wrap-up)、小标题、反复出现的关键词、特殊印刷的斜体字和粗体字等前景化的信息中挖掘原文的关键信息。在内容传达的准确性和完整性方面,引导学生用在原文做标记,做页边注释,灵活使用框架式笔记、思维导图等各种记笔记手法,更有效地标记重点信息,取舍内容,如实体现原文的侧重点。

在语言表述方面,要求学生用自己的语言凝练、准确地再现原文要旨、核心内容和观点态度。有些学生因对自己的语言水平缺乏信心而拘泥于原句的表达,可以建议学生在撰写具体内容的阶段把原文置于视线之外,根据自己对原文的全面理解,先以思维导图简明呈现原文的脉络路径,建立要点间的关联,进而在此基础上形成自己的语言表达。同时引导学生在写出文献概述的第一稿后进行第二次,甚至第三次的语言转化,在确保忠于原文意思的前提下让语言表达进一步摆脱原文的束缚,切实从内容核心上去再现原文精要。

本章的一个难点是在对较长篇幅原文进行文献概述时所涉及的阅读量较大,例如对长达几十页的研究论文的概述,这需要花费较多的阅读时间。有教师表示"练习的量还是挺多,所以时间安排上要处理妥当"。改善的方法包括预留较多时间,课前提前发原文给学生预读,让他们上课时可以把更多精力放在合作学习、探讨难点、思考解惑、取长补短上。此外,引导学生有意识地调用之前学习阶段所接触过的各种快速阅读技巧,避免逐字逐词的阅读,结合积极思考的深度阅读,在短时间内快速抓住原文主要内容。

教师普遍反馈本章的教学达到预期目标,能使学生收获较充实的学习成果。有教师总结,文献概述的课"设计得很合理,内容充实,对概述技巧、步骤介绍得很清晰,理论与操练相结合能帮助学生更好理解和掌握这一技巧"。由于本章所处理的原文语言单位的跨度较大,教师在学习者的语言材料长度、语言处理难度递增时应及时提供适当的引导,正如有教师提议的:"在讲文献概述中的记笔记技巧)(note taking skills)和写作技巧(writing skills)时如果结合例子讲解,能够帮助学生理解。"针对不同的学习内容,平衡好放手让学生独立探究和为学生提供适时帮助的关系,可让学生更有信心地去探索新知,在容许试错的氛围中提升技能。

附录11.1 学习任务

(一) 学习任务一

Directions:Summarize the following long sentences.

1. Blood based tests such as PSA screening start with the advantage that the initial screening test does not require expensive equipment (such as spiral CT machines for lung cancer screening), unpleasant preparation (such as the bowel prep for colonoscopy), exposure to radiation (such as mammography), or clinical skills (such as the Pap smear). (Golemis et al.,2018,p. 890)

2. Based on these calculations, they estimated that replication rate was sufficient to explain risk for a large number of cancer types that were described as replicative and that prevention was unlikely to be productive for these tumors, which could be ascribed to "bad luck." (Golemis et al.,2018,p. 886)

(二) 学习任务二

Directions:

1. Read through an excerpt from Frankel (2008, p. 13) and write a one-paragraph summary for this section with the summary writing skills you have just learnt.

2. Exchange with a teammate and revise each other's summary writing.

The excerpt:

America has changed dramatically during recent years. Not only has the number of graduates in traditional engineering disciplines such as mechanical, civil, electrical, chemical, and aeronautical engineering declined, but in most of the premier American universities engineering curricula now concentrate on and encourage largely the study of engineering science. As a result, there are declining offerings in engineering subjects dealing with infrastructure, the environment, and related issues, and greater concentration on high technology subjects, largely supporting increasingly complex scientific developments. While the latter is important, it should not be at the expense of more traditional engineering.

Rapidly developing economies such as China and India, as well as other industrial countries in Europe and Asia, continue to encourage and advance the teaching of engineering. Both China and India, respectively, graduate six and eight times as many traditional engineers as does the United States. Other industrial countries at minimum maintain their output, while America suffers an increasingly serious decline in the number of engineering graduates and a lack of well-educated engineers.

(三) 参考答案

学习任务一

1. Blood-base tests are favored for the affordable equipment, convenience, freedom from radiation and clinical accessibility.

2. They regareded replication rate as a substantial contributor to many cancer types caused by ill luck.

学习任务二

In a 2008 Faculty Newsletter article, "Change in Engineering Education: The cost of sacrificing fundamentals," MIT Professor Emeritus Ernst G. Frankel expresses his concerns regarding the current state of American engineering education. He notes that the number of students focusing on traditional areas of engineering has decreased while the number interested in the high-technology end of the field has increased. Frankel points out that other industrial nations produce far more traditionally-trained engineers than we do, and believes we have fallen seriously behind. (Brennecke, 2019, p23)

参考文献

Brennecke P, 2019. Academic Integrity at MIT: a handbook for students. MIT Office of the Vice Chancellor.

Frankel EG, 2008. Change in education: The cost of sacrificing fundamentals. MIT Faculty Newsletter, XX, 5, 13.

Golemis EA, Scheet P, Beck TN, et al., 2018. Molecular mechanisms of the preventable causes of cancer in the United States. Genes & Development, 32: 868-893.

Hyland K, 1999. Academic attribution: Citation and the construction of disciplinary knowledge. Applied Linguistics, 20: 341-367.

Swales JM, 1990. Genre analysis: English in academic and research settings. Cambridge: Cambridge University Press.

Swales JM, 2014. Variation in citational practice in a corpus of student biology papers: From parenthetical plonking to intertextual storytelling. Written Communication, 31(1): 118-141.

Swales JM, Feak CB, 2000. English in today's research world: a writing guide. Ann Arbor: The University of Michigan Press.

Swales JM, Feak CB, 2004. Academic writing for graduate students: essential tasks and skills. 2nd ed. Ann Arbor: The University of Michigan Press.

World Association of Medical Editors (WAME), 2004. Recommendations on publication ethics policies for medical journals. Archives of Medical Research, 35: 361-367.

第三篇

综合能力训练：专业情境化任务

第十二章 综述写作(上)
——文献汇总与思路形成

杨 苗 刘佳佳

一、对教学主题和教学思路的解读

同为学术写作体裁,和研究论文相比,综述写作在 EAP 研究领域受到的关注非常少(这方面重要的论著见 Feak 及 Swales,2009)。但是因为撰写综述是每位研究者的"必经之路",所以综述写作是研究生语言课程中最常见的学习任务(Teramoto 及 Mickan,2008;Woodward-Kron,2003)。综述写作是学术英语教学的难点,目前我国多个出版社出版的学术英语教材,对学术听力、学术口语、学术阅读和研究论文写作都有涉猎,但鲜有专门针对综述写作的教材。

综述写作是本课程几经尝试之后形成的最核心的内容,我们先后在本科高年级学生和研究生中设置综述写作选修课,经过反复试讲和修改,最终形成目前综述写作的教学内容和思路。在本课程中,综述写作与多文本阅读、同义转化技巧、概述技巧结合在一起,授课时数 20 小时,构成了课程 1/4 的内容。

因为内容繁多,特辟两章专讲综述写作。本章聚焦如何从文献中寻找综述写作的思路,逐步形成写作的框架,主题内容包括分析和评价文献、建立进化式阅读笔记、构思综述的写作框架。下一章则侧重如何在综述写作中"表述己见",呈现作者对该研究主题的见解、结论和建议。通过这几部分的学习和训练,学生逐步阅读、整合、构思、写作和修改,最终撰写一篇完整的综述。

(一) 教学主题

1. 分析和评价文献:撰写文献综述的第一个目的是展示自己能够深入了解某一特定领域的研究历史和现状,从广度和深度两方面体现出来(Hart,1998)。检索、分析和评价相关文献,是撰写综述的第一步。本章重点介绍了 CRAAP 文献评价原则(Jones 及 Barry,2014),CRAAP 分别代表时效性(currency),相关性(relevance),权威性(authority),准确性(accuracy)和目的性(purpose)。

2. 建立进化式阅读笔记:文献综述通过评价性地讨论该研究主题的不同理论、方法和观点,最终目的是形成自己的见解,用于支持自己对研究主题和研究方法的选择,并阐述自己的研究所能做出的贡献。因此,综述必须有非常清晰的逻辑思路(clear line of argument),而清晰的思路需要借助有效的文献阅读笔记来形成。边阅读文献边做笔记,笔记经历三个阶段的演变,最终会成为综述的写作框架。这三个进化阶段是:注释文献 1,即描述与总结文献;注释文献 2,即建立文献间联系;注释文献 3,即形成自己的见解、构思综述提纲。

3. 构思综述的写作框架：我们把综述的写作框架比喻为建筑工地上的脚手架（scaffold），"脚手架"由两大要素组成为纵向的支柱，即 sequence of ideas；横向的踏板，即 important details。我们在简介综述的三大部分（即前言、主体和总结）之后，详述每一部分的重要语步（moves）和主体部分的组织方法（organizing schemes），并讲解如何构思和撰写段落。

（二）教学思路

在开始教授综述写作的同时，我们要求学生定下自己的研究主题。随着教学内容的展开，学生在课程指导下开始检索分析文献，撰写阅读笔记，形成自己的思路。为减轻学生的负担，将学习难度控制在学生可以接受但又需要努力才能达到的水平，同时也为了适当减轻老师的工作量，我们要求学生在指定的六大医学人文主题中选题和阅读文献（相关主题的选择和文献库的建立详见第二章的介绍），学生可以根据初步文献阅读的结果进一步检索文献。这样就把老师在辅导学生综述写作过程需要了解的研究领域限定在六个。而让学生自由选择主题的结果，往往是有多少学生就有多少个研究主题，老师无法一一了解这些主题，就很难在思路和内容上指导学生。限定六个主题还有一个好处，每个班级的学生自然形成六个主题组，非常适合在课前课后安排小组讨论，互相切磋。

另外，我们需要给学生足够多的时间来阅读和评估文献，并完成阅读笔记（即注释文献），否则课堂上讲再多也是纸上谈兵。我们将多文本阅读技巧与综述写作结合起来，因此可以很好地将课堂教学与实践结合起来。我们在讲完评判性阅读技巧之后布置注释文献1，讲完整合性阅读技巧后布置注释文献2，讲完综述的写作框架后布置注释文献3，每次完成作业的时间都是两周，每完成一次作业都安排课堂展示和讨论的时间。我们还要求学生从写注释文献开始就严格遵守文献引用的学术规范，充分运用概述与总结技巧，文内引用和文末参考文献都规定采用 Vancouver 格式（大多数医学国际期刊规定的格式）。其他院校可以根据学生的不同专业规定选用的文献格式。

二、教学案例设计

（一）教学目标

1. 学生能进一步学习和运用多文本阅读技巧，尤其是评估和综合运用文献的技巧。
2. 学生能运用评判性笔记与思维导图构思写作思路。
3. 学生能明确文献综述的主要结构和各主要部分的写作思路和内容。

（二）教学内容

1. What is literature review?

教学内容	注解
❖ **What is literature review?** ✓ a critical discussion showing insights into differing arguments, theories and approaches ✓ a synthesis and analysis of the relevant published work, linked at all times to your own purpose and rationale	此部分主要强调综述不是对原有文献的简单回顾，而是以作者对文献的见解为导向，对文献进行有目的的选择、梳理、分析和整合

(续表)

教学内容	注解
❖ **Steps in writing literature review** 1. Literature searching, analyzing and evaluating 2. Multi-textual reading to identify relationship in the literature and connect your ideas into them 3. Scaffolding and structuring your literature 4. Writing effective introduction, main body and conclusion 5. Writing effective abstract 6. Proofreading and editing for standard academic language	
❖ **What makes a good literature review?** ✓ Open-minded 　• Compare and contrast different authors' views on an issue ✓ Integrative 　• Note areas in which authors are in disagreement 　• Highlight exemplary studies 　• Group authors who draw similar conclusions 　• Show how your study relates to previous studies or the literature in general 　• Conclude by summarizing what the literature says ✓ Critical 　• Criticize aspects of methodology 　• Highlight gaps in research	此处借用(Caulley,1992)的标准,将一篇好的综述应具有的特点归纳为三点:开放性、整合性与评判性

2. Analyzing and evaluating literature

教学内容	注解
❖ **The CRAAP Principles** ✓ C for currency: the timeliness of the information ✓ R for relevance: the importance of the information for your needs ✓ A for authority: the source of the information ✓ A for accuracy: the reliability, truthfulness, and correctness of the content ✓ P for purpose: the reason the information exists	CRAAP 原则是非常有效的文献评估策略,如果课堂时间允许,在简单讲解五个原则之后,可以借用 Jones 及 Barry (2014)的 CRAAP 测验设计一个课堂练习

3. Evolving the reading notes

教学内容	注解
❖ **How do your reading notes evolve?** 1. DESCRIBE and SUMMARIZE each selected article	

2. DEMONSTRATE how concepts in the literature relate to the results of studies and ESTABLISH how the literature is connected 3. IDENTIFY relationships in the literature and CONNECT your own ideas to them	文献阅读笔记随着阅读深度的增加会一步步进化。学生需要在理解和评价文献的基础上，逐渐形成自己的观点，在多文本间建立联系，最终以自身观点为主线，援引多个文献来源形成写作思路，这是我们在第九章讲到的整合阅读的最终目的。要达到这些目的，需要学生按照这三个步骤构建自己的文献阅读笔记
❖ **What notes do you take step by step?** ✓ Annotated Bibliography 1: Describe & summarize ✓ Annotated Bibliography 2: Demonstrate & establish ✓ Annotated Bibliography 3: Identify & connect	我们要求学生先后完成三份注释文献，作为三个阶段的阅读笔记的具体成果。在课堂上我们会使用前一届学生的作品作为例子，让学生分析讨论笔记要包含的要点（课堂学习任务一、二、三）。下面课后作业部分会介绍三种注释文献的详细要求
❖ **Using thinking maps to demonstrate connection** ✓ Several commonly used thinking maps to display eight logical relationships: circle diagram, tree diagram, star diagram, horizontal tree diagram, circle diagram & network diagram (Kress & van Leeuwen, 1996; Martinec & van Leeuwen, 2008)	我们在第九章强调运用思维导图呈现整合性阅读的结果，在完成注释文献2时我们重新强调了这个重要的视觉工具，感兴趣的教师也可详细参考Hart(1998)第六章

4. Scaffolding your literature review

教学内容	注解
❖ **Scaffolding your literature review** ✓ Poles: sequence of ideas in a well-structured manner ✓ Boards: important details	在这里我们借助"脚手架"这个概念来讲解综述写作的结构
❖ **General structure of a literature review** ✓ Introduction ✓ Main body ✓ Conclusion	
❖ **Moves in the introduction (CARS model)** 1. Begin with a rather general description of your topic 2. Highlight its importance by suggesting it is interesting, problematic, or otherwise relevant 3. Establish that a review of the literature is valuable in understanding important aspects of your research area 4. Clarify the scope and overall organization of the review	这里我们引用了Feak及Swales (2009)对综述前言的语步分析结果，介绍综述前言一般应该包含的四个重要组成部分。在介绍四个语步之前，安排学生完成课堂学习任务四
❖ **The main body** ✓ Important concepts/development at different stages/different aspects of analysis, etc. ✓ Well structured ✓ Logically developed, leading to the conclusion	
❖ **Organizing schemes of main body** ✓ Chronological (time): early to later studies	

(续表)

教学内容	注解
✓ Geographical: research carried out in different locations ✓ Perspectives of authors: position taken, "school of thought" ✓ Method: how the research has been done ✓ Topical/thematic: presented in sequence *Notes*: *There can be a combination of different organizing schemes.*	综述主体部分的组织方法(Swales, 2004), 在学生完成注释文献2和3的时候已经基本确定下来, 这些组织方法与上文提到的各种思维导图一一对应
❖ Developing academic paragraphs-two important elements ✓ Coherence (for idea development) 1. Definition 2. Process 3. Classification 4. Comparison and contrast 5. Exemplification 6. Cause-effect ✓ Cohesion (for linkage between sentences/paragraphs) 1. Reducing clumsy repetition 2. Increasing flow and link through cohesive devices 3. Using effective and various citation	综述的主体部分由各段落组成, 段落写作要兼顾逻辑性(coherence)和衔接性(cohesion)。这里我们借用 Swales 及 Feak(2012)总结出来的六种段落发展模式, 结合上文提到的8种思维导图, 告诉学生如何构思和撰写段落, 并且向学生强调: 逻辑性和衔接性的要求和写作策略同样适用于整篇综述
❖ Moves in the conclusion 1. Summary of the point of view (including important aspects of analysis/discussion) 2. Implications 3. Pointing out the research gap/limitations and providing suggestions for future research	

(三) 课堂学习任务

任务一

任务内容　学生阅读注释文献1范例,分析作者对文献的评价。

任务要点　学生依据 CRAAP 的原则,分析作者是否对文献进行全面的评价。

任务完成形式/师生互动形式　学生先完成阅读,之后分组讨论,各小组发言,教师总结注释文献1的写作要求,并解释评分标准。

任务二

任务内容　学生阅读注释文献2范例,分析作者如何建立起文献之间的联系,并评价优缺点。

任务要点　学生需要重点分析思维导图所体现的文献间联系,并判断作者是否已经形成自己的观点,并以此贯穿整个思维导图。

任务完成形式/师生互动形式　学生先完成阅读,之后分组讨论,各小组发言,教师总结注释文献2的写作要求,并解释评分标准。

任务三

任务内容 学生阅读注释文献3范例,分析作者如何搭建全文的框架。

任务要点 学生需要重点分析综述的主体部分如何发展,是否水到渠成地得出结论。

任务完成形式/师生互动形式 学生先完成阅读,之后分组讨论,各小组发言,教师总结注释文献3的写作要求,并解释评分标准。

任务四

任务内容 学生阅读一篇综述的前言(Capella,et al.,2011),分析其语步。

任务要点 学生在回顾研究论文的前言的语步之后,依照类似的方法划分综述前言的语步。

任务完成形式/师生互动形式 学生先完成阅读,之后老师以提问的形式检查任务完成情况,总结后正式介绍 Feak 及 Swales(2009)的语步分析结果。

(四)课后作业

1. 学生在学完评判性阅读后,完成注释文献1,要求如下:

Please select articles that you have read in depth and found important for your literature review. **Take notes for EACH article**. Your notes should include three parts.

Article 1

A. Concisely sum up the <u>main idea</u> of the article or the <u>main concepts/aspects</u> discussed in the article that is closely related to your writing topic.

B. Assess its validity, reliability and relevance to your topic.

C. State how you are going to use/cite it in your literature review later.

Article 2...

Article 3...

Article 4...

2. 学生在学完整合性阅读后,完成注释文献2,要求如下:

Annotated Bibliography 2 will be written after you finish Annotated Bibliography 1 in which you sum up and evaluate all important literature in your own way. The purpose of Annotated Bibliography 2 is for you to <u>**cross-refer to and forge connection in between different texts**</u>.

A. Write briefly about how your point of view is informed by the literature reading so far.

B. Analyze and synthesize the information by using techniques of cross-reference and forging connection in between different texts. Write a thinking map that show the connection between the multiple articles and how your point of view or your purpose of literature review emerges from this connection.

3. 学生在学完综述的写作框架后,完成注释文献3,要求如下:

The purpose of Annotated Bibliography 3 is to <u>**identify relationship in the literature and connect your own ideas into them**</u>.

Sketch an outline for your literature review. The outline should be a well-structured framework for you to display the interrelationship you have developed from the literature and argue for your point of view on the research topic.

(五) 学生作业点评

Annotated Bibliography 1:

Medical students' attitudes and perceptions on abortion: a cross-sectional survey among medical interns in Maharastra, India

A. 8% of maternal mortality is attributed to unsafe abortion in India, and research showed that improved attitudes and increased knowledge increase safe risk of abortion. The research was to explore attitudes toward abortion among medical interns in Maharastra, India. A cross-sectional survey was conducted among 1996 medical students. The conclusion showed that opposed attitudes toward abortion and misconceptions about the legal regulations were common in medical students in India. However, attitudes and knowledge toward abortion among them could be improved by educational inclusion, which potentially increase safe risk of abortion.

B. The study consisted of 1996 medical students. A cross-sectional survey was put into use and the result was evaluated with a structured questionnaire, which indicated on a 5-point Likert scale. The questionnaire consisted of three sections covering sociodemographic background, the student's perception of his/her educational program characteristics regarding sexual and reproductive health and training, and attitude statements on contraception and abortion. In my opinion, the questionnaire is effective to attain the aims of the research. Statistical Package for Social Studies (SPSS) 21 software was used.

C. The paper can be a very good supplement to my research topic. In late writing, I will use it to state the necessity of educational inclusion on abortion, which potentially decrease maternal mortality that attributed to unsafe abortion.

点评：
1) 这位学生对研究的背景、目的、方法和结果做了非常扼要的介绍。
2) 对该文献的评价非常不到位，只尝试评价研究方法的有效性，但没有写出任何依据（见划线部分句子）。
3) 对该文献将如何用到自己的综述有初步可行的看法。
4) 文献目录没有按照规定的 Vancouver 格式写出来。

Annotated Bibliography 2:

A. Write briefly about how your point of view is informed by the literature reading so far.

As time goes on, the acceptance of euthanasia among the European public shows a more polarized trend, which suggests that a macro-intervention at the population level may promote the acceptance of euthanasia. To prove this conjecture, further study is needed.

The legalization of euthanasia has both support voices and opposed voices. Advocates believe that... (I will make it specific in my final work); While opponents believe that Poor doctor-patient relationship, Patient's autonomy and diagnosis, Physician's professionalism, etc. are the reasons why euthanasia should not be legalized.

B. Write a thinking map that show the connection between the multiple articles and how your point of view or your purpose of literature review emerges from this connection.

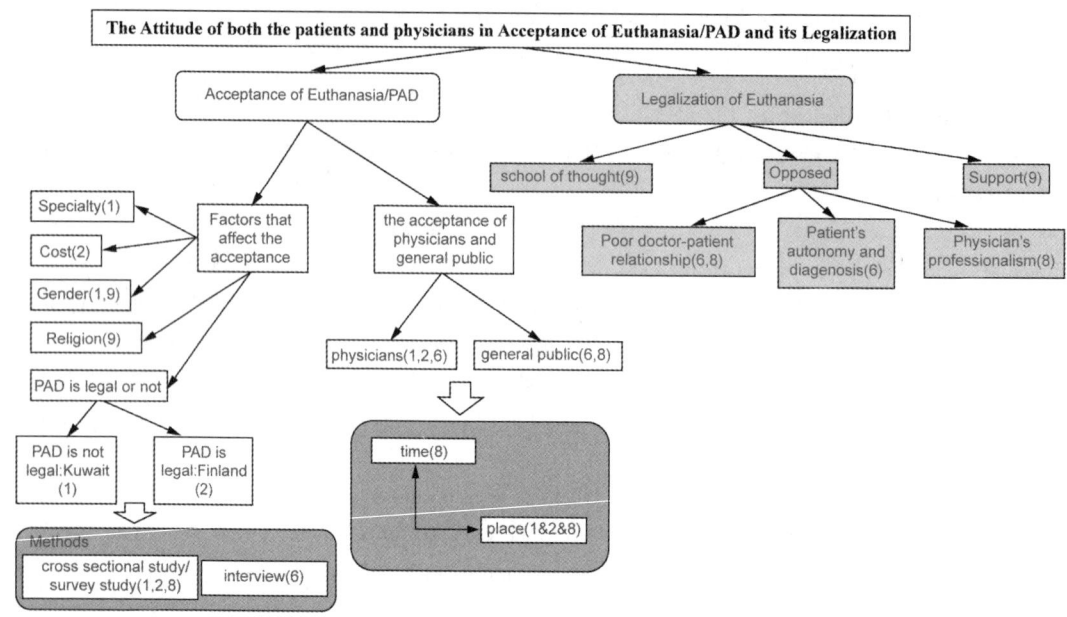

点评：这位学生对有关安乐死的接受度和合法化的文献做了非常详尽的梳理，对两个主题都做了全面的总结，比如接受度又分为影响接受的因素和医生群体与普通民众的接受度对比，合法化又分为影响合法化的思潮、支持与反对的原因。但是不足之处在于这两个主题相互独立，似乎没有任何联系。作者似乎只为了总结文献而写导图，并没有融入自己的见解，因此也无法看到作者写综述的目的。这一点从她对第一个问题的回答可以看出来。

Annotated Bibliography 3：

Sketch an outline for your literature review.

1. Introduction

1.1 The overall circumstance and trend of teenager smoking.

1.2 The purpose of writing this article

2. Study of relevant smoking factors

2.1 Study of advertising and teenager smoking

2.2 Study of cigarette packing with teenager smoking

2.3 Study of warning with smoking

3. Discussion

3.1 The measures made to control the teenager smoking

3.2 The limitation of this research

4. Conclusion

In order to control teenager smoking, we can increase the number of anti-tobacco advertising while decrease their contact to pro-tobacco advertising. We can provide some education to help them understand health risk of smoking. So they can resist the influence of smoking friends or family members. Reducing pressure is also helpful to prevent smoking. Additionally, we can modify the design of cigarette packing, remove brand elements including color and imagery and add some health warnings to reduce the attraction of the cigarettes to the teenagers.

点评：这位学生虽然没有写出其综述的写作目的，但从主体的内容和结论部分可以看出其目的是探讨防止青少年吸烟的广告策略，也反映了他在写注释文献3时已经很清楚自己的写作内容和思路。美中不足的是前言部分的语步不够清楚,只列出对研究主题的宽泛的介绍,没有将研究主题细化到反烟草广告及其重要性,即前言的提纲里缺乏第二和第三个语步。

三、课程反馈

(一) 学生反馈意见

我们要求学生运用思维导图分析文献,呈现多文本阅读成果,并且一步一步构思综述思路。问卷调查发现,在 276 名参与问卷的学生中,89% 的学生认为这种方法对他们有大帮助,71% 的学生觉得自己很感兴趣,也很投入地运用这种方法,73% 的学生自评学习收获很大,同时约 58% 的学生认为使用这种方法进行学习有难度。这说明了使用思维导图梳理、整合文献,构思写作框架,是有效的学习方法,很值得提倡,但同时对半数以上的学生来说还有一定的难度,需要老师的及时指导和反馈。

三个注释文献是本章最重要的学习任务,学生对它们的认可度也非常高,大约 85%～87% 的学生认为这对分析文献撰写综述很有帮助。在写到具体学习收获时,他们主要认为注释文献帮助他们从纷杂的文献中整理思路:"注释文献为我后续的写作提供了一个更为清晰的思路,也可以说是改变了我对整理复杂资料的想法""我一直认为阅读文献是很枯燥的事情,而且看完也没有什么头绪,通过思维导图和注释文献的方式可以把自己想要的内容找出来,沿着思维导图去阅读文献,对于提高阅读文献的效率很有帮助"。三个注释文献是进化式阅读笔记,从描述与总结文献开始,然后建立文献间联系,最后形成自己的见解和综述提纲,学生对综述的构思是一步一步发展起来的。"把一篇综述的完成分成几个具体的步骤,一步一步完成,这对于综述的构思和拓展非常有用"。

(二) 教师反馈意见

进行本章内容的教学之后,我们发现对学生注释文献的及时反馈至关重要。因为每班有 30～40 名学生,不可能一一给予及时、详细的反馈意见,我们采用小组讨论、班级展示和点评的方法评讲注释文献。这样做点评难免不够全面,或者没有突出重要问题,而且总有一些学生上课不够专注、学习松懈,没有在听完点评之后修改注释文献。我们发现有些学生分析、评价文献深度及广度不够,在还没有形成自己的看法时就写出文献的思维导图和综述的提纲(如以上学生作业点评所示),造成的结果是写出来的综述仅仅是简单总结文献,没有自己的真知灼见。因此,有必要改善作业反馈机制,在课堂集中点评之后增加同侪互评和修改的环节,提高修改效率,帮助学生真正建立进化式的文献阅读笔记。

附录 12.1 注释文献 1 范例

Gardiner P, Kemper KJ, Legedza A, Phillips RS. Factors associated with herb and dietary supplement use by young adults in the United States. BMC Complement Altern Med. 2007;7:39.

A. The study examined the overall prevalence and pattern of herbs and dietary supplement (HDS) use and its association with certain lifestyle/behavior factors as well as the disclosure rate of HDS use to health care professionals among young adults aged from 18～30 by analyzing data from a 2002 national health interview survey. The results reported that 17% of the respondents used HDS in the last 12 months and the demographic factor associated with higher DS use included older age, higher income, higher education level and being non-Hispanic others such as Asian and American Indian. Current smoking, high activity level, moderate/heavy alcohol use and prescription medicine use were the identified behavioral factors related to higher HDS use. In addition, only 24% of the HDS users disclosed the use of HDS to a healthcare professional.

B. Palua Gardiner is from the Department of Family Medicine, Boston University Medical School. Kathy J Kemper (MD, MPH) is from the Department of Pediatrics, Public Sciences and Family and Community Medicine, Wake Forest University School of Medicine. Anna Legedza and Russell D Phillips are from the Division for Research and Education in Complementary and Integrative Medical Therapies, Harvard Medical School. This peer-reviewed article was published in BMC Complementary and Alternative Medicine (JIF: 2.109) on Nov. 30, 2007.

The strengths of the study were that it involved ample participants and the national health interview survey was the principal source of information in the U.S. on the health of civilian. However, as this study only focused on non-vitamin-non-mineral HDS use and the self-reported data dated back to 2002, the results should be interpreted with caution and not be generalized to other cases of DS use.

C. The findings of the predictors of DS use in this study differed from other studies due to its excluding vitamin and mineral from the research and thus will not be included in the later synthesis writing. With regards to the concurrent use of HDS with prescription medicine and the disclosure rate of HDS to health care professionals, the results were similar to others and will be cited in their respective discussion section. In addition, young adults' response to the adverse reactions of DS use was also mentioned in the study, which will be referenced in the discussion of people's response to the adverse effect of DS in later writing.

附录12.2 注释文献2范例

A. My point of view that has been informed by the literature:

Abortion is discussed in the 11 articles, of which four are about health care providers and the rest are about medical students. I want to explore medical students' attitudes toward abortion and abortion education. Therefore I chose article b、c、d、f、h、i、j. I found the different trends between developing and developed countries. In developing countries like India, medical students do not have adequate legal knowledge about abortion, are lack of clinical training and seriously influenced by traditional ideas. Therefore, it is difficult to carry out abortion services. In developed countries such as the United States, Norway and other countries, medical students are more open to abortion. It is easy for medical students to have a positive attitude toward abortion and abortion education. In order to ensure the safety of abortion, abortion education should be carried out at the stage of medical students' study. It is necessary to clarify the value of abortion, eliminate misunderstandings and provide more clinical training for medical students.

B. My thinking map:

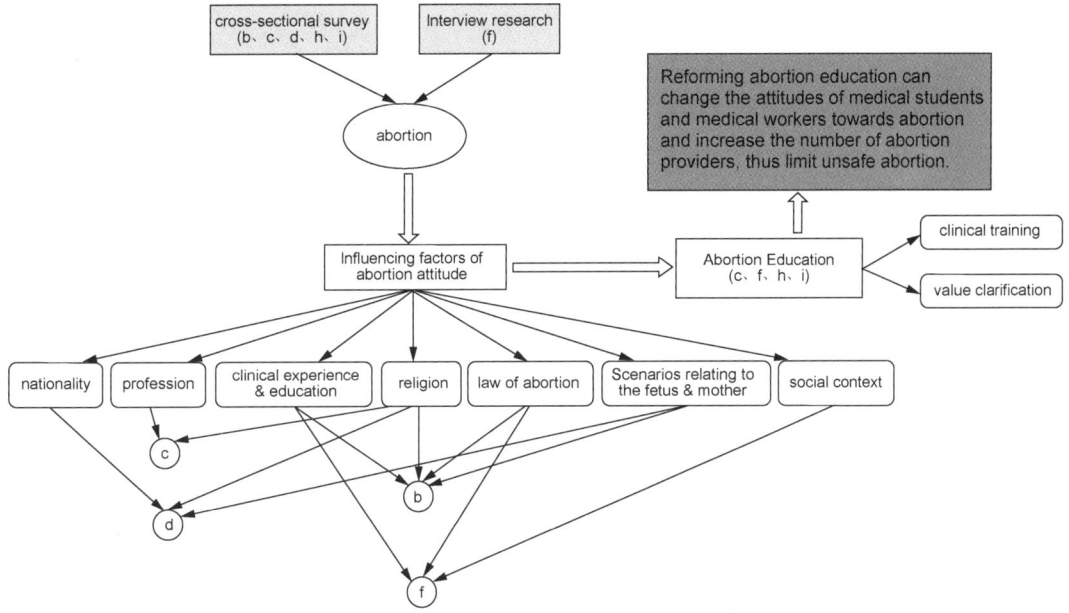

附录12.3 注释文献3范例

The outline of my literature review:

1. Introduction

1.1 Prevalence and trends of abortion services worldwide

1.2 Influence factors for attitudes toward abortion: religion, nationality, clinical experience & education and so on

1.3 The current situation of abortion education and its importance

1.4 The purpose and structure of my review

2. Influence factors for attitudes toward abortion

2.1 Religion

2.2 Clinical experience & education

2.3 Law of abortion

2.4 Scenarios relating to the fetus & mother

2.5 Profession

2.6 Nationality

2.7 Social context

3. Attitudes toward abortion education and its prospect

3.1 The relationship between abortion and abortion education

3.2 Prospects for abortion education

4. Summary/conclusion

Reforming abortion education can change the attitudes of medical students and medical workers towards abortion and increase the number of abortion providers, thus limit unsafe abortion. (I will improve my conclusion later.)

参考文献

Capella, et al. ,2011. A review of the effect of cigarette advertising, International Journal of Research in Marketing. 28: 269-279.

Caulley DN, 1992. Writing a critical review of the literature. Bundoora: La Trobe University.

Feak CB, Swales JM, 2009. Telling a research story: Writing a literature review. Ann Arbor: University of Michigan Press.

Hart C, 1998. Doing a literature review: releasing the social science research imagination. London: Sage Publication.

Jones MLB, Barry M, 2014. Detecting CRAAP: evaluating information sources. https://core. ac. uk/download/pdf/36765859. pdf.

Kress G, van Leeuwen T, 1996. Reading Images: The Grammar of Visual Design. London: Routledge.

Martinec R, van Leeuwen T, 2008. The Language of New Media Design. London: Routledge.

Swales J, 2004. Research genre: explorations and applications. Cambridge: Cambridge University Press.

Swales J, Feak C, 2012. Academic writing for graduate students: Essential tasks and skills. 3rd ed. Michigan series in English for academic & professional purposes. Ann Arbor: University of Michigan Press.

Teramoto H, Mickan P, 2008. Writing a Critical Review: Reflections on Literacy Practices. Language Awareness, 19(1): 44-56.

Velarde O, 2018. The 8 Types of Thinking Maps and How They Help Visualize Ideas. https://visme. co/blog/thinking-maps.

Woodward-Kron R, 2003. Critical analysis and the journal article review assignment. Prospect, 18 (2): 20-36.

第十三章 综述写作(下)
——表述己见

杨　苗　刘佳佳

一、对教学主题和教学思路的解读

在第十二章,我们介绍了如何从文献中寻找综述写作的思路,逐步形成写作的框架。我们指出,综述不是对原有文献的简单回顾,而是以作者撰写综述的目的为导向,对文献进行选择、梳理、分析和整合,其最终目的是呈现作者对该研究主题的见解、结论和建议。所以好的综述自始至终都必须以作者的观点为主线,在引用各家之言"百鸟争鸣"时,作者自己的"声音"一直是统领思路的主角,最终水到渠成,得出结论。因此,表述己见是综述写作的一个重点。

和现有研究的发现(Hirvela 及 Belcher,2001;Matsuda 及 Tardy,2007)一致,我们在教学中发现表述己见是学生的一大难点,很多学生仅对文献进行梳理和汇总,没有进行深度的分析和评价,因而写出来的综述流于表面,缺乏自己的见解。本章介绍综述写作技巧,聚焦于如何在写作中表述己见。我们强调三大策略:使用多样化引用策略、多进行解释性阐述、加入个人评价。

(一) 教学主题

使用多样化引用策略:本书第十章和十一章专门讲述如何教授同义转化技巧和概述技巧,并且对引用策略的使用目的和各种引用策略都有简单的介绍,本章主要凸显为何引用策略能够帮助作者表述己见。从语言使用的层面看,引用策略能帮助作者用自己的方式引述他人观点,从而避免抄袭。从交流的层面看,引用策略向读者交代了参考文献的来源。从认知的层面看,引用策略不仅引述他人观点,还表述作者对所引用文献的看法,这就是 Bakhtin(1978)提出的双重表述(double-voicing)。对引用策略的研究表明,不管是直接引用,还是转述、概述或整合,只要能有机地融入作者自己的写作思路,就能帮助作者表达见解(Hyland 及 Jiang,2017;Hu 及 Wang,2014)。具体的引用格式,如嵌入式或非嵌入式(Swales,1990 及 2014),大段引用还是零星引用(Hu 及 Wang,2014),对是否有效表达见解是有影响的。在各种引用策略中,汇报动词(reporting verbs)起了重要的作用,因此也是本教学主题要包括的内容。

(二) 进行解释性阐述

解释性阐述(interpretation)指的是作者对已有的研究和观点进行诠释和解读,属于综述写作中的论证元素。根据 Hart(1998)的分类,对研究主题的论述可分为知识基础元素(knowledge-based elements)和论证元素(argumentational elements)。前者以描述和介绍为主,包括介绍前人研究、重要定义、概念和理论,对定义或概念的发展进行梳理,找出其他研究者认为重要的研究议题。后者以诠释和评判为主,包括对已有研究和观点进行诠释和解读,找出已有研究的优劣或存在的问题,提出解决问题的方法。要求进行解释性阐述,是鼓励学生脱离对文献的表层总结、开始深入探讨研究主题的第一步。要帮助学生做到这一点,我们除了以已发表的综述论文中的文段作为例子进行文本分析、让学生明白何谓解释性阐述之外,还需要介绍相应的语言表述技巧。

(三) 加入个人评价

个人评价(critique)与解释性阐述同属论证元素,要求作者对已有研究的优劣进行评判,找出存在问题,甚至提出解决问题的做法。只有做到这一步,作者才能真正在综述里"发声"。同样,为帮助学生意识到这样做的重要性和实现的方法,我们需要以已发表的综述论文为范例进行分析。

教学思路:这部分的教学主要介绍引用策略、解释性阐述和个人评价的使用目的及方法,以及相关语言技巧。我们在课堂上挑选已发表论文的综述段落让学生进行分析和学习,课后布置学生写一个小章节,一般包括2~3个段落,然后再在课堂上进行互评,点评的重点就放在是否运用了表述己见的策略。

二、教学案例设计

(一) 教学目标

1. 学生能有效运用各种引用策略来表达自己对引用文献和研究主题的看法。
2. 学生能在综述写作中对他人研究进行解释性阐述,体现自己对文献的理解和评判。
3. 学生能通过对现有文献的分析和评判,对研究主题提出自己的见解或得出结论。

(二) 教学内容

1. Using various citation strategies

教学内容	注解
❖ **Citation** ✓ developing argument persuasively and effectively ✓ establishing authority and credibility ✓ establishing your voice and acknowledge sources of your voices	这部分向学生解释引用策略的使用目的和方法,然后让学生完成学习任务一。我们挑选已发表论文的综述段落,让学生分析该文段使用的引用策略。以下其他课堂任务均使用同样的综述段落
❖ **Citation—at language level(to avoid plagiarism)** ✓ Quotation ✓ Paraphrasing ✓ Summarizing ✓ Synthesizing	
❖ **Citation—at communicative and cognitive level** ✓ To report the source material ✓ To indicate the author's position or stance towards the cited material	

(续表)

教学内容	注解
❖ **author-focused & information-focused** ✓ Integral citation-author-focused ✓ Non-integral citation-information-focused	第十一章概述技巧里详述过这两种文内引用方式(Swales,1990),这里略述

❖ **Reporting verbs**
✓ Verb which are used to talk about or report on other people's work
  1. To indicate the cited author's personal viewpoint;
  2. To indicate your viewpoint regarding what the cited author says;
  3. To indicate the cited author's viewpoint regarding other literature.
	我们发给学生一份讲义(Velliaris及Miller,2009),里面有对汇报动词的解释和分类,分类依据之一是语气强弱,依据之二是语法结构(后接介词结构、名词/动名词还是that从句)。此处完成课堂任务二

2. Moving from descriptive to interpretive

教学内容	注解
❖ **Knowledge-based elements in the review** ✓ A description of previous work on the topic (leading concepts/definitions/theories) ✓ A description of how definitions/theories were developed/operationalized ✓ Identification and description of matters other researchers have considered important	这部分向学生解释如何进行解释性阐述。根据Hart(1998)的分类,介绍解释性阐述和描述性阐述之间的差异,并介绍具体的语言技巧
❖ **Argumentational elements in the review** ✓ Interpretation of what previous work has found ✓ A description of what you find strong (strength critique) or weak (deficit critique) in previous work ✓ A solution you propose to solve the problem	
❖ **Language skills to move from descriptive to interpretive** ✓ This shows/suggests/highlights/implies that... ✓ This is important/significant because... ✓ This calls attention to... ✓ Importantly, this suggests that... ✓ ...illustrates/points to/suggests the need to...	

3. Responding with critique

教学内容	注解
❖ **Responding to the literature with critique** ✓ Comments of what you find strong (strength critique) or weak (deficit critique) in previous work ✓ A solution you propose to solve the problem	这部分向学生解释如何在综述中加入个人评价，然后让学生完成学习任务三
❖ **Language skills to respond with critique** ✓ For strength critique 　• In this milestone/groundbreaking/wide-ranging/pivotal study... 　• This was significant/influential in that... 　• ... correctly argues that... ✓ For deficit critique 　• A question that needs to be asked, however, is that... 　• A weakness in this argument, however, is that... 　• One of the limitations is that... 　• This approach fails to take... into account. ✓ For proposing a solution 　• This study would have been more useful if it had... 　• The findings may have been more applicable if it had...	这部分语言技巧参考 The University of Melbourne Academic Skills（n.d.）网络教学资源 Writing the Literature Review

（三）课堂学习任务

任务一

任务内容　学生阅读两段段综述写作文本，分析其中使用了哪些引用策略。

任务要点　学生在分辨出不同的引用策略之后，还要分析作者如何通过引用这些文献来支持或表明自己的观点。

任务完成形式/师生互动形式　学生先独自完成阅读与分析，教师邀请一些学生发表意见，引导全班进行讨论。

任务二

任务内容　学生阅读段综述写作文本，识别其中使用的汇报动词并分析其用意。

任务要点　学生在识别出汇报动词之后，还要分析作者如何通过使用这些汇报动词来表达对该引用文献的评价或者所引用研究者对他人文献的看法。

任务完成形式/师生互动形式　学生先独自完成阅读与分析，教师邀请一些学生发表意见，引导全班进行讨论。

任务三

任务内容　学生阅读段综述写作文本，分析哪些地方以描述与介绍为主，哪些地方以诠释和解读为主，哪些地方加入个人评价。

任务要点　学生在辨析描述、解释和评价三个层面的写作目的时,要意识到这三个层面如何交错出现,以形成富有逻辑的、连贯的论述。

任务完成形式/师生互动形式　学生先独自完成阅读与分析,教师邀请一些学生发表意见,引导全班进行讨论。

（四）课后作业

1. 一般要求作业

Write 2 to 3 paragraphs on your literature review topic. Your writing should include：

（1）various citations of the relevant studies；

（2）your description, interpretation and critique of the studies；

（3）your own point of view concerning the topic.

2. 更高要求作业

Select a research topic and write a literature review (about 1500 words). You can review the articles recommended by the teacher, but you are highly suggested to search and select other articles for your reference.

授课教师可以根据课时安排选择一般要求或更高要求作业。如第十二章介绍,在本课程中,我们把综述写作与多文本阅读、同义转化技巧、概述技巧结合在一起,授课时数20小时,课程的阶段大作业即综述写作。因篇幅过长,本章仅点评了一般要求作业,没有对整篇综述的作业进行点评,仅在附录13.2附上评分标准供授课教师参考。

（五）学生作业点评

Example 1

Cigarette packaging contains rich information. Twelve studies in different countries have shown an increase in knowledge following the implementation of graphic and text warnings for cigarettes [10,12]. The increased knowledge covered many aspects, including the knowledge of the components of cigarettes, the effects of smoking on various organ systems, the health effects of secondhand smoke and so on [10].

A study indicated that removing as much brand information as possible from cigarette packages, such as colors, brand fonts and images, may reduce positive associations of cigarette brand image among teenagers, which influencing adolescents' perceptions [9]. The study also found that larger graphic warning labels reduced perceptions of positive pack characteristics among established smokers, experimenters, and susceptible non-smokers [9].

点评：该学生对文献的论述大部分属于描述性阐述,并没有对相关研究进行解读,也没有分析各文献之间的联系。所采用的汇报动词如show、indicate和find都属中性词,仅介绍他人研究的发现,并没有表述自己的讲解。

Example 2

The importance of reliable information source for DS is self-evident. Misinformation may undermine efficacy of DS or even induce undesirable effects [11]. A study of American consumers from two geographic locations reported physicians to be the most common source for DS information [7], but other studies disagreed with such a finding. A nationwide survey of Japanese college students identified the Internet as the most common source, followed by stores, television and advice from family, with information from healthcare providers being one of the lowest sources [12]. The Internet was also the commonest source in a survey of pregnant women from Croydon University Hospital [13] and in a study of people living with HIV/AIDS [9]. ***These studies***, *however, were limited in their study design as they were all cross-sectional study and only involved specific groups in the general population. Nonetheless, the relative lack professional recommendations of DS and the prominent role of the Internet in disseminating DS information were highlighted, calling attention to stricter scrutiny of online DS information* as large disparity was observed between the strength of causal inference among published articles and those widely shared on social platforms [14], which may contribute to poor health outcomes like increased costs and injuries [15]. In addition, healthcare practitioners, especially physicians and pharmacists, are advised to receive adequate training in DS[1,7,16] to be a more reputable source of scientific information and to promote more efficacious usage of DS.

点评：该学生有效地运用本单元的三种策略表述己见。在介绍他人研究内容的同时，加入了自己的解读与评价（见斜黑体部分），尤其是整合文献，在不同的研究之间建立联系（见划下划线部分）。所采用的汇报动词有中性的，如 report, identify 和 observe；有负面评价的，如 were limited 和 only involve；有正面评价的，如 were highlighted。

三、课程反馈

（一）学生反馈意见

在综述中表述己见对学生来说难度较大，在 2017 级参与问卷的 276 学生中，有 65％认为这部分的学习内容很难，是综述写作所有学习内容中最难的，因此有学生建议在课程中增加这方面的训练。但与其他学习内容一样，高达 87％的学生认为这对他们很有帮助。我们综合分析了学生对本章内容的具体评价，发现在综述写作中强调多样化的引用策略和对文献的评判，不仅培养了学生的批判性思维能力、发现问题的能力，对他们学术思维的塑造也起了作用。以下摘取一些学生对这部分内容的反馈：

"引用文献诠释自己观点，培养了我的批判性思维，让我在看医学论文文献时不仅仅去吸收知识，并且思考，拥有自己的独立观点和有创造性的理解，这对于我们的科研创新能力有很大帮助。"

"这个学习过程中锻炼了我总结概括并进一步发现问题的能力，有助于我日后在临床或者科研领域中发现问题。"

"我觉得作为医学相关人员，写论文是必然的。但是在阅读过程中，我发现一些注水文章，这种不负责任的文章伤害了科研界的生态，也警示我要好好做研究。"

"这改变了我对英语论文的看法，需要更加严谨以及合适的引用。"

"综述的学习改变了我对学术研究的看法，学术研究不仅仅是数据的处理就可以，还要考虑方方面面的影响。"

"这改变了我原先认为科研重在实验或调查过程的看法，认识到了科研文章撰写的重要性。"

（二）教师反馈意见

所有参与授课的教师都同意"表述己见"是学生综述写作的一大弱点，具体表现在三方面：一是写出来的内容太宽泛，没能就一个切入点集中进行综述，因此缺乏深入的分析；二是虽然能够梳理文献，但是综述以描述性阐述为主，缺少述评（interpretation 及 critique）；三是虽然表达了自己的观点，但缺乏依据和合理的论证。

针对这些问题，我们认为在教授这部分内容时要引导学生学习更多综述范例，包括已经发表的综述论文和以前学生的范文，并且在学生完成自己的综述后增加互评互改的时间，使得他们有机会运用实例分析"表述己见"策略的运用,同时改进自己的写作。为此,我们需要调整教学进度,在学生每完成一个综述结构(即前言、主体和结论)之后,都安排教师反馈和同侪反馈的时间。当然,这对课程的设置提出很大挑战。我们在课程中分配给文献阅读和综述写作的时间只有10周,很难安排大量的讨论时间。令人欣喜的是,这门学术英语课程在中国大学MOOC(慕课)"学校云"成功上线之后,我们使用了线上线下混合式教学的方法,"硬核"的写作策略和语言技能通过视频和材料发给学生课前观看和阅读,因此有更多的面授课时间用于讨论和交流。

附录13.1 课堂任务

(一)原综述论文文本

Perhaps because of the complex association between exposure to advertising and smoking (e. g., Klitzner, Gruenewald, & Bamberger, 1991), the large body of extant research on the effectiveness of cigarette advertising has generated equivocal conclusions on this subject. On the one hand, some investigators concluded that cigarette advertising perpetuates or increases consumption by enticing new smokers, by inducing former smokers to relapse, which hinders smokers' efforts to quit, and by acting as an external cue to smoke, which increases the level of consumption (e. g., Cohen, 2000; Pechmann & Knight, 2002; Pollay, 1989). These conclusions correspond with the increasing number of lawsuits filed against tobacco manufacturers and advertisers (see, for example, Byrnes & Carey, 2004). On the other hand, other researchers report that cigarette advertising merely enhances the brand loyalty and brand-switching behaviors of established smokers (e. g., Calfee, 2000; Smith, 1990).

Because the findings from the previous decades of research are inconsistent and because there is no consensus regarding the relationship between advertising and smoking, scholars have attempted to consolidate the research findings in this area by utilizing meta-analyses. Probably the most noteworthy meta-analysis on this topic to date was published by Andrews and Franke (1991), who examined 48 time-series analyses of cigarette industry aggregate sales as a function of aggregate advertising and other variables (i. e., price) in the period from 1933 to 1990... Andrews and Franke found that cigarette advertising effects were consistent with a market evolution perspective... However, Andrews and Franke's meta-analysis concentrated solely on aggregated (i. e., econometric) data and, thus, excluded brand-level data, cross-sectional studies, and estimates based on survey results. Similarly, Gallet and List (2003) focused exclusively on aggregated data in their review, which comprised a total of 86 studies. Notably, a majority of the studies included in Gallet and List (2003) did not specifically examine advertising but instead provided insight on other variables related to consumption, such as price and income.

(Capella, et al., 2011, p. 269)

(二) 参考答案

任务一

Two main citation strategies are used in this excerpt: synthesizing and summarizing. There are four places of citation in the first paragraph, all of which use synthesizing skills to provide evidences for main findings in previous research. The three places of citation in the second paragraph use summarizing skills to sum up the research methods or findings from a specific study.

任务二

The excerpt uses various reporting words, most of which indicate a neutral position to evaluate or conclude other research, such as "conclude", "report", "find" and "examine". But some reporting verbs, while used with certain adverbs or adjectives, imply the author's negative evaluation (e. g. "did not specifically examine" and "focus exclusively on") and some display the author's interpretation of the cited literature (e. g. "has generated equivocal conclusion", "correspond with" and "have attempted to consolidate").

任务三

In the following graph, the interpretive texts are highlighted in light grey, and those which respond with deficit or strength critique are highlighted in dark grey, while the unmarked texts are mainly descriptive. Please also note that in the last but one and two sentences, the author is also implying a solution to more reliable meta-analysis: the data that have been excluded in previous meta-analysis should be included. In this excerpt, the layers of three rhetorical functions (descriptive, interpretive, and critique) are interlaced into logical, coherent and powerful discussion of previous research.

> **INTERPRETIVE**
> Perhaps because of the complex association between exposure to advertising and smoking (e.g., Klitzner, Gruenewald, & Bamberger, 1991), the large body of extant research on the effectiveness of cigarette advertising has generated equivocal conclusions on this subject. On the one hand, some investigators concluded that cigarette advertising perpetuates or increases consumption by enticing new smokers, by
> **DESCRIPTIVE**
> inducing former smokers to relapse, which hinders smokers' efforts to quit, and by acting as an external cue to smoke, which increases the level of consumption (e.g., Cohen, 2000; Pechmann & Knight, 2002; Pollay, 1989). These conclusions correspond with the increasing number of lawsuits filed against tobacco
> **INTERPRETIVE**
> manufacturers and advertisers (see, for example, Bymes & Carey, 2004). On the other hand, other researchers report that cigarette advertising merely enhances the brand loyalty and brand-switching behaviors of
> **DESCRIPTIVE**
> established smokers (e.g., Calfee, 2000; Smith, 1990).
> Because the findings from the previous decades of research are inconsistent and because there is no
> **INTERPRETIVE**
> consensus regarding the relationship between advertising and smoking, scholars have attempted to

consolidate the research findings in this area by utilizing meta-analyses. Probably the most noteworthy meta-analysis on this topic to date was published by Andrews and Franke(1991) [CRITIQUE], who examined 48 time-series analyses of cigarette industry aggregate sales as a function of aggregate advertising and other variables(i.e., price) in the period from 1933 to 1990....Andrews and Franke found that cigarette advertising effects were consistent with a market evolution perspective... [DESCRIPTIVE] However, Andrews and Franke's meta-analysis concentrated solely on aggregated (i.e., econometric) data and, thus, ex dude d brand-level data, cross-sectional studies, and estimates based on survey results. [CRITIQUE(implying a solution)] Similarly, Gallet and List (2003) focused exclusively on aggregated data in their review, [DESCRIPTIVE] which comprised a total of 86 studies. Notably, a majority of the studies included in Gallet and List (2003) did not specifically examine advertising but instead provided insight on other variables related to consumption, such as price and income. [CRITIQUE]

附录 13.2 综述写作评分标准

		1	2	3	4	5
A Content	A1 Relevance	Not relevant to topic	Topic is not fully addressed	Some studies included are irrelevant to topic	Reviews studies that are generally relevant to the topic	Reviews studies that are highly relevant to the topic
	A2 Currency	Currency is unreasonable	A lot of studies included are with unreasonable currency	Some studies included are with unreasonable currency	Most studies included are with reasonable currency	All studies included are with reasonable and meaningful currency
	A3 Reliability	Fails to provide sources	A lot of studies included are from unreliable sources	Some studies included are from unreliable sources	Most studies included are from reliable sources	All studies included are from highly reliable sources
B Thinking	B1 Structure	Has almost no evidence of structure	Lacks focus and/or structure	Has a generally organized structure	Has a generally clear and well-organized structure	Sustains a clear and well-organized structure

（续表）

		1	2	3	4	5
	B2 Logicality	Has almost no logic in development of paragraphs	Lacks logic in development of paragraphs	Development of paragraphs is somewhat logical	Development of paragraphs is generally logical	Development of paragraphs is rigorously logical
	B3 Writer's voice	Has almost no writer's voice	Lacks writer's voice	Somewhat presents writer's voice	Presents adequate writer's voice	Presents well thought-out writer's voice
C Language and communication	C1 Accuracy	Use of vocabulary and grammar is problematic and consistently interferes with communication	Use of vocabulary and grammar frequently interferes with communication	Use of vocabulary and grammar expresses meaning with acceptable clarity	Use of vocabulary and grammar expresses meaning clearly	Use of vocabulary and grammar expresses meaning precisely
	C2 Cohesion	Has almost no use of cohesive devices, ideas not linked	Lacks cohesive devices to connect information and ideas	Information and ideas are somewhat connected with some use of cohesive devices	Information and ideas are connected with use of cohesive devices	Information and ideas are well connected with effective use of cohesive devices
	C3 Academic features	Inappropriate to communicate for academic purposes	Inadequate to communicate for academic purposes	Somewhat demonstrates features of academic written language	Adequately demonstrates features of academic written language	Appropriately and well demonstrates features of academic written language

参考文献

Bakhtin MM, 1981. // Bakhtin MM, Holquist M, Emerson C, et al. The dialogic imagination: Four essays by. Austin: University of Texas Press.

Capella et al., 2011. A review of the effect of cigarette advertising. International Journal of Research in Marketing, 28: 269-279.

Hirvela A, Belcher D, 2001. Coming back to voice: The multiple voices and identities of mature multilingual writers. Journal of Second Language Writing, 10(1-2): 83-106.

Hart C, 1998. Doing a literature review: releasing the social science research imagination. London: Sage Publication.

Hu G, Wang G, 2014. Disciplinary and ethnolinguistic influences on citation in research articles. Journal of

English for Academic Purposes, 14: 14-28.

Hyland K, Jiang F, 2017. Points of reference: Changing patterns of academic citation. Applied Linguistics. Epub ahead of print, 31 May 2017.

Matsuda PK, Tardy CM, 2007. Voice in academic writing: The rhetorical construction of author identity in blind manuscript review. English for Specific Purposes, 26(2): 235-249.

Swales JM, 1990. Genre analysis: English in academic and research settings. Cambridge: Cambridge University Press.

Swales JM, 2014. Variation in citational practice in a corpus of student biology papers: From parenthetical plonking to intertextual storytelling. Written Communication, 31(1): 118-141.

The University of Melbourne Academic Skills. (n. d.). Writing the Literature Review [2019-11]. https://www.youtube.com/user/UoMAcademicSkills/videos.

Velliaris D, Miller J, 2009. Reporting verbs. The University of Adelaide [2019-11]. https://www.york.ac.uk/students/studying/skills/integrity.

第十四章 研究计划书

杨 苗

一、对教学主题和教学思路的解读

撰写研究计划书对许多本科生来说是陌生的,因为他们鲜有机会接触研究,更谈不上写研究计划书。我们之所以将其纳入课程内容,首先,是因为汕头大学医学院许多本科生从一年级开始学习写研究计划书(《医学科学推理》选修课程的要求),还有大约20%的学生在二年级的时候经遴选参加暑期自主设计研究性实验课,需要完成临床研究设计(中英文版),所以将其纳入课程内容能满足学生的专业学习需求。其次,在我们的课程规划里,研究计划书上接综述写作,下接壁报研究,是引导学生由文献阅读、综述写作到形成自己研究的重要环节。

研究思维是学术英语课程一个重要内容,是批判性思维在专业领域的具体运用。在本课程中,我们对学生研究思维的培养始于文献阅读与分析,初步运用于综述写作,撰写研究计划书则帮助他们进一步思考研究的本质,并形成更为连贯的思维过程。但在教授这部分内容时,学术英语老师遇到最大的质疑是能否胜任教授不同专业的学生写研究计划书。在学术英语教学和科研领域,大家长期纠结于这个问题:该由英语老师还是专业老师来教学术英语写作课?英语老师的劣势在于不了解其他专业的背景知识和研究现状,布置的作业可能脱离真实的专业场景(Huang,2017)。和专业老师合作教学当然是上上之选,但在现实中合作教学成本很高,不合实际。我们的做法是从选用素材到任务设计、作业评估等方面都多与专业老师交流、请教。研究思路在任何一个领域大致相同,起始于研究问题,终结于研究结论。我们在讲述如何写研究计划书时,关键在于把研究计划书各部分内容之间的内在逻辑联系阐述清楚,以"为什么要以这样的顺序写(why)""每部分一般写什么内容(what)""怎么样写好每部分内容(how)"这样的次序安排上课内容。至于不同专业对研究计划书的不同要求,属于微观差异,往往可以通过和学生或者专业老师讨论达成共识,事实上这并非英语老师教学的最大障碍。

本章的教学主题有两个:视研究计划书为论证过程(research proposal as a process of argumentation)和视研究计划书为学术作品(research proposal as a product)。我们首先将撰写研究计划书视为一个论证的过程,强调构思过程中的逻辑思维,其次才强调其作为成品应该具备的基本内容和写法。

(一)教学主题

1. 研究计划书——一个论证过程:我们首先将研究计划书书视为论证"what""how"和"why"的过程,可以避免学生肤浅地认为研究计划书就是一个简单描述研究计划的文本,因而忽略其背后体现的严密逻辑。此部分的教学主题主要强调研究计划书应该围绕三个核心问题来写。一是研究想要回答什么问题("what");二是研究尝试如何回答问题,即使用何种研究方法("how");三是研究有何意义或贡献("why")。对这三个核心问题的回答必须环环相扣,才能形成内在的逻辑连贯性。

2. 研究计划书——一个学术作品:将研究计划书作为一个最终写作成品来看,不管研究主题属于哪个研究领域,也不管提交研究计划书的目的在于完成学位论文还是申请科研项目,都会包含这些基本内容,如标题页面、前言、文献综述、研究设计与方法、研究意义、参考文献。这些内容依次回答以上三个核心问题,每一部分的写作目的和内容都非常明确。

(二) 教学思路

讲述研究计划书的构思过程往往很抽象,需要借助具体研究案例加以说明。其次,学生很难在上完两次课后就写出一个研究计划书,需要将本章内容与上下两章(综述写作和学术壁报)的学习内容联系起来完成,所以预留给学生完成和修改计划书的时间就要多一点,课堂上也要安排学生对各自的研究计划书进行点评。

二、教学案例设计

(一) 教学目标

1. 学生能了解研究计划书在专业学习或学术研究中的作用、撰写的思路、基本内容构成和写作要求。

2. 学生通过运用之前文献综述的成果构思自己的研究、形成研究计划并规范地表述出来,进一步学习学术研究的本质和逻辑思维。

3. 学生通过撰写研究计划书综合运用学术阅读和写作技巧。

(二) 教学内容

1. Research proposal——contexts and purposes of usage

教学内容	注解
❖ **Two contexts to use** ✓ The university context——approval of research proposal leading to research as part of requirement for an academic degree ✓ The research grant or funding context——application for research funds	此部分通过介绍研究计划书使用的场景、主要内容和评判标准,先帮助学生了解何谓研究计划书
❖ **Three central questions to answer** ✓ What is the research trying to find out (research questions)? ✓ How does the research propose to answer its questions (research methods)? ✓ Why is this research worth doing (research significance)?	

(续表)

教学内容	注解
❖ **General judgments** ✓ Is the proposed research feasible and doable? ✓ Is the research worth doing? ✓ Can the candidate do it?	

2. Research proposal as a process of argumentation

教学内容	注解
❖ **Research proposal as a process of argumentation** ✓ Different parts fit together ✓ The logic behind the study (what—how—why)	此部分强调研究计划书背后的逻辑思维，主要讨论为什么必须先有研究问题，才有研究方法，即"what"问题如何主导了"how"问题。在"what"问题上，最重要的是如何区分五个层次的"研究问题"，从宽泛到明确，由抽象至具体，最终水到渠成地引入研究方法（即"how"问题）。建议教师找具体的研究为例，分析五个层次的问题，也可以参照 Punch(2000)一书里所举的例子(pp24-26)
❖ **Distinguishing five levels of concepts and questions** ✓ Research area：general，stated in one or a few words ✓ Research topic：more specific，falling within the area ✓ General research question(s)：general & abstract，not directly answerable ✓ Specific research question(s)：specific，detailed and concrete，directly answerable ✓ Data collection question(s)：asked to collect data to answer research questions	完成此部分的讲解后，安排课堂任务一。任务讲义见 Kouwenhoven(2015)，参考答案见附录14.1。因这部分内容是学习难点，附录里对学生容易混淆的问题也进行了分析

3. Research proposal as a product

教学内容	注解
❖ **A basic structure** ✓ Title page ✓ Introduction ✓ Literature review ✓ Research design and methods ✓ Implications and contribution to knowledge ✓ Reference list or bibliography	此部分介绍研究计划书的基本内容
❖ **Title page** ✓ Proposed title ✓ Author's name ✓ Supervisor ✓ Institution	

（续表）

教学内容	注解
❖ **Introduction** √ Introducing the topic √ Giving background and context √ Outlining problem statements and research questions	此部分内容用于回答第一个核心问题：What is the research trying to find out?
❖ **Literature review** √ Providing a summary of previous related research √ Analyzing their strength and weakness √ Giving a justification of your research	文献综述是对第一个核心问题的进一步论证，需要从三个方面阐述相关文献：① 哪些文献与研究相关？② 研究主题与相关文献是什么关系，即如何契入研究现状？③ 如何运用相关文献论证研究计划？ 需要注意的是，社科类的研究计划书经常把文献综述作为独立一部分来写，但理工科类的计划书常把文献综述作为前言的一部分。授课教授应该清楚告诉学生这种学科差异，并说明本单元所提供的范例属理工科模式
❖ **Research design** √ A statement of overall approach and relevant strategies √ Practical steps: data sources; tools and procedures; data collection schedule; potential obstacles; data analysis e.g. This study adopted a case-study approach combining different methods to illuminate the 10-year EMI program from various angles... Data were collected from students' test scores, survey responses and focus group discussions. Teachers completed surveys and focus groups. (Yang, et al., 2019)	此部分内容用于回答第二个核心问题：How does the research propose to answer its questions? 对研究方法的概述（statement of overall approach）能帮助学生把握研究的本质、区分研究类型、辨别研究策略。此处老师除了从别人已经发表的论文中援引例句外，还可以让学生自己写类似的表述，完成课堂任务二。任务讲义见Kouwenhoven(2015)，参考答案见附录14.1
❖ **Implications and contribution** √ to knowledge in the area √ to policy considerations √ to practitioners	此部分内容用于回答第三个核心问题：why is this research worth doing? 此处可简单提及其他可能包括的内容，如研究的局限性及相应措施，或者计划如何获得研究参与者的知情同意等。如有必要，可以加上附录，附上预研究/预实验的报告，或比较详细的数据收集日程表

4. From outline to draft—discussion and peer review

教学内容	注解
❖ Discussion—outline of the research proposal ✓ Each group introduce the outline to the whole class ✓ Comments and questions are invited from other groups to arouse discussion ✓ Each group revise the outline based on the results of discussion	此部分介绍为配合完成本单元作业而安排的课堂讨论和同侪反馈活动。讨论内容主要是学生自己的习作,所以这里不提供讲义,但可参考一份研究计划书大纲的范例(附录14.2)
❖ Peer review—draft of the research proposal ✓ The drafts are exchanged and reviewed in between different groups before the class ✓ Each group present the comments on another group's draft ✓ Each group revise the draft based on the results of discussion	

(三)学习任务

任务一

任务内容　学生快速阅读一篇研究论文(Kouwenhoven,et al.,2015),分析五个层次的研究问题(研究领域、研究主题、总研究问题、细化研究问题、数据收集问题)。

任务要点　引导学生重点阅读前言、文献综述和研究方法部分的内容,分析作者如何由抽象到具体表述这些问题,并以思维导图的形式呈现。

任务完成形式/师生互动形式　学生先独立阅读,然后分组讨论,之后老师以提问的形式检查任务完成情况。

任务二

任务内容　学生快速阅读任务一的论文,用1~2个句子写出该研究所使用的研究方法和策略。

任务要点　引导学生重点阅读研究方法部分的内容,寻找与研究方法和策略相关的关键词。

任务完成形式/师生互动形式　学生独立写出句子,老师邀请部分学生朗读句子并加以点评。

(注:指定学生阅读的论文见 Kouwenhoven,et al.,2015,练习答案见本章附录14.1。)

(四)课后作业

以小组为单位,基于学术写作课程里文献阅读和综述写作的收获,设计一个与医学人文话题相关的研究计划书。也可以基于专业课程或实验研究的收获,设计一个与医学研究相关的研究计划书(研究计划书评分标准见附录14.3)。

(五)学生作业点评

这篇作为范例的研究计划书是汕头大学医学院一组2016级的学生完成的(林颖怡 等,

2019),入选 2019 年中国大学生国际研讨会并做学术报告[①]。我们获得各位作者的同意在此使用其为范例。

Title: A Structural Equation Modeling Approach to Advance Directives Acceptance in China

Abstract

Advance directives (ADs) document patient's instruction on future medical care in case of disease aggravation. Enlightened by a pilot study suggesting the potentiality of practicing ADs in China, this study aims to investigate the relationships between five predictors of ADs preference (family functioning, knowledge of palliative care, treatment self-determination, quality of life and Chinese culture) and ADs acceptance. Questionnaires containing six adapted scales will be administered to 300 patients and their family members in China's hospitals. Exploratory and confirmatory factor analysis will be employed to validate the measurements and the hypothesized model will be tested with structural equation modeling. The results may be of significant reference value for the application of culture-sensitive ADs in China and even in other culturally-connected countries.

Key words: Advance directives, China, Structural equation modeling

Introduction

Advance directives (ADs) are formal documents that nominate the patients' substitute decision maker and/or detail their wishes regarding life-sustaining treatment through a living will[1,2], in the event that their decision-making ability becomes compromised due to terminal illness or cognitive impairment. They are widely considered to be essential tools in protecting patient autonomy, particularly at the end of life[3]. Previous studies also suggest that ADs play a critical role in improving patient and family satisfaction with hospital care and reducing the incidence of post-traumatic stress in surviving relatives[4,5.] Unlike other countries (e.g. Australia[6], Canada[6], Germany[7], the United States[8] and Singapore[9]) where ADs have been legislated, the prevalence of ADs remains relatively low in China[10-12]. However, as China became an aging society at the end of the 20th century and the medical expenditure has been increasing rapidly ever since[13], there is growing interest about palliative care and the practice of ADs. The Beijing Advance Directive Promotion Association was established with the approval of the Beijing Civil Affairs Bureau in 2013[14] and this organization is dedicated to sowing seeds of education about how ADs can improve the care of terminally ill patients[12].

Over the years, multiple research has been conducted to investigate the predictors of ADs preference among patients or nursing home residents in China, from which five prominent predictors may be extracted for further evaluation. From Wuhan and Hong Kong study[10,15], the knowledge of palliative care and treatment self-determination were two significant factors that facilitated peoples' decisions to complete ADs. Another study in Sun Yet-sen University Cancer Center, however, identified good family support as a possible risk predictor for positive attitude toward ADs[16]. Furthermore, the moral perspective of end-of-life care is influenced primarily by Confucianism[17] in China and mixed results were observed regarding the impact of Chinese culture on ADs in research from both Western and Eastern countries[18]. Some reported that participants welcomed the idea of ADs[12,19,20] while others suggested that ADs, as traditionally conceived, were met with indifference and negativity[21]. It was also noted that socio-demographic characteristics such as age, education level and quality of life were associated with ADs preparation[22]. Nonetheless, there is no available study that demonstrates the possible pathways of how these predictors can affect people's acceptance of ADs in

---

[①] 该研究计划书的前期研究也是这组学生在本课程完成的作业,其研究参加首届全国大学生科研英语演讲比赛,获得本科组全国特等奖,获奖视频见 http://sentbase.com/cn5mrp/?content-app-v=&p=3419。

China. Additionally, in a pilot study on the feasibility of ADs implementation in China among health care providers (No=118), the practice of ADs was deemed as an arduous task but with promising prospect, reinforcing the necessity of exploring possible interactions between multiple key predictors of ADs.

Objectives

This study aims to investigate the relationships between five predictors of ADs preference (family functioning, knowledge of palliative care, treatment self-determination and Chinese culture) and ADs acceptance and to identify the main factors influencing people's attitude toward ADs in China.

Methods

Online questionnaires containing a socio-demographic section and six scales, measuring family functioning (BFRS)[23], knowledge of palliative care (PaCKS)[24], treatment self-determination (IPAS)[25], quality of life (QOLS)[26,27], Chinese culture with emphasis on death and filial piety (modified from AVS[28,29]) and advance directives acceptance (Chan et al.[30]), will be administered to collect quantitative data on 300 patients and their family members in Guangdong hospitals. The six scales are adapted from previous research and will be translated into Chinese. Given the general lack of awareness of ADs in mainland China, all participants will be introduced to the concept of ADs before completing the questionnaire. Structural equation modeling (SEM) will be used for factor analysis and path analysis. In particular, the reliability and factor structures of the measurements will be assessed using Cronbach's alpha (α) and exploratory factor analysis (EFA) in the preliminary study respectively. In the main study, confirmatory factor analysis (CFA) will be utilized to validate the measurements and the hypothesized structural model of the six variables will be tested via SEM.

Possible findings and implications

The SEM results might quantify the interplay among the five predictors of ADs preference and demonstrate how they influence the overall acceptance of ADs, thus providing a unique insight into Chinese perspective on end-of-life decision as well as an alternative means of identifying the main factors accounting for ADs acceptance. It is hypothesized that Chinese culture and knowledge of palliative care are the two strongest predictors of ADs. The study finding, therefore, may be of significant reference value for the development of specific ADs tailored to Chinese people's beliefs to facilitate broader discussion of ADs in Chinese society. In addition, developing countries that share similar culture values with China may also benefit from the results by modifying the tested model based on national conditions to formulate a suitable version of ADs for themselves.

Hypothesized model

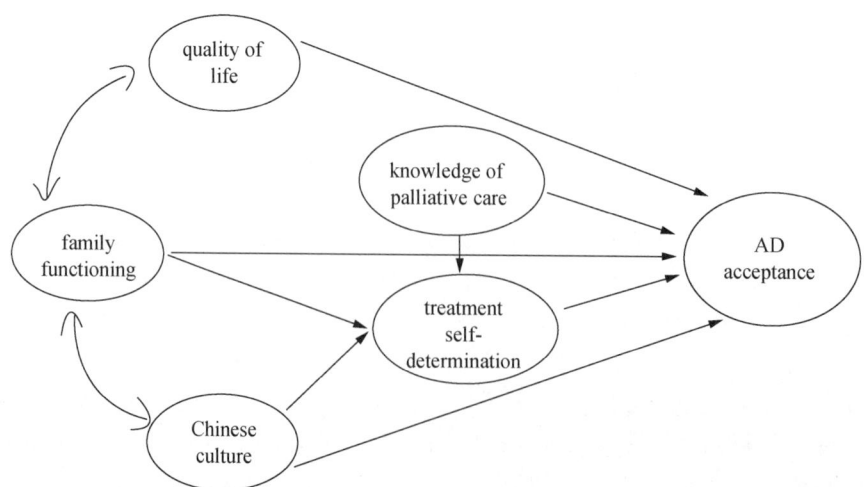

References

1. Silveira MJ, Kim SY, Langa KM. Advance directives and outcomes of surrogate decision making before death. N Engl J Med. 2010 Apr 1;362(13): 1211-8. PubMed PMID: 20357283. PMCID: PMC2880881.
2. Hannon B, Swami N, Pope A, Rodin G, Dougherty E, Mak E, et al. The oncology palliative care clinic at the Princess Margaret Cancer Centre: an early intervention model for patients with advanced cancer. Support Care Cancer. 2015 Apr;23(4): 1073-80. PubMed PMID: 25281230.
3. O'Sullivan R, Mailo K, Angeles R, Agarwal G. Advance directives: survey of primary care patients. Can Fam Physician. 2015 Apr;61(4): 353-6. PubMed PMID: 25873704. PMCID: PMC4396762.
4. Detering KM, Hancock AD, Reade MC, Silvester W. The impact of advance care planning on end of life care in elderly patients: randomised controlled trial. BMJ. 2010 Mar 23; 340: c1345. PubMed PMID: 20332506. PMCID: PMC2844949.
5. Chan CWH, Wong MMH, Choi KC, Chan HYL, Chow AYM, Lo RSK, et al. What Patients, Families, Health Professionals and Hospital Volunteers Told Us about Advance Directives. Asia Pac J Oncol Nurs. 2019 Jan-Mar;6(1): 72-7. PubMed PMID: 30599019. PMCID: PMC6287378.
6. Brown M. The law and practice associated with advance directives in Canada and Australia: similarities, differences and debates. J Law Med. 2003 Aug;11(1): 59-76. PubMed PMID: 14526727.
7. Wiesing U, Jox RJ, Hessler HJ, Borasio GD. A new law on advance directives in Germany. J Med Ethics. 2010 Dec;36(12): 779-83. PubMed PMID: 21112938.
8. Brown BA. The history of advance directives. A literature review. J Gerontol Nurs. 2003 Sep;29(9): 4-14. PubMed PMID: 14528744.
9. Tay M, Chia SE, Sng J. Knowledge, attitudes and practices of the Advance Medical Directive in a residential estate in Singapore. Ann Acad Med Singapore. 2010 Jun;39(6): 424-8. PubMed PMID: 20625616.
10. Chung RY, Wong EL, Kiang N, Chau PY, Lau JYC, Wong SY, et al. Knowledge, Attitudes, and Preferences of Advance Decisions, End-of-Life Care, and Place of Care and Death in Hong Kong. A Population-Based Telephone Survey of 1067 Adults. J Am Med Dir Assoc. 2017 Apr 1; 18(4): 367 e19- e-27. PubMed PMID: 28214237.
11. Cheng HWB. Advance Care Planning in Chinese Seniors: Cultural Perspectives. J Palliat Care. 2018 Jan 1: 825859718763644. PubMed PMID: 29569520.
12. Ting FH, Mok E. Advance directives and life-sustaining treatment: attitudes of Hong Kong Chinese elders with chronic disease. Hong Kong Med J. 2011 Apr;17(2): 105-11. PubMed PMID: 21471589.
13. Chen Y, Chen L, Wang Q, Xu X, editors. The Research of Medical Expenditure in China. Education and Management; 2011 2011//; Berlin, Heidelberg: Springer Berlin Heidelberg.
14. Kang L, Liu X-H, Zhang J, Shan P-Y, Wang J-P, Zhong P, et al. Attitudes Toward Advance Directives Among Patients and Their Family Members in China. Journal of the American Medical Directors Association. 2017 2017/09/01/;18(9): 808. e7-. e11.
15. Ni P, Zhou J, Wang ZX, Nie R, Phillips J, Mao J. Advance directive and end-of-life care preferences among nursing home residents in Wuhan, China: a cross-sectional study. J Am Med Dir Assoc. 2014 Oct; 15 (10): 751-6. PubMed PMID: 25066002.
16. Zhang Q, Xie C, Xie S, Liu Q. The Attitudes of Chinese Cancer Patients and Family Caregivers toward Advance Directives. Int J Environ Res Public Health. 2016 Aug 11; 13(8). PubMed PMID: 27529264. PMCID: PMC4997502.
17. Li LB. Clinical review: Ethics and end-of-life care for critically ill patients in China. Crit Care. 2013 Dec 4;17(6): 244. PubMed PMID: 24313980. PMCID: PMC4057346.
18. Lee MC, Hinderer KA, Kehl KA. A Systematic Review of Advance Directives and Advance Care Planning

in Chinese People From Eastern and Western Cultures. Journal of Hospice & Palliative Nursing. 2014;16(2).

19. Wong SY, Lo SH, Chan CH, Chui HS, Sze WK, Tung Y. Is it feasible to discuss an advance directive with a Chinese patient with advanced malignancy? A prospective cohort study. Hong Kong Med J. 2012 Jun;18(3): 178-85. PubMed PMID: 22665680.

20. Chan HYL, Pang SMC. Let me talk—an advance care planning programme for frail nursing home residents. Journal of Clinical Nursing. 2010 2010/11/01;19(21-22): 3073-84.

21. Bowman KW, Singer PA. Chinese seniors' perspectives on end-of-life decisions. Soc Sci Med. 2001 Aug;53(4): 455-64. PubMed PMID: 11459396.

22. del Pozo Puente K, Hidalgo JL-T, Herráez MJS, Bravo BN, Rodríguez JO, Guillén VG. Study of the factors influencing the preparation of advance directives. Archives of Gerontology and Geriatrics. 2014 2014/01/01/;58(1): 20-4.

23. Fok CC, Allen J, Henry D, People Awakening T. The brief family relationship scale: a brief measure of the relationship dimension in family functioning. Assessment. 2014 Feb;21(1): 67-72. PubMed PMID: 22084400. PMCID: PMC3292682.

24. Kozlov E, Carpenter BD, Rodebaugh TL. Development and validation of the Palliative Care Knowledge Scale (PaCKS). Palliat Support Care. 2017 Oct;15(5): 524-34. PubMed PMID: 28025952.

25. Stiggelbout AM, Molewijk AC, Otten W, Timmermans DR, van Bockel JH, Kievit J. Ideals of patient autonomy in clinical decision making: a study on the development of a scale to assess patients' and physicians' views. J Med Ethics. 2004 Jun;30(3): 268-74. PubMed PMID: 15173361. PMCID: PMC1733851.

26. Dantas RAS, Ciol MA. Flanagan Quality of Life Scale. In: Michalos AC, editor. Encyclopedia of Quality of Life and Well-Being Research. Dordrecht: Springer Netherlands; 2014. p. 2284-8.

27. Burckhardt CS, Anderson KL. The Quality of Life Scale (QOLS): reliability, validity, and utilization. Health Qual Life Outcomes. 2003 Oct 23;1: 60. PubMed PMID: 14613562. PMCID: PMC269997.

28. Kim B, R. Atkinson D, H. Yang P. The Asian Values Scale: Development, Factor Analysis, Validation, and Reliability1999. 342-52 p.

29. Kim B, Hong SH. A Psychometric Revision of the Asian Values Scale Using the Rasch Model2004. 15-27 p.

30. Chan CWH, Wong MMH, Choi KC, Chan HYL, Chow AYM, Lo RSK, et al. Prevalence, Perception, and Predictors of Advance Directives among Hong Kong Chinese: A Population-based Survey. Int J Environ Res Public Health. 2019 Jan 28;16(3). PubMed PMID: 30696082. PMCID: PMC6388376.

点评：

这是一篇出色的研究计划书，每一部分的内容都非常到位，充分回答了三个核心问题：研究想要回答什么问题，研究尝试如何回答问题，研究有何意义或贡献。研究背景部分由研究主题AD（advanced directive，即为病人准备的预先说明书）的定义入手，介绍国外使用现状和研究现状，然后介绍国内AD的使用情况和对AD接受度影响因素的相关研究。文献引用翔实，清楚列出各种影响因素，并指出对多种因素的交互影响进行研究的必要性。此研究背景通过文献综述充分论证进行本研究的必要性，研究目的水到渠成地呈现。研究方法部分介绍了所采用的六份问卷和结构方程建模（SEM）的统计方法。在预期研究结果的同时介绍了一个预期模型，这是根据现有文献对各个影响因素的描述所预测的SEM的建模结果，体现了这组学生对相关研究的深入了解和对SEM统计方法的熟练掌握。这些并非泛泛而谈的预期研究结果与意义，正体现了研究计划的必要性、可行性和研究者的执行能力。

在语言表述方面，该计划书使用规范、正式的学术语言，表述清晰、准确、简洁，文内引用文献符合要求。

三、课程反馈

（一）学生反馈意见

本单元参与反馈的学生达 302 人，约 86% 认为撰写研究计划书对他们未来的专业的学习和发展很有帮助，约 79% 表示对这部分的学习很投入，约 75% 表示学习收获很大。另外，55% 的学生认为通过这些学习其科研思维能力有所提高，16% 的学生认为有很大提高。不少学生意识到学习撰写研究计划书对以后的科研工作有很大帮助，有的学生写道："研究计划书的学习，对将来自己准备其他实验项目的申请或论文的准备都有帮助。"有的学生甚至表示："学习撰写研究计划书，阅读了相关研究的文献，对科研产生了兴趣，觉得未来可以往学术研究方向走。"还有的学生将所学内容进行横向联系，发现"研究计划书的撰写的提纲和文章的摘要不完全相同，这是我之前没有注意到点的"，说明我们将研究计划书作为独特的学术体裁纳入课程，并运用体裁教学法进行教学，确实能提高学生的体裁意识，为他们在课程结束之后的自主学习和专业发展打下基础。而同时有 47% 的学生认为本单元的学习难度很大，尤其是关于 5 个层面的研究问题的分析，容易混淆。但学生表示，经过老师的点评和讲解后，这些概念清楚了，对于研究计划书中的研究背景、研究目的和研究方法的写作很有帮助。

（二）教师反馈意见

学生对本单元学习内容的接受度和认可度这么高，得益于思路严谨、由简入繁的内容安排。我们把原来对学生来说比较陌生、颇有挑战性的学术写作任务分解为若干小任务，使学生可以逐步领会、掌握。学生完成的小任务总结如下：

1. 阅读一篇已发表的研究论文，总结其五个层面的研究问题并用一句话写出研究方法概述。
2. 写出与自己研究相关的五个层面的研究问题和研究方法概述。
3. 写出研究计划书大纲并在全班汇报、讨论。
4. 分别写出计划书各个主体部分并在全班汇报、讨论。
5. 完成计划书初稿并进行同侪反馈。
6. 修改定稿。

整个教学过程长达 5 周，给了学生充分的时间思考自己要进行的研究。因为他们完成计划书后要真正进行研究，然后形成壁报报告，所以研究设计必须具有科学性和可行性，而不是纸上谈兵。

授课老师也反映研究计划书的教学难点在于对不同层次的研究问题的厘清，学生能否掌握这些概念主要体现在计划书的研究背景、研究目的和研究方法三大主体部分。我们使用范例（附录 14.2）展示 5 个层面的研究问题如何在计划书大纲里一一展现（图 14.1），然后引导学生以同样的研究思路去分析自己的计划书大纲。之后又对计划书的研究背景和研究目的进行语步分析（图 14.2），这样把科研思维和语言表述紧密联系起来，让学生学会如何厘清研究思路，如何进行简明扼要的表述。

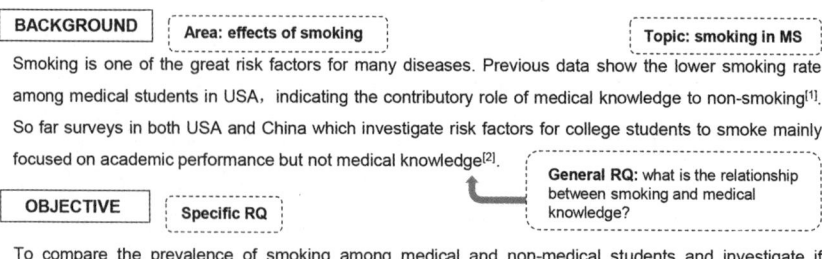

图 14.1　研究计划书大纲五个层面的研究问题分析

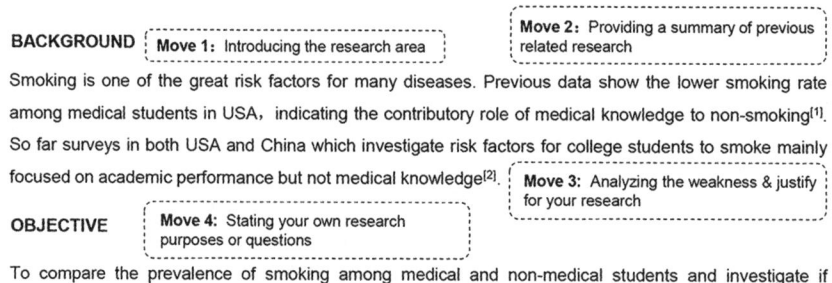

图 14.2　研究计划书大纲研究问题和目的语步分析

附录 14.1　课堂学习任务答案与问题分析

任务一参考答案

research area：euthanasia

research topic：physicians' attitudes towards euthanasia

general research question(s)：What are the opinions of physicians about euthanasia in patients who are unable to communicate?

specific research question(s)：What are the opinions of physicians and members of the general public in the Netherlands on euthanasia in patients with advanced dementia?

data collection question(s)：What data can be collected concerning the respondents' age, sex, education, occupation and two questions about the case: Is the physician's act legal in the Netherlands? Do you personally agree with the physician's act?

完成任务一时学生易混淆后面三个层次的研究问题。General research questions 比较宽泛，没有明确具体的研究对象和研究地域，只有大致的人群，因而 not directly answerable。

对 general research questions 的论述,一般出现在研究论文前言第二个语步,即 summarizing previous research。specific research questions 则进一步明确具体的研究对象和研究地域,是在具体分析前人研究的空白、指出存在问题(即前言第三个语步:preparing for present research—gap indications & question raising)之后才出现,属前言第四个语步(introducing present research)(Swales,2011)。学生容易将宽泛的研究问题等同于具体的研究问题,如以下例子:

例 1

general research question(s):What are the opinions of physicians and the general public on euthanasia in patients with advanced dementia?

specific research question(s):What are the opinions of physicians and the general public on the acceptability of euthanasia in patients with advanced dementia?

data collection questions 在研究方法部分出现,是收集数据时所提的非常具体的问题,这一点在看别人的论文时比较容易把握。但有些学生写出自己的研究问题时误会为需要把具体问卷或访谈的所有问题一一列出。我们需要帮助学生分析这些问题背后体现的概念(construct),并根据概念将问题概括出来,才能形成"data collection questions"(例 2)。这样的讨论和分析能有效帮助学生理清研究思路:必须由重要概念入手设计问卷的主要结构,而不是想到什么问题就列出来,毫无章法。

例 2(a):修改前的数据收集问题

(1) Do college students think it necessary to maintain health such as keep fit during self-quarantine?

(2) Do college students collect information from medical professionals?

(3) Will college students share their knowledge about how to maintain health during self-quarantine with others?

(4) What is college students' opinion towards the rumors on the Internet (e.g. drink hot water can kill virus)?

(5) What will college students do if their family members/relatives are adopting some methods that has been proved wrong to prevent viral infection?

(6) Do college students wear mask in public before the virus spread to their city?

(7) Do college students use dietary supplements to enhance resistance to infection of the virus?

例 2(b):修改后的数据收集问题

(1) What is college student's source of information regarding health management during epidemic period?

(2) What preventive methods are used by college students during epidemic period?

(3) What roles do college students play in the anti-coronavirus campaign?

任务二参考答案

The current research is a qualitative study conducting interviews among respondents who were purposively sampled from Dutch general public, physicians and nurses, with a balanced distribution of age, education and gender.

对研究方法的概述能帮助学生把握研究的本质、区分研究类型、辨别研究策略。计划书大纲里面的研究方法部分其实就是这样的概述。我们发现学生这个任务都完成得很好（如例3），只有个别组写出了太多研究方法的细节，"只见树木不见林"，反而无法让人了解研究方法的概貌（如例4）。

例3

The study will adopt a qualitative research to illustrate the relationship between students' organ donation-related knowledge and attitude towards organ donation of Shantou university. Data concerning age, major, knowledge and attitude towards organ donation will be collected from an online questionnaire designed by the researcher.

例4

We will find Apps in two main platforms: Ying Yong Bao (Android) and AppStore (iOS). Data collection will be performed by one reviewer, with the support and supervision of a second reviewer using the keyword "diabetes". Apps that meet inclusion criteria will be selected. Another 2 investigators will download the Apps and record the major functions, the latest update date, target user, security statement, support data, and information source. After that, we will...

附录14.2 研究计划书提纲范例

Title: Medical Knowledge Contributes to Non-Smoking

Background

Smoking is one of the great risk factors for many diseases. Previous data show the lower smoking rate among medical students in USA, indicating the contributory role of medical knowledge to non-smoking[1]. So far surveys in both USA and China which investigate risk factors for college students to smoke mainly focused on academic performance but not medical knowledge[2].

Objective

To compare the prevalence of smoking among medical and non-medical students and investigate if medical knowledge contributes to reducing tobacco use.

Methods

An online cross-sectional questionnaire will be used to gather quantitative data on the smoking situation and medical knowledge among college students in Guangdong Province. Convenient sampling will be adopted to include both medical and non-medical students in the survey.

Possible findings and implications

Smoking rate of non-medical students may be significantly higher than medical students due to less knowledge about smoking and health risks. This research will suggest effective health education about smoking and contribute to decreasing cigarette used among college students.

References

[1] Ho J Y, Fenelon A. The Contribution of Smoking to Educational Gradients in U. S. Life Expectan-

cy. Journal of Health & Social Behavior,2015,56(3):307.

[2]Chen X,Tang X,Stanton B,et al. Cigarette smoking among medical students in China and modifiable risk factors for smoking prevention. Health Education,2012,112(4):333-349.

附录 14.3 研究计划书评分标准

	Items	1	2	3	4	5
A Content & Thinking	A1 Background	No research background is introduced	The research background is introduced, but too simple to explain the relevant context and literature	The research background is not fully addressed, and some important development of ideas is missing	The research background is well addressed to lead to the current research purposes	The research background is fully addressed and the current research purposes are strongly justified
	A2 Objectives	No research objectives are introduced	The research objectives are introduced with vagueness or ambiguity	The research objectives are introduced, but not specifically related to the research topic	The research objectives are introduced clearly and specifically, but not logically developed from the research background	The research objectives are introduced clearly, specifically and logically
	A3 Methods	No research methods are introduced	The research methods are introduced, but too simple or vague to explain how the research will be done	The research methods are introduced clearly, but not with adequate details	The research methods are introduced clearly and adequately	The research methods are introduced clearly and adequately, with specific and practical plan for implementation
	A4 Possible findings /implication	No possible findings and implications of the research are introduced	The possible findings are introduced without any discussion of the implications or significance of the research	Both possible findings and implications are introduced, but too simple to address the research purposes	Both possible findings and implications are introduced clearly	Both possible findings and implications are introduced clearly and robustly

（续表）

Items		1	2	3	4	5
	A5 References	No references are included	References are included, but not with required Vancouver format	Important references are cited and included in required Vancouver format		
B Language and communication	B1 Accuracy	Use of vocabulary and grammar is problematic and consistently interferes with communication	Use of vocabulary and grammar frequently interferes with communication	Use of vocabulary and grammar expresses meaning with acceptable clarity	Use of vocabulary and grammar expresses meaning clearly	Use of vocabulary and grammar expresses meaning precisely
	B2 Cohesion	Has almost no use of cohesive devices, ideas not linked	Lacks cohesive devices to connect information and ideas	Information and ideas are somewhat connected with some use of cohesive devices	Information and ideas are connected with use of cohesive devices	Information and ideas are well connected with effective use of cohesive devices
	B3 Academic features	Inappropriate to communicate for academic purposes	Inadequate to communicate for academic purposes	Somewhat demonstrates features of academic written language	Adequately demonstrates features of academic written language	Appropriately and well demonstrates features of academic written language

参考文献

Huang JC, 2017. What do subject experts teach about writing research articles? An exploratory study. Journal of English for Academic Purposes, 25: 18-29.

Kouwenhoven P, Raijmakers N, van Delden J, et al., 2015. Opinions about euthanasia and advanced dementia: a qualitative study among Dutch physicians and members of the general public. BMC Medical Ethics, 16 (7). http://www.biomedcentral.com/1472-6939/16/7.

Punch K, 2000. Developing effective research proposal. London: SAGE Publications.

Swales JM, 2011. Aspects of Article Introductions. Ann Arbor: University of Michigan Press.

Yang M, O'Sullivan PS, Irby DM, et al., 2019. Challenges and adaptations in implementing an English-medium medical program: a case study in China. BMC Medical Education, 19 (15). https://doi.org/10.1186/s12909-018-1452-3.

林颖怡，王齐，黄陶然 等, 2019. A Structural Equation Modeling Approach to Advance Directives Acceptance in China. 第五届中国大学生国际学术研讨会. 同济大学, 上海.

第十五章 学术壁报

李晓玲 余 凡

一、教学主题和教学思路

学术壁报是国际学术交流的重要手段之一,于1974年在美国首次出现(Maugh,1974)。制作和运用壁报和演示文稿(如 PowerPoint)的技巧是参加学术交流必备的视觉素养(visual literacy)(Forsyth 及 Waller,1995)。随着国际间交流合作机会日渐增加,学会撰写、制作符合国际惯例的学术壁报已成为学生必须掌握的重要学术技能之一。本章教学内容通过向学生阐述学术壁报的内涵和重要意义,介绍学术壁报的格式、内容和语言特点及学术壁报的设计和撰写步骤等,整合前期课程所教授的学术语言特征、学术阅读技巧与学术写作技巧等学术语言技能,使学生得到一次综合能力训练。

(一) 教学主题——学术壁报

国际学术会议的交流方式一般包括大会专题或主旨报告(keynote speech)、分场口头报告(oral presentation)和壁报报告(poster presentation)。专题或主旨报告通常由特邀的相关领域有造诣的专家来做,而分场口头报告和壁报报告是一般参会人员的主要交流方式。由于时间关系,能够受邀做口头报告的人数比较有限,因此通过壁报展示研究成果成为专业人员提升自我、建立学术联系、扩大学术影响的重要交流方式。壁报用直观的图像、图表及精简的文字说明展示主要的研究结果,让感兴趣的参会者在几分钟内就可以了解作者的研究发现和结论,并且可以与作者面对面地交流。然而,要从展示区的众多壁报中脱颖而出,吸引更多参会者的目光,单纯依循会议制作规范是不够的,必须结合精练准确的语言、简洁明了的内容、系统的图表组合及美观的版面设计。本章教学内容是介绍学术壁报的撰写要点及学术壁报报告的技巧,以帮助学生掌握这一国际学术交流手段。

(二) 教学思路

本章对学术壁报做一整体介绍,先从学术壁报的概念和使用目的入手,再对学术壁报各项内容逐一说明:① 学术壁报的构成,包括标题、正文(引言、方法、结果、讨论等)和参考文献;② 撰写步骤,包括起草、写作(标题特点、内容选择、语言特点、插图和图表的写作要点等)、设计(版面布局、文字样式、色彩选择等);③ 壁报报告的技巧和注意的事项。中间穿插了若干小组讨论和学习任务:包括分析所给样例的标题、引言、方法、讨论等部分的内容构成;对比四个壁报标题,分析其各自的优劣;对所给论文的前言部分进行改写,使其符合壁报要求;划出所给论文的讨论部分的中心意思,并对其进行改写,使其符合壁报要求;分析所给若干壁报样例的优劣;讨论学术壁报报告和学术口头报告的不同点。最后通过组织综合性学习活动(integration activities)、同伴互评(peer review)、师生会议(teacher-student conference)等帮助学生完成本章节的最终作业,其中分为一般要求作业和更高要求作业。一般要求作业是学生从教师提供的 6 个主题共计 12 篇学术论文中选择一篇进行阅读,将各部分按壁报要求进行改写,设计制作成一份壁报,并模拟壁报报告环节进行汇报。一般要求作业适合大学本科低年级学生。更高要求作业是学生把自己在其他专业科目中所做的研究或调查及获得的研究结果用壁报的形式撰写出来,并模拟壁报报告环节进行汇报。更高要求作业适合大学本科高年级学生和研究生。

壁报制作和报告的技巧非常重要,很多大学为学生提供专项培训。本章作者也参阅了一些网络资料,并将比较可靠和有用的网址列在参考文献里供读者参考。

二、教学案例设计

(一)教学目标

1. 了解学术壁报的格式、内容和语言特点。
2. 恰当运用归纳、总结等阅读技巧提炼出所读学术文章的要点。
3. 恰当运用转述、概述等引用策略撰写学术壁报各部分内容。
4. 根据学术壁报的内容要求和语言特点撰写各部分内容。
5. 根据学术壁报的格式制作出符合国际惯例的学术壁报。
6. 运用壁报报告技巧进行口头汇报。

(二)教学内容

1. Structure and content of a research poster

教学内容	注解
❖ **Academic poster: what is it?** ✓ A poster is an enlarged graphic display of research work. ✓ The aim of a scientific poster is to convey scientific information and views in a *visual* format, to an interested audience.	由学术壁报的定义和使用目的入手。
❖ **Structure of a poster** ✓ Banners ✓ Contexts 　• Introduction/Background 　• Objective/Hypothesis 　• Methods/Research design 　• Results/Findings 　• Conclusions/Discussion 　• Limitations/Future directions 　• Acknowledgement (Optional) 　• References	这部分讲解学术壁报的各部分内容,包括标题、正文(引言、方法、结果、讨论等)、参考文献。中间穿插四个小组讨论:讨论分析所给范例的标题、引言、方法、讨论等部分的内容构成。小组讨论一的讲义见附录15.1。

2. How to create a research poster

教学内容	注解
❖ **Your poster design should enable a reader to answer these questions easily**: ✓ What is it about? ✓ Where is the take-home message? ✓ Where do I begin reading? ✓ Where's the conclusion? ❖ **Poster components in order of importance**: ✓ the title → the aims & conclusion → results → methods→discussion ❖ **Don't put your conclusion at the bottom!**	此部分介绍学术壁报的设计原则

❖ **Steps in creating posters**
✓ Step 1：Read the guidelines or instructions & decide on format
✓ Step 2：Determine and gather content
   • Title
   • Language
   • Content selection
   • Graphics
✓ Step 3：Design a visually appealing display
   • Make a sketch
   • Layout
   • Font types and sizes
   • Color
✓ Step 4：Edit ruthlessly
	这部分讲解学术壁报的制作步骤，包括起草、写作（标题特点、内容选择、语言特点、插图和图表的写作要点等）、设计（版面布局、文字样式、色彩选择等）。中间穿插若干小组讨论和学习任务：对比四个壁报标题，分析其各自的优劣（小组讨论二）；对所给论文的前言部分进行改写，使其符合壁报要求（任务一）；划出所给论文的讨论部分的中心意思，并对其进行改写，使其符合壁报要求（任务二）；分析所给若干壁报样例的优劣（任务三）。小组讨论和学习任务讲义分别在附录15.1和附录15.2

3. How to deliver a research poster

教学内容	注解
❖ **What is Poster Presentation**? ✓ The oral presentation of research information based on academic poster, always by individuals or representatives of a research team at an academic conference ✓ Held in a separate room or area of the tradeshow floor ✓ Researcher answering questions posed by the passing conference participants ✓ Display time ranging from several hours to several days ❖ **What are the poster sessions like**? ✓ Social and interactive settings → loud, chaotic & exciting	此部分由学术壁报报告的定义入手，进而讨论分析学术壁报报告与学术口头报告的区别

(续表)

教学内容	注解
❖ **Poster Presentation vs. Oral presentation** ✓ Poster presentation 　• Present mainly visually 　• Limited space for presentation (usu. less than 1 m^2) 　• Allowing more interpersonal communication ✓ Oral presentation 　• Present mainly orally 　• Limited time for presentation (15～20 minutes) 　• Allowing more public discussion	
❖ **Preparing your Poster Presentation** ✓ Plan a 3～5 minutes presentation to accompany your poster ✓ Your verbal presentation should align with your visual presentation ✓ Be prepared for frequent interruptions. Viewers will ask you questions as you go along ❖ **Delivering your Poster Presentation** ✓ Put the poster on your left as you look at your audience ✓ Stand straight and look confident ✓ Make eye contact periodically with each individual ✓ Start with the big picture ✓ Emphasize your project goal ✓ Walk the viewers through all your poster ✓ Allow viewers to approach as close as they need to see the poster and hear what you are saying, so do not stand in the middle ✓ Make sure that you end with a take-home message ❖ **How to give an effective poster presentation** ✓ Rule 1：Don't read your poster. Don't stare at your poster. Use your poster as a visual tool and engage with your viewers ✓ Rule 2：Be prepared. Expect questions ✓ Rule 3：Don't put everything on the poster. Bring supplementary materials, copies of your poster, and your contact message with you. Deliver them to viewers if necessary ✓ Rule 4：For questions that go beyond the scope of your research or you don't have an answer on the spot, do not make up an answer, but reply honestly. Or give the viewer your contact card and suggest for later discussion	这部分讲解壁报报告的技巧和注意的事项。中间穿插课堂活动：观看北卡罗莱纳州立大学研究生院制作的有关壁报报告技巧的视频片段（Hess, et al., 2013）

(续表)

教学内容	注解
✓ Rule 5：Put your viewers first. When viewers come up to the poster, politely excuse yourself from the side conversation, introduce yourself, and make yourself available for questions	

4. Integration activities

教学内容	注解
❖ Discussion 3～1：Rewrite the title for your poster ✓ Each person in the group writes a title for the poster ✓ Share with your teammates and explain why you think it is appropriate ✓ After discussion, vote for the best one ✓ Try to revise/polish/improve the best one (Feel free to keep your own one if you think the original one is better. Provide reasons) ❖ Discussion 3～2：Peer Review the Introduction Section ✓ Exchange your draft of Introduction section and the original text with other groups ✓ Do peer review, focusing on content • Does the draft include all the key points? • Are all the key points expressed concisely and precisely? ❖ Discussion 3～3：Draft & revise ✓ Each member revises a section for your poster • Round 1：Focus on content • Round 2：Exchange with other members. This time, focus on grammar and vocabulary. ✓ Submit your poster draft (including title, all the sections, graphs, references). ❖ Discussion 3～4：Each group provides at least 3～4 questions for each poster after reading the abstract of the original article.	这部分在各小组已经完成壁报初稿之后进行，通过四个综合性学习活动或同伴互评（小组讨论三）加深学生对各种技巧的理解，帮助他们修改初稿。讨论讲义见附录15.1

（三）学习任务

任务一

  任务内容 对所给论文的前言部分进行改写，使其符合壁报要求。

  任务要点 学生应通过对所给论文的前言进行"语步分析"，并结合壁报写作的语言特点及壁报前言部分应包含的要点信息恰当地进行内容选择。

任务完成形式/师生互动形式　学生独立完成任务,之后老师以提问的形式检查任务完成情况,引导学生了解壁报写作的语言特点及如何进行内容选择。

任务二

任务内容　划出所给论文的讨论部分的中心意思,并对其进行改写,使其符合壁报要求。

任务要点　学生应通过对所给论文的讨论部分进行"语步分析",并结合壁报写作的语言特点及壁报讨论部分应包含的要点信息恰当地进行内容选择。

任务完成形式/师生互动形式　学生独立完成任务,之后老师以提问的形式检查任务完成情况,引导学生了解壁报写作的语言特点及如何进行内容选择。

任务三

任务内容　分析所给若干壁报样例的优劣

任务要点　阅读比较真实的壁报样例,并从格式、内容和语言特点等方面来分析其优劣。

任务完成形式/师生互动形式　学生独立完成任务,之后老师以提问的形式检查任务完成情况,并进行点评,使学生能更直观地了解壁报的格式、内容和语言特点。

(四) 课后作业

1. Design and write a poster based on the article you selected. Your poster should include all important elements (Introduction, Methods, Results/ Findings and Discussion/ Conclusions/Implications, References, Acknowledgement, etc.) and visual tools (tables, graphs, pictures, etc.) to display the key research information academically, concisely and attractively.

Format of the final project:

(1) Poster size: A2 (420mm * 594mm)[①]

(2) Left-justification

(3) Suggested Font size of the text

Title section	Font size(B)
Title	70~75
Headings	45~55
Text	35~45
Graph text	20~25

2. Plan a 8-minutes (6 minutes for presentation, 2 minutes for Q & A) presentation to accompany your poster. Your verbal presentation should align with your visual presentation. Be prepared for questions.

壁报报告评分标准见附录15.3。

---

① 在正式的学术会议中,壁报的尺寸比 A2 大得多,我们的课程壁报规定为 A2 大小,一是节约印刷成本,二是节约展示的空间,使壁报报告在一般的教室里也可以进行。

三、案例使用反馈

(一) 学生反馈意见

完成了本单元内容以后,大部分学生(参与课程反馈的学生总数为279人)明确表示他们对学习做壁报比较感兴趣(64.9%),精力投入比较大(69.87%),认为这对他们未来专业学习和发展有帮助(67.55%),学习收获很大(66.23%)。有同学写道:"这一项课程内容设置得非常好!使我学会了学术壁报的基本制作和形式。"有的同学表示:"制作学术壁报是一件挺辛苦但也能学到不少东西的事情。需要花费很多时间在阅读文献和设计问卷等方面,而最后的文字也需要花不少精力和时间,但能学到如文字语言特点、内容提炼等知识或技能。"他们表示可以学到很多东西,如了解海报的格式、特点、内容,懂得提炼文章的要点,学会小组内如何分工及交流,以及如何制作海报。而且,在把自己的研究制作成海报的任务中,他们还对自己的研究重新反思,表示"感觉问卷的设置和数据的获取与分析不太专业",有的对自己研究的主题,调查目的及研究方法通过阅读文献、小组讨论的形式再进一步完善。

对于该单元的内容学习,学生还是感觉较有难度(难度均值是3.5,介于"3-难度适中"与"4-有困难"之间)。有不少同学反映:"如何用规范的学术语言去制作学术海报,是那时候遇到最大的困难。"有的同学觉得阅读原文是一个很大的挑战,但更多的同学表示,阅读原文并不难,如何提炼要点及转述更加困难。而且要"用到比较专业的词汇和句子,难度比较大"。也有同学反映排版难度较大,或者与同伴沟通,达成共识较难。有同学这样总结,"最困难的是寻找和阅读相关文献,即开题—查找—提炼—筛选,这些过程都需要组员的意见统一,求同存异,大家不同的意见比较多,所以统一意见是最困难的;其次是文献的提炼,阅读能力和主题确定都与之相关"。这句话几乎涵盖了他们反映的所有难题。

总的来看,他们的问题有两个方面,第一与自身能力有关,就是来自语言能力和思维能力的挑战,体现在阅读原文,提炼要点,以及展示研究成果上。这个正是整个单元,乃至课程的重点,就是让学生在学习中语言和思维相助相长。关于这个方面的挑战,教师应该给予更多的指导。例如,如何提炼要点,如何使用规范的学术语言转述或陈述,多给学生这方面的训练和示例。第二方面与沟通协调能力相关,这体现在他们与同伴合作上如何就选题、设计、撰写和排版达成一致意见。这是每次团队合作都需要面临的挑战,可以让学生自己锻炼、摸索;同时教师也需要及早发现问题并提供及时指导,可以通过开展组内与组间讨论,甚至班间的同伴互评等形式,师生一起针对各种例子进行交流点评。

(二) 教师反馈意见

本节课的内容分为两大部分,第一是学术壁报的内容和语言,第二是学术壁报的版面设计。内容和语言方面的教学重点是帮助学生了解学术壁报的整体框架以及各个部分的要素。如壁报的 Introduction 部分里有 Research background, Gap, 以及 Objectives; 在 Conclusions 里有 main findings, limitations, 以及 forward-looking statements 等等。在此基础上,学生要学会对原文献各个部分的内容有所取舍,然后使用自己的语言简洁且有逻辑地呈现研究最重要的信息。教学难点之一是提高学生的信息提炼能力,要突出重点,让观众记住核心内容,而不是面面俱到,以至于版面过度拥挤,让观众感觉信息过于密集而失去阅读的兴趣。难点二是提高学生的语言能力,要规范、简练又完整地表达信息。在壁报版面设计的教学中,重点是让学生设计既符合学术规范,专业性强,又有视觉冲击力、吸引力的壁报。难点是帮助学生在规范性和创意之间取得平衡。

针对以上的重点和难点,建议是:① 让学生多做、多评、多改。因为在过往的教学中发现,学生有时对别人的点评很到位,但自己做的时候会比较粗心。所以需要多修改,在细节中打磨、提升。② 教学设计上不要急于把所有的内容和理论都放在一次课里面。条件允许的情况下,宁可慢一点,一次课一个重点,效果会更好。例如,第一次课先讲内容和语言,然后布置相关作业让学生完成;第二次课针对他们的作业的内容进行点评,让学生修改;第三次课再讲版面设计,然后再完成作业,点评。这样让学生能够更好地消化并掌握。总之,佳作示范、作品点评、同伴评议、教师及时反馈,这些方法是师生都认可的有效方法。本章提供的课堂讨论、学习任务和课后作业比较多,授课教师可以根据课时和学生能力水平选用。

(三)学生作业点评

1. 阅读他人文献,做学术壁报(一般要求作业)

作业点评1

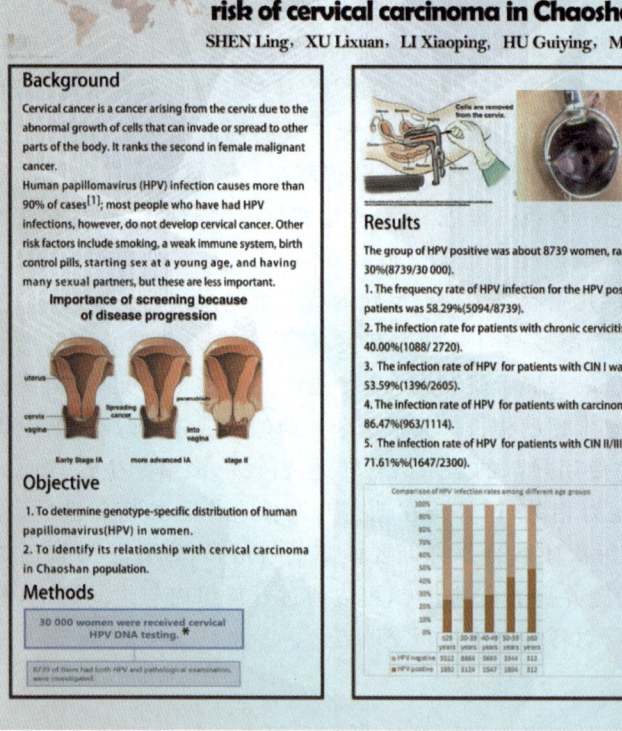
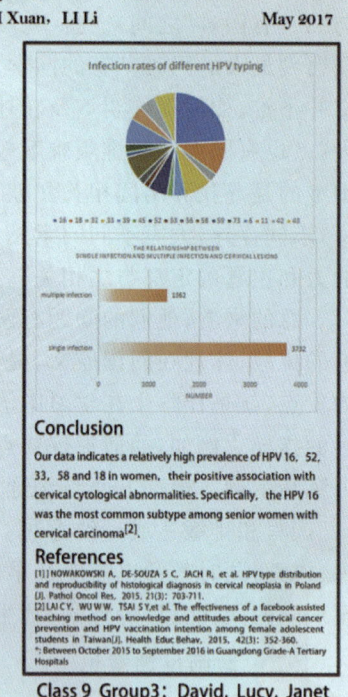

点评:

优点分析

(1) 选取文献主题立足当地(潮汕地区),关联性和时效性都比较强,较易为目标观众理解。

(2) 整体风格简洁、明快。图片切题而又清晰生动,能引发观众兴趣、加深印象。

(3) 内容提炼取舍得当,既忠于原文又再现原文要点。

(4) 结构相对完整,能包括海报大部分的结构要素。各部分之间联系紧密、明晰。

(5) 语言表达简明扼要。

(6) 图文结合,比例合理,内容分为三栏,排版均衡,留白恰当。

缺点分析

(1) 文末可加上 Acknowledgements 的信息。

(2) Background 和 Conclusion 需分为要点(bullet points)表述。

(3) 有个别语言瑕疵,例如该海报 Methods 中提到的 30,000 women were received cervical HPV DNA testing 这句中的"were received"应改为主动语态的"received."

(4) HPV 这个缩略语的正确书写规范,应是在 Background 部分首次出现时采用完整拼写形式"human papilloma-virus"后面紧跟着用括号加缩略语(HPV)的格式,然后下文都统一用缩略形式,而非在延迟到 Objectives 部分再采用该格式。

(5) Results 的图表要加 Fig 1,2,3 的标签。

注:该壁报基于原文献 Shen,et al.,2017。

作业点评 2

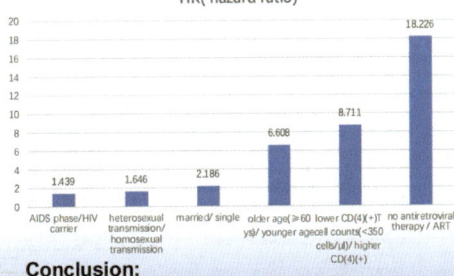

点评:

该壁报所选主题适合目标观众的能力水平,但有待改进的空间较大:

(1) 完全复制所选取的原文语言表述,没有在理解原文的基础上,采用适当的策略以自己的语言归纳表述原文内容。

(2) 结构不够完整,缺少 Background、References、Acknowledgments 等部分。

(3) 排版虽然分为三栏,但各部分比例不协调,位置不当(例如 Objective,位置过于靠上,中间栏又过窄),排列不整齐,整体结构显得凌乱,缺乏专业感。

(4) 把"红丝带"的标志放在壁报中间最显著位置,所占空间很多。相比之下,Results 部分的图表太小,也缺乏必要的文字说明。应该把更多的空间留给 Results。

注:该壁报基于原文献 Li et al.,2017。

2. 使用学术壁报展示自己的研究（更高要求作业）

作业点评1

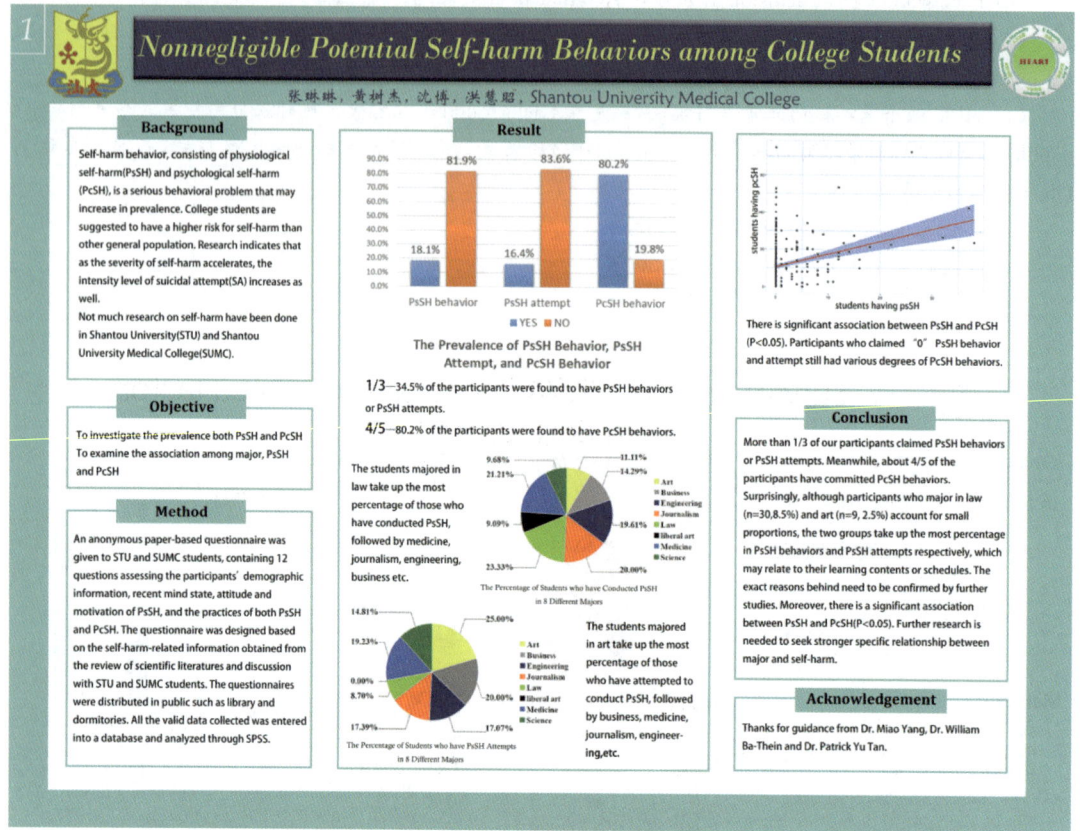

点评：

优点分析

（1）研究主题是社会所关注的大学生自我伤害行为，时效性强，对社会和教育均有参考价值。研究对象为就读学校的大学生，数据收集方便，针对性强，对目标观众有吸引力。

（2）内容提炼取舍得当，结构相对完整，编排合理，图表选择有代表性。

（3）语言表述规范清晰。

建议

（1）内容呈现可以适当使用要点，不要单一地使用段落，这样阅读起来更加方便。

（2）单复数要注意，例如，Objective 不止一个，需要复数。同理，Method、Result、Acknowledgement，由于这些标题下要点不止一个，需要使用复数形式。

（3）Results 的图表要加 Fig 1,2,3,4 的标签。

作业点评 2

Delayed Sleep and Classroom Performance of Medical Students.

Background
Delayed sleep is common in medical students because of busy schedules.[1] Most studies have been about classroom performance while few has been done on the relationship between delayed sleep and classroom performance.[2,3]

Objectives
- To investigate delayed sleep and classroom performance of medical students.
- To provides scientific basis for improving classroom efficiency
- To improve classroom performance of medical students.

Methods
1. Questionnaire:
   - Web-based
   - 8 questions including grand, major, the time of falling sleep, and the information of classroom performance.[4]
   - Measure attention and persistence of participants.
   - Basis of LBS (learning behavior scale[4])
2. Data analysis: SPSS version 20
3. Participants:
   - 45 medical students in SUMC.
   - 7 freshmen, 36 sophomores and 2 juniors.
4. Informed consent: from each participant.

Results

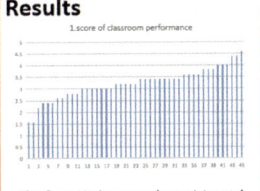

The figure1 shows each participants' classroom performance score.

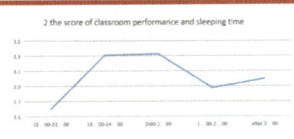

The figure2 shows that as sleep time delay, class performance scores decrease, proving that delayed sleep can reduce class performance. Interestingly, classroom score of 22:00-23:00 is significantly lower than others. It seems that sleep early would also reduce classroom performance.

Reference
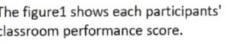

Conclusion
- The survey shows that delayed sleep decrease the performance of medical students in class, and worsen sleep can affect medical students' classroom performance. Besides, some delayed sleeping students are still performing effectively in class.
- The limitation of this survey is that the heavy learning task in medical life leads to the over-hasty filling of the questionnaire and the insufficient number of questionnaires.
- Further research to identify the long term effects of delayed sleep, such as psychological impact and academic performance.

点评：

该壁报优点是壁报的各要素结构完整，表述清晰，配色明快悦目。但尚有较大提升空间，尤其在语言表述方面。具体建议如下：

（1）标题结尾不应该有句号，另外，建议改为 *The Relationship between Delayed Sleep and Classroom Performance in Medical Students* 更为确切。

（2）Objectives 标题以下内容为分点，每一行末应该使用分号，或者不使用标点符号。另外，第一个研究目标过于空泛，而第二和第三个研究目标重复。

（3）Conclusion 的第一点最后一句"Besides, some delayed sleeping students are still performing effectively in class"表述与上文逻辑有矛盾。根据 Figure 2 的说明，建议改为"However, early sleep (before 22：00) seems to reduce classroom performance"。

（4）对研究的不足之处，表达过于冗长，偏向中式英语。建议改为"The limitations of the study are the small number of respondents and a limited validation of the self-reported sleep data"。

（5）"Further research to..."该句结构不完整，缺少谓语，而且"academic performance"在这里与"psychological impact"并列，也有逻辑问题。建议改为"Further research could be undertaken to identify the long term effect of delayed sleep, such as the psychological impact on academic performance in the future"。这样修改是避免了句子头重脚轻，符合句末重心原则，而且从逻辑上也更合理。

（6）Reference 应该是复数。

（7）排版分布需要调整，Objectives 和 Methods 的位置最好对调。Reference 应该置于海报下方。

附录15.1 课堂讨论

小组讨论一

1. Look at the banners, point out its components.

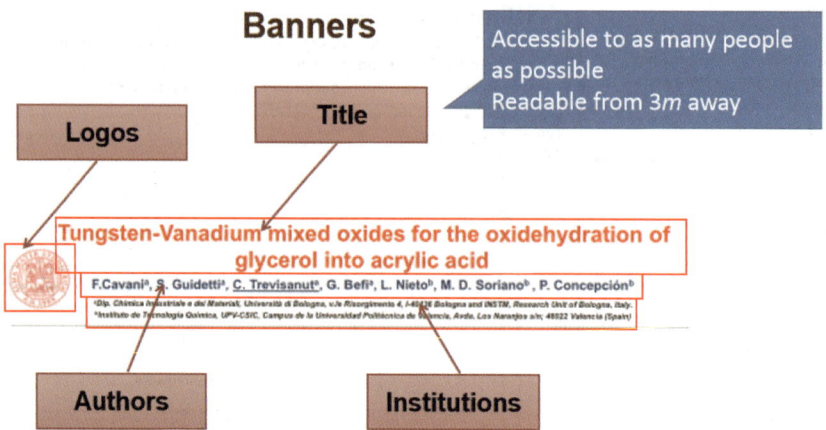

2. Read the following Introduction of a poster and answer.

(1) How do junior doctors learn the Newborn and Infant Physical Examination?

(2) What is the structure of an introduction?

Introduction

The newborn and infant physical examination (NIPE) is part of the newborn screening programme in the UK, performed between birth and discharge from hospital. It is a routine job for neonatal junior doctors at SHO (Senior House Officer) level.

The process is taught during medical school, and at the start of every neonatal job, in a variety of ways. The UK National Screening Programme has an e-learning module, and gives advice on ongoing training, and the London School of Paediatrics advises completion of a workplace-based assessment to complement this.

There is minimal research into the teaching and learning of the NIPE, with most studies comparing doctors to other multidisciplinary team members rather than educational techniques. This project aimed to assess neonatal SHOs' experience of teaching styles in their postgraduate education on the NIPE, including what they found enjoyable and useful.

3. Identify the elements of a method section by reading the following samples.

Examples of Quantitative Research

Methods

Online questionnaires were used to gather quantitative and qualitative data on SHO experiences of teaching styles.
The survey was sent to all neonatal SHOs working at a tertiary level neonatal unit over the course of a year (18 doctors), with a final response rate of 44%.

Methods

- Pre and post course questionnaire
- Modified Spielberger State-Trait Anxiety Inventory[4,5]
- Data collected anonymously, analysed using Excel
- Means were compared using student t-test (p-value <0.05)
- Free text comments analysed into themes using a pragmatic approach to framework analysis

Example of Qualitative Research

Methods

- Used salient belief elicitation from RAA to identify participants' perceived barriers to eating fruits and vegetables.
- Face-to-face, 20-30-minute, semi-structured interviews were conducted with 182 adults and 221 middle school students using computer-assisted interviewing software, as part of a larger study on several eating and physical activity behaviors.
- Participants were asked one of three questions:
  1. "What might make it hard for you to eat at least 2 cups of dark green leafy vegetables every week for the next three months? (n=137)"
  2. "What might make it hard for you to eat at least 2 cups of orange vegetables every week for the next three months? (n=126)"
  3. "What might make it hard for you to eat fruit every WEEK DAY for the next three months? (n=140)"
- Content analysis was used to identify categories of salient circumstances. Chi-square tests compared adults to youth on frequency of mentioning barriers.
- The study was approved by the Indiana University, Bloomington Committee for the Protection of Human Subjects (Study #05-10563)

4. Identify the elements of a conclusion section.

CONCLUSIONS & IMPLICATIONS

- Participants were most aware of interventions that were recommended in UWCCC patient education materials (oral care, baking soda-salt water rinses, pain medication, ice cubes, soft bland diet), or that were prescribed by a care provider (magic mouthwash, topical antibiotics, acyclovir).
- Very few participants (< 25%) actually used any of the self-care interventions, but among those used, most were rated as at least moderately effective.
- Study limitations include the small sample size, inclusion of participants who may not have experienced mucositis, potential confusion between mouth sores and cold sores (oral herpes), and uncertainty in whether or not participants had received mucositis education from the clinical care providers.
- Further research is needed to document the effectiveness of various self-care interventions for mucositis. Nurse clinicians can provide targeted education to increase patients' awareness and use of strategies found to be effective.

小组讨论二

1. Read the following titles and determine which one(s) you like best.

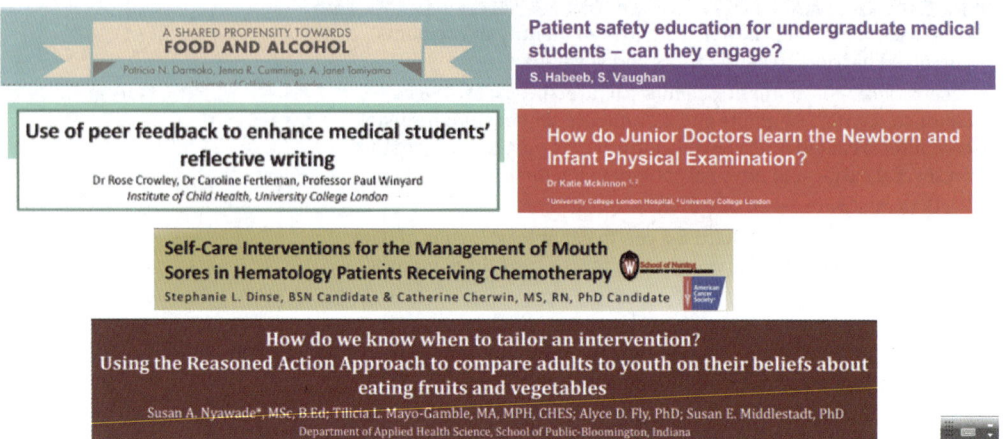

2. Comment on the following titles.

Mechanism Of Airway Constriction and Secretion Evoked by Laryngeal Administration of SO_2 in Dongs

Evidence That Reflex Effects of SO_2 Are Mediated By Afferent Endings in the Upper Airway

Are Reflex Effects of SO_2 Mediated By Afferent Endings in the Upper Airway?

How Does SO_2 Affect the Upper Airway?

小组讨论三

1. Revise the title for your poster.

◇ Title：_____

◇ Abstract：

Steps：

(1) Each person in the group writes a title for the poster.

(2) Share with your teammates and explain why you think it is appropriate.

(3) After discussion，vote for the best one.

(4) Try to revise/polish/improve the best one. (Feel free to keep your own one if you think the original one is better. Provide reasons.)

◇ **Title of the selected article:**

Stu. Name	Title for poster	Tick

◇ **Revise the best title:** _____
◇ **Revised version:** _____

2. Peer Review the Introduction Section (between two groups)

Preparation: Each group provides the original text of your RA to another group; and exchanges the draft of "Introduction" section with each other.

Steps:

Conduct peer review, focusing on the content.

(1) Does the draft include all the key points? (E. g. : necessary general background info. , research gap, purpose, hypothesis, etc.)

(2) Are all the key points expressed concisely and precisely?

◇ Partner Group's title: _____

◇ Partner Group's draft of "Introduction" section:

◇ Feedback (suggestions) for your partner group:

3. Draft & revise in your own group

Each member revises a section for your poster, including Introduction, Methods, Results/Findings, Conclusions/Discussions.

Round 1: focus on content

Round 2: focus on grammar and vocabulary

Main Process:

(1) Select a different section from round 1.

(2) Identify the errors of each section using "Editing marks" provided. Mark it on the

copy of your draft. (Note: don't correct them yet!)

(3) With the peer-review editing suggestions done, start correcting the identified errors and revising your draft together. (Discuss with teammates when necessary, such as different opinions, asking questions, etc.)

(4) Submit the revised version as a group.

\multicolumn{2}{c|}{Editing Marks for Identifying Errors}	
WW	Wrong Word
WF	Wrong Form
WO	Word Order
WT	Wrong Tense
Sp	Spelling mistake
Unc. ?	I have no idea what you are trying to say.
Awk.	Your words are grammatically correct, but it is difficult to understand what you mean.
Run-on	Your sentence is too long and needs to be broken up into more than one sentence.

◇ Original draft of **Introduction**: (**Writer**: _____ **Reviewer**: _____)

◇ Revised version of **Introduction**: (**Writer**: _____)

◇ Original draft of **Methods**: (Images are preferred)
(**Writer**: _____ **Reviewer**: _____)

◇ Revised version of **Methods**: (Images are preferred) (**Writer**: _____)

◇ Original draft of **Results**：(Images are preferred)
(**Writer**：_____ **Reviewer**：_____)

◇ Revised version of **Results**：(Images are preferred) (**Writer**：_____)

◇ Original draft of **Discussion(s)/Conclusion(s)/Implication(s)**
(**Writer**：_____ **Reviewer**：_____)

◇ Revised version of **Discussion(s)/Conclusion(s)/Implication(s)** (**Writer**：_____)

附录 15.2 学习任务讲义

1. Rewrite the introduction part for a poster.

Low concentrations of SO_2 cause bronchoconstriction in asthmatic patients. Since low concentrations of SO_2 may be totally absorbed in the upper airways and since the upper airways appear to be very sensitive to SO_2, we have explored the possibility that SO_2 evokes reflex effects by engaging afferent nerves in the upper airways.

2. Read the excerpt of a discussion about the student contact sheets taken out from the Discussion & Findings section from a research paper. Underline the central ideas. Rewrite it to make an effective paragraph in the Findings section of a poster.

Because a member of the research team distributed the first contact sheet and gave students instructions on how to complete it, and because subsequent reminders were given to all four teachers and delivered to students in the same way, we can be reasonably confident that students completed the forms in the same ways in both traditional and computer classes. And yet the computer students consistently reported more contacts than their counterparts in the traditional classes.

Moreover, as one teacher noted, students in the computer classroom may not have been recording as many contacts as they probably had: "I don't know if they're writing those kinds of contacts [chatting in class about their papers] down on their contact sheet. Probably not. They see it as really normal interaction" (Caitlin, Interview Two). The teachers all noted that in the computer classroom students seemed much more comfortable talking to each other, and that most of the student-student talk focused on writing issues and papers-in-progress.

The computer setting, then, appears to have contributed to a greater extent than did the traditional setting to students "willingness to share their writing openly and to elicit peers" and teachers' commentary on their writing as it developed.

(Kiefer, et al., 1994-2012)

3. Below are a number of posters created by SUMC[①] undergraduates. Go through each poster to highlight its greatest strengths and areas where there is room for improvement.

Sample 1

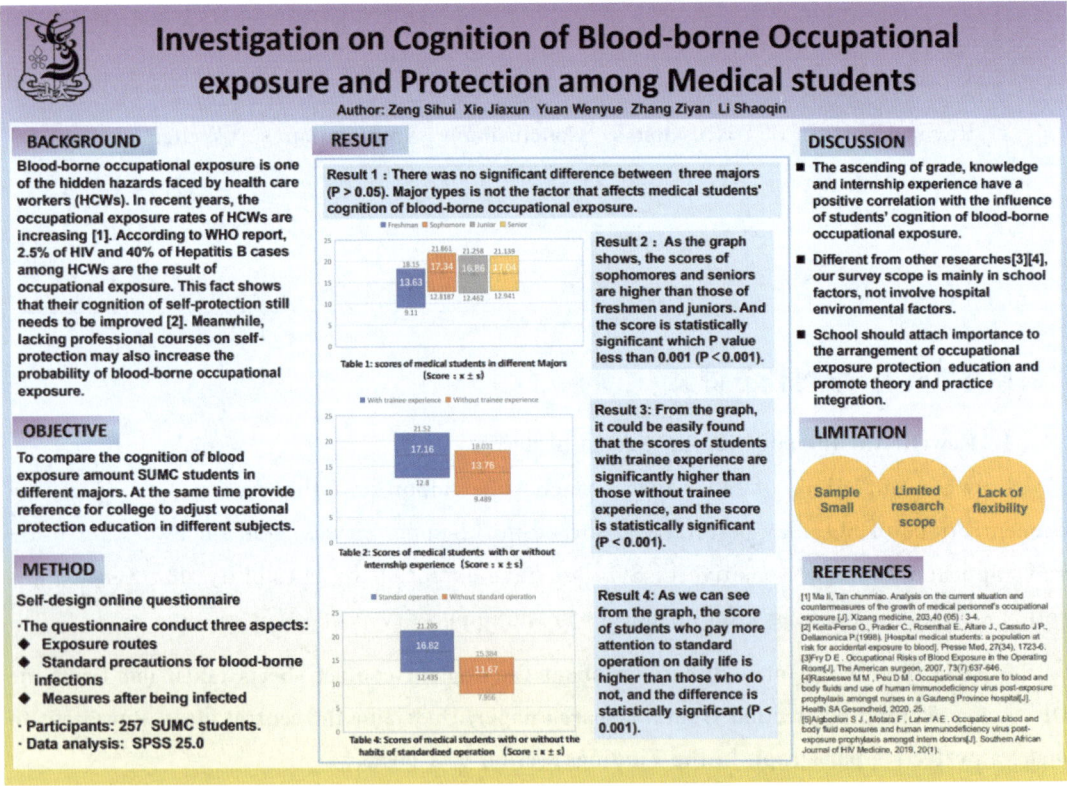

---

① Shantou University Medical College

Sample 2

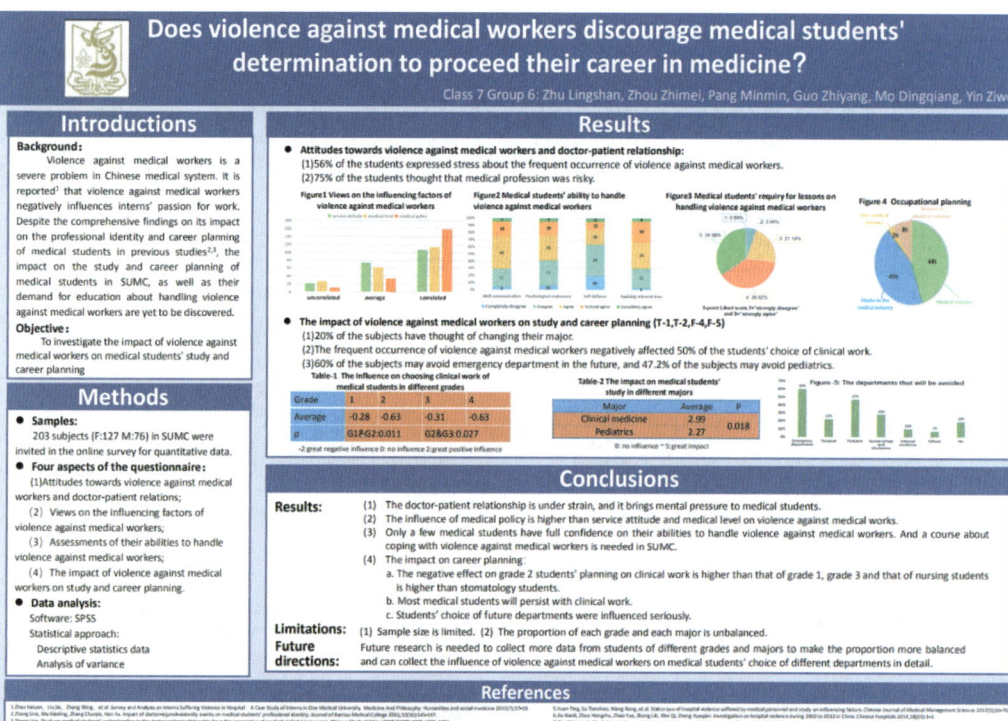

Sample 3

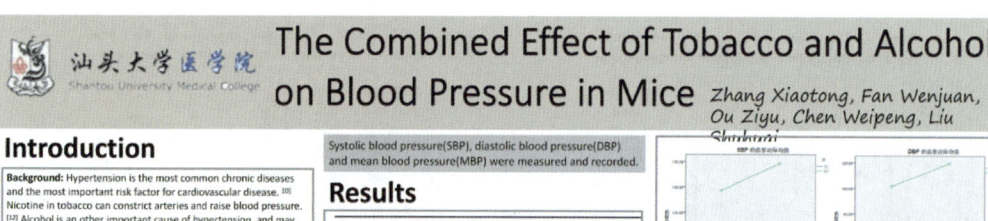

Sample 4

The Relationship between Knockdown TKT Expression Level and Functions of Esophageal Squamous Cancer Cells

Raj, Raphael, Walker, Vaya, Allen

Introduction

- Transketolase (TKT) is a key enzyme in the non-oxidative pathway of the pentose phosphate pathway, which is involved in the synthesis of ribonucleic acid and NAPDH, and returns the excess pentose through this reaction to the metabolic pathway of glycolysis for reuse.
- Previous studies have shown that TKT is associated with ovarian and esophageal cancer metastasis and lower survival rates in patients.
- To response these results, we hypothesized that the reduction of TKT gene expression could lead to reprogramming of tumor cell metabolism, thereby reducing the proliferation, invasion and metastasis of tumor cells in esophageal squamous cell carcinoma (ESCC).

Methods

- KYSE150 cell line of esophageal squamous cell carcinoma was used as the research material.
- TKT-si-1, TKT-si-2 and NC cells were transfected into the tktsi-1, tktsi-2 and NC groups respectively, compared with the blank group.
- Wound healing experiment, Transwell experiment and MTS experiment were carried out, so as to understand the influence of TKT expression level on cell function.

Results

Figure 1. TKT-Flag sequencing results : The TKT gene was successfully linked to the plasmid.

Figure 3. The results of wound healing experiment: TKT gene down regulation can reduce mobile ability of cancer cells.

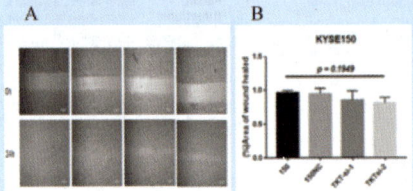

Figure 2. The results of MTS: TKT gene down regulation can reduce proliferation of cancer cells.

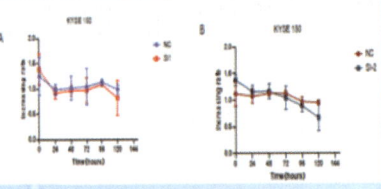

Figure 4. The results of transwell experiment: TKT gene down regulation can reduce transfer ability of cancer cells.

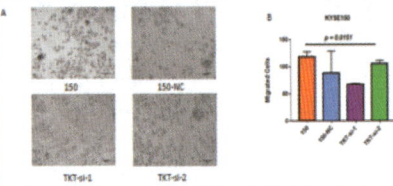

Conclusions

The proliferation and mobility of esophageal squamous cancer cells which TKT gene were knocked down, were lower than that of the control group, although the effect was not obvious.

Limitations:
- The operation of the experiment was not rigorous as expected.
- The functional status of esophageal cancer cells was not stable.
- The lack of multiple experiments.

TKT inhibition may be a useful strategy to intervene in cancer cell invasion and metastasis, which may lead to a better prognosis for ESCC patients, but further research is still needed.

Acknowledgements

This work was supported by Biological and Molecular Chemistry Laboratory of Shantou University Medical College.

Sample 5

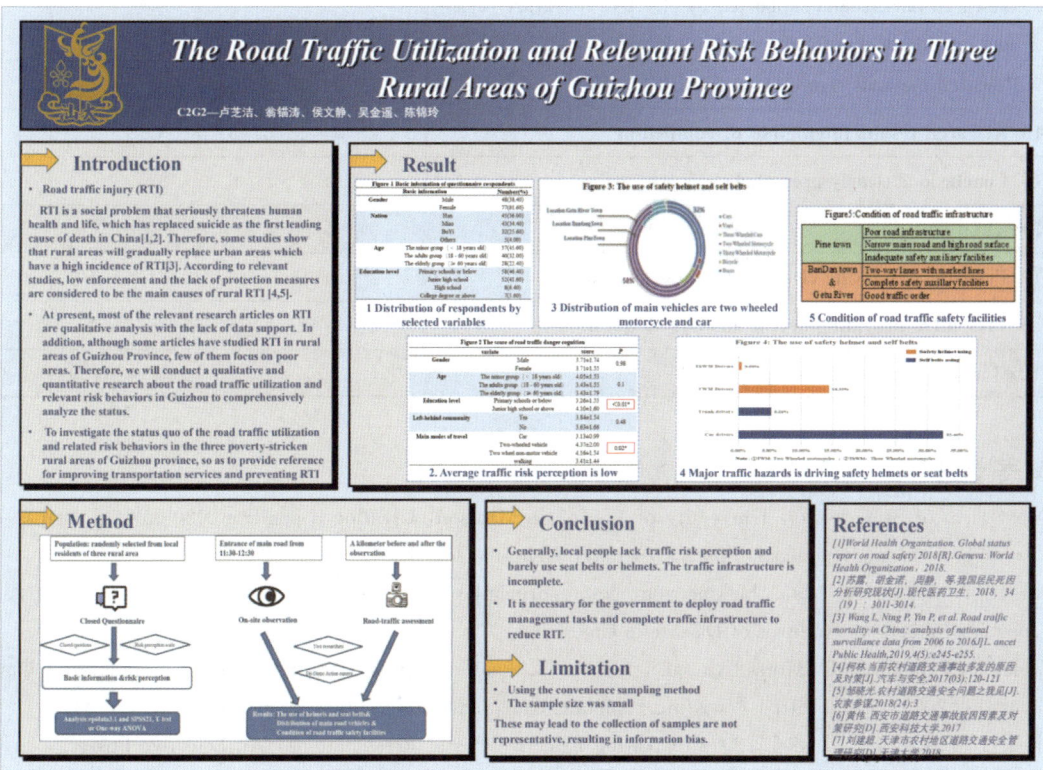

附录15.3 壁报报告评分标准

Criteria for Poster Presentation

Presenter _____

Poster Title _____

Rater _____

Note: Please select a proper number to evaluate the poster; the bigger the number, the higher your evaluation. Please circle first and then add up the total.

Format & Appearance 32%									
1. Clear progression of information	1	2	3	4	5	6	7	8	
2. Consistency of style, terminology, and symbolism	1	2	3	4	5	6	7	8	
3. Figures and text easy to read and pleasing to eye	1	2	3	4	5	6	7	8	
4. Appropriate use of colors	1	2	3	4	5	6	7	8	
Content 48%									
6. Good grammar with correct use of tenses, voices and sentence structures	1	2	3	4	5	6	7	8	
7. Words/expressions proper for academic written style	1	2	3	4	5	6	7	8	

(续表)

8. Research background supported by effective literature review and leading to significant research objectives	1　2　3　4　5　6　7　8	
9. Research methods rigorously described	1　2　3　4　5　6　7　8	
10. Research results intelligible & compelling	1　2　3　4　5　6　7　8	
11. Conclusions clearly presented	1　2　3　4　5　6　7　8	
Presentation　20%		
12. Presenters speaking clearly and enthusiastically	1　2　3　4　5　6　7　8　9　10	
13. Presenters providing decent answers to questions	1　2　3　4　5　6　7　8　9　10	
Total score		

参考文献

Department of Bacteriology:University of Wisconsin-Madison, Creating a poster [2020-05-17]. https://writing.wisc.edu/Handbook/PosterPresentations.html#samples.

Forsyth B, Waller A, 1995. Making your point: principles of visual design for computer aided slide and poster production. Archives of Disease in Childhood, 72: 80-84.

Kiefer K, Palmquist M, Barnes L, et al., 1994-2012. Poster Sessions. Writing@CSU. Colorado State University [2020-05-17]. https://writing.colostate.edu/guides/guide.cfm? guideid=78.

Hess G, Tosney K, Liegel L, 2013. Creating Effective Poster Presentations: An Effective Poster. North Carolina State University. https://projects.ncsu.edu/project/posters.

Li Y, Wang J, He S, et al., 2017. Survival time of HIV/AIDS cases and related factors in Beijing, 1995-2015. Chinese Journal of Epidemiology, 38(11): 1509-1513. doi: 10.3760/cma.j.issn.0254-6450.2017.11.014.

Maugh TH, 1974. Poster sessions: A new look at scientific meetings. Science, 184(4144): 1361.

Shen L, Xu L, Li X, et al., 2017. Prevalence of human papillomavirus genotypes and associated risk of cervical carcinoma in Chaoshan population. Carcinogenesis, Teratogenesis & Mutagenesis, 29(3): 226-229.

第三部分

课程评估

第十六章　课程评估

杨　苗　林常敏

课程评估是实施每门课程的必要步骤。Cronbach(1963)认为课程评估有三个目的：改善课程、对学习者进行筛选或评定、管理调控(学校或教师评估)。我们对学术英语课程进行评估，主要是出于第一个目的——改善课程，即评判教材、教学内容和方法是否达致满意的课程效果，并提出改进之处。本章先依据形成性评价和课程嵌入式评估介绍本课程的评估框架，并一一解释评估的主要内容，然后介绍针对本课程进行的两个研究，对课程的教学效果进行初步评估。

一、课程评估框架

（一）形成性评价法

形成性评价近年来被大量运用于学习评估，但这个概念的提出者Scriven(1967)一开始是将形成性评价用于课程评估，他认为在课程的发展阶段，形成性评价为课程的形成和优化提供了反馈和指导意见。我们的学术英语课程共分四个阶段，安排在四个学期进行。在每个阶段的备课和上课期间，教学团队持续进行在线讨论，从备课内容、教材和活动设计，到上课的体会、学生表现等都广泛交流意见。这些意见有的很快就用于接下来的教学中，有的则用于阶段性教学后的课程内容修改。在完成每个阶段的教学之后两周内，我们都会通过问卷收集学生对课程的反馈意见，这些意见也很快用于改进教学和课程。

（二）课程嵌入式评估法

我们采用了基于课堂教学的课程嵌入式评估法(course-embedded assessment)。和学习结束时才进行的评估不同，嵌入式课程评估将学习和评估融为一体。根据McConnell及Doolittle(2012)的定义，课程嵌入式评估通过课程活动和作业进行，聚焦学生的学习收获，而学习收获不仅来自学习成果，也来自学习过程；不仅包括量化评分，也包括质性描述；不仅包括知识和技能层面的能力表现，也包括认知、行为、情感层面的收获。

Course-embedded assessment is implemented through the judicious use of course assignments and activities. Valid course assignments and activities are those that align directly with the course's learning outcomes, pedagogical practices, course content, and student characteristics. These assignments may be formative or summative, qualitative or quantitative, and cognitive, behavioral, social, or affective. (McConnell及Doolittle, 2012, p.95)

（三）课程整体评估框架

我们参照McConnell及Doolittle(2012, p.100)的嵌入式课程评估框架，结合自身课程的具体情况，设计了以下评估框架(图16.1)。

我们在前期研究分析了医科生和执业医师的英语学习需求(杨苗，2017)，又分别在本书

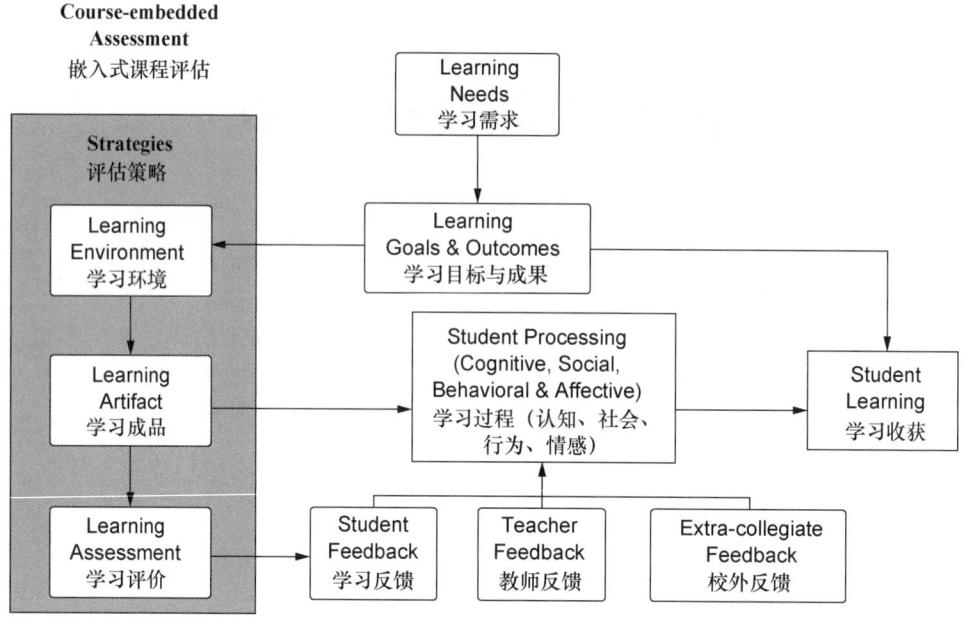

图 16.1　嵌入式课程评估框架

第一章和第二章讲述了学术英语课程的理论基础和课程设计，形成课程的具体目标，即三位一体（英语语言能力、专业信息素养和批判性思维能力）的批判性学术素养培养目标，以及具体的能力培养成果（图 1.1 和表 2.1）。这些构成嵌入式课程评估策略的环境要素。

学习成品与学习评价是嵌入式课程评估策略的另外两个要素。学生在课程四个学习阶段分别完成学术口头报告、学术壁报报告、文献综述和研究建议书等专业情景任务（表 2.2）。在评估这些任务时，我们都以学生的语言能力、专业信息的运用能力及思维能力作为评分的主要维度（详细评分标准见各章附录）。

另外，每个阶段课程结束之后，我们都会进行课程反馈调查，主要了解学生在学习过程中对每个学习主题的认知和投入程度，主要包括以下几方面：

（1）这个学习主题对我未来专业的学习与发展是否很有帮助。
（2）这个学习主题对我而言难度是否很大。
（3）我对这个学习主题是否很感兴趣。
（4）我在这个主题学习中是否很投入。
（5）我从这个主题学习中是否收获很大。

我们根据每届学生的反馈情况调整教学内容的安排和学习进度，尤其关注学生对挑战性比较大的学习内容（如文献综述和学术壁报）的反馈。经过两轮课程的调整和改善，学生对内容的接受度越来越高，学习收获也越来越大。以文献综述为例，使用同样的评分标准评分，在第一轮课程中，85 分以上的学生占比是 24%，在最近两轮教学中分别是 32% 和 37%。

每一届学生完成课程学习之后，我们都会询问他们在整个课程学习中的收获。最近一次问卷数据所显示的自评能力得到提高的学生比例为学术听力 65%、口语 77%、阅读 91%、写作 87%、科研思维 81%，尤其是后面三种能力，自评有较大提高的学生达到 25% 左右（图 16.2）。

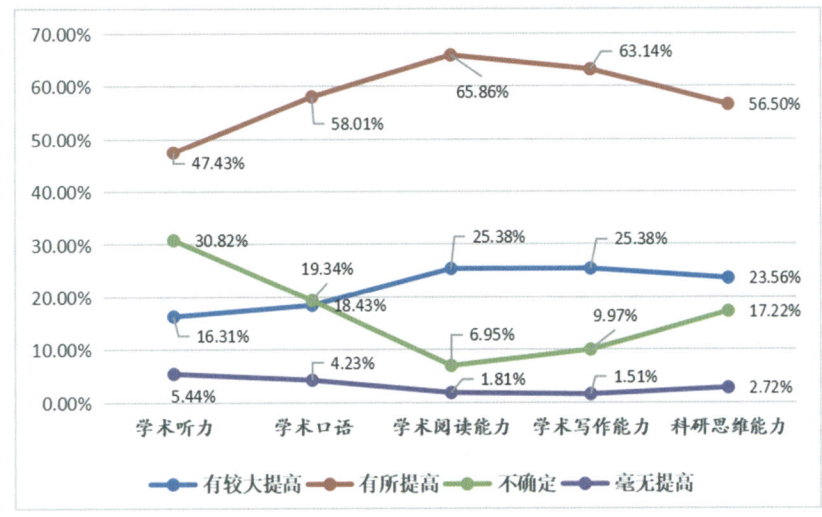

图 16.2 学生自评课程的学习收获

我们请学生用三个词形容学术英语课程,将学生列出的词语进行词频分析,发现出现频率最高的词是实用、专业、有趣;其次是严谨、团队合作、有难度和学术(图 16.3)。这些描述与我们在课程设计之初对课程的定位非常一致。令人欣慰的是,即使课程具有较大难度,学生仍然认为是"有趣"的,说明课程同时激发了学生的学习兴趣,这是成功的教学带来的学习体验。

图 16.3 学生对课程的描述形成的词频云图

教师的课程反馈则比较零散,每个学习阶段开始时都会集中讨论课程安排和教案,上课期间则借助邮件和即时通讯软件等工具共同备课和交流意见,每个学习阶段结束时都会再次集中讨论,根据学生课程反馈的数据修改该阶段的教案。教师对每个学习主题的教学反馈意见,我们在每章都择重点做了介绍。本书所展示的课程整体内容安排和各章具体的教学思路都是在经过两轮课程实施后逐步修改形成的,这真正体现了形成性课程评估的精髓和意义。

校外课程评估意见主要借助举办主题工作坊、邀请参加者回答问卷获得。课程负责人分别在"第五届中国学术英语教学研究会年会暨第四届学术英语亚洲国际研讨会"(同济大学,2019 年 5 月)和"外语教师发展工作坊"(东北大学,2019 年 7 月)做了题为"EAP Curriculum as a Praxis of Critical Negotiation and Action"的工作坊,并邀请与会教师参加课程的校外评估问卷调查。共46位高校英语教师回答了问卷,其中28位正从事学术英语教学,8位正准备加入此教学行列。所有教师都认同本课程拟定的大学生学术英语学习需求,其中阅读英语文献和撰写研究报告得到100%的认可,其次是撰写并发表论文(94%)、听学术讲座(88%)、做口头报告或壁报报告(88%)、撰写研究计划书(75%)。有半数的教师认为本课程的内容设置能很好地满足学生需求,另一半教师认为能基本满足学生需求。约80%的与会教师认为课程应该更强调学术听力训练。在对学术英语教师的能力要求方面,与会教师认为最首要的是理解学科研究思维的能力(80%),其次是具备英语学术能力(76%)和了解相关学术体裁、学术规范和学科信息(70%)。教师们认为本课程对学生而言最具挑战性的是培养学科研究思维,50%的教师认为他们的学生会非常喜欢这门课程,32%认为学生会有点喜欢这门课程。简而言之,笔者的校外同行对本课程有比较高的认可度,会后很多教师表示想了解更多的课程细节,以便用于本校教学。

我们鼓励、支持学生参加学术活动和竞赛,将从课程学到的内容运用到真正的学术交流活动中。近年,学习本课程的学生共有11人次在国际学术会议上做报告,在全国各项学术活动或赛事中共获奖102项,以下是其中几项重要的赛事。

2018年　学生参加2018年首届"中国大学生5分钟科研英语演讲比赛",在全国决赛中取得了2项特等奖、4项一等奖、3项二等奖、2项三等奖的优异成绩。

2019年　9位学生获邀参加2019年第五届国际大学生学术研讨会,获3项全国最佳研究计划奖,4项优秀海报论文奖,4位同学因现场出色的表现,获优秀报告奖。

2019年　学生参加第二届"中国大学生5分钟科研英语演讲比赛",在全国决赛中取得了2项特等奖、5项一等奖、13项二等奖的优异成绩。

2019年　学生参加第三届"北大医学·教育论坛"研究论文投稿,共获得3项一等奖,4项二等奖,1项优秀奖。

2020年　学生参加第三届"中国大学生5分钟科研英语演讲比赛",在全国决赛中取得了2项特等奖、3项一等奖、6项二等奖和7项三等奖的优异成绩。

学生的学术素养和科研能力还表现在积极参加科学研究、发表专业论文上。2018年以来,完成本课程学习的本科生以第一作者发表SCI论文27篇,总影响因子达到84.554。

二、课程评估实践

我们在实施课程的同时也积极开展课程研究,在此简单介绍两项研究,一项是关于课程三位一体能力的理论建模(林颖怡 等,2020)(图16.4),另一项则初步论证了课程对学生三位一体的能力的有效培养(杨苗 等,2017)。

(一) 以医科生为主体的学术素养理论建模研究

该研究在医科生($N=386$)中进行测试和问卷调查,获取学术英语、信息素养和批判性思维三方面的数据进行结构方程建模,探讨了三种能力之间的关联性。研究采用皮尔森学术英语测试(Pearson Test of English Academic)的写作和阅读部分用于测试学生的学术英语能力,使用信息素养评价量表(参照2000年版《高等教育信息素养能力标准》)测量学生的信息管理能力,使用加州批判性思维人格倾向测量表测量学生的批判性思维能力。研究使用IBM SPSS Statistics 25.0进行统计描述和问卷信度分析,使用IBM SPSS AMOS 24.0进行验证性因子分析和结构方程模型的界定和执行。

研究结果显示：批判性思维对学术英语的影响为 0.135，其比例占 79.9%，在信息素养的一个维度（评价信息，ILS3）和学术英语之间起中介效应，中介效应值为 0.034，比例占 20.1%（表 16.1）。与信息素养相比，批判性思维对学术英语能力的直接影响效应更为显著，效应值为 0.135（$p<0.05$），说明批判性思维在一定程度上可正面预测学术英语能力。研究初步结论是批判性思维在整个学术素养的理论模型构建中起到了中坚作用，它既对学术英语有直接正面的预测效应，又导介了信息素养与学术英语之间的关系。研究对学术英语课程的启示是，对学生批判性思维的培养可能会有效促进其学术英语水平的提高，学术英语课程应着重培养学生的通用批判性思维能力，同时利用翻转课堂、网络平台及融入专业知识等方式促进批判性思维和专业思维的融合，提高学生的信息素养。

表 16.1　模型直接间接影响效应分解（林颖怡 等，2020，p3）

影响路径	标准化效应值	比例
ILS3→批判性思维→学术英语	0.034	20.1%
批判性思维→学术英语	0.135	79.9%
批判性思维→学术英语总效应	0.034＋0.135＝0.169	—

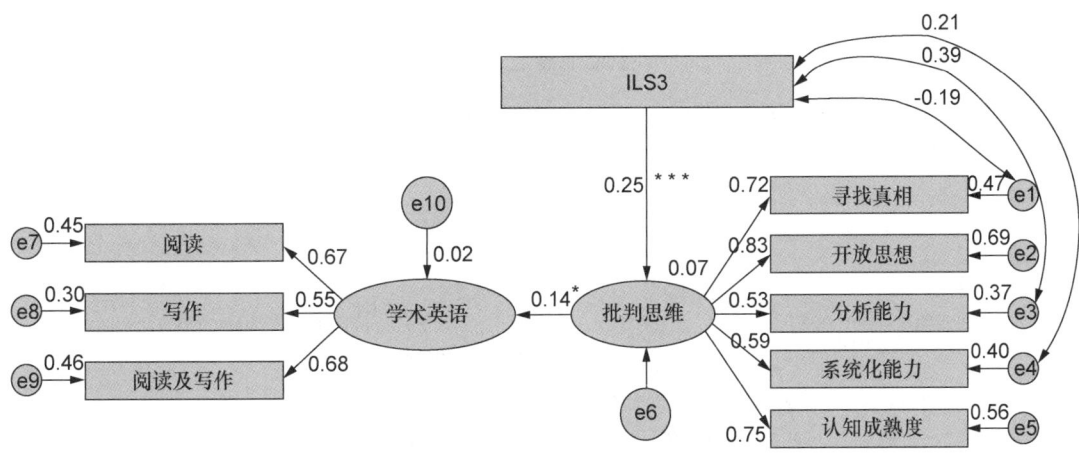

图 16.4　理论模型及路径系数（林颖怡 等，2020，p2）

（二）医学院校大学英语教学中依托信息管理的批判性学术素养培养实证研究

该研究分两个部分。第一部分在 2014 级全体七年制医科生中进行（$N=195$），具体设计是在学生进入课程学习之前和完成一年的学习之后分别进行信息管理能力和批判性思维能力（这两份量表与前一个研究相同）的前测和后测。第二部分在学生学习了一年学术英语课程之后，在全级中随机抽取一个班的学生（$N=30$）进行个案研究，设计一个评价量表，从专业信息运用、语言能力体现和思维能力三个方面评价学生的综述写作，以便分析语言、学科信息和思维三者在学习过程中的交互作用和对学习效果的影响。

研究结果显示，专业信息管理能力的总分前后测有显著统计学差异（$p=0.000$）。在五个分项能力中，获取信息、评价信息和运用信息的前后测得分有统计学差异，说明学生在这三方面进步较大（图 16.5）。批判性思维能力的总分前后测也有显著统计学差异（$p=0.000$）。在七个分项能力中，开放思想、认知成熟度和求知欲望得分较高（分项得分大于 45

分),只有自信心("对自己的理性分析能力有把握")的增长没有统计学差异,这是唯一一个分项得分未满40分的特质,说明学生这方面表现较弱(图16.6)。

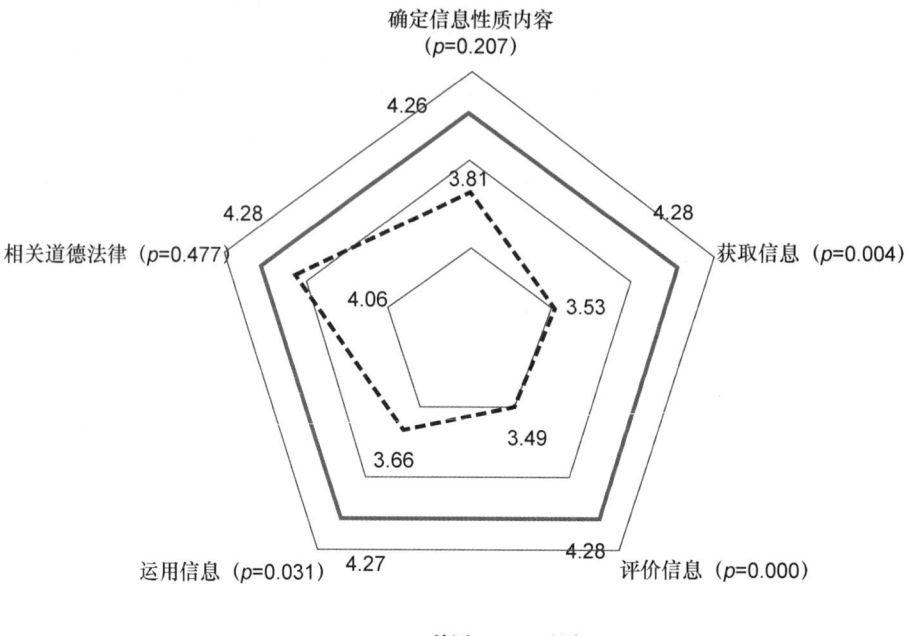

图 16.5　信息管理能力前后测对比(杨苗 等,2017,p.110)

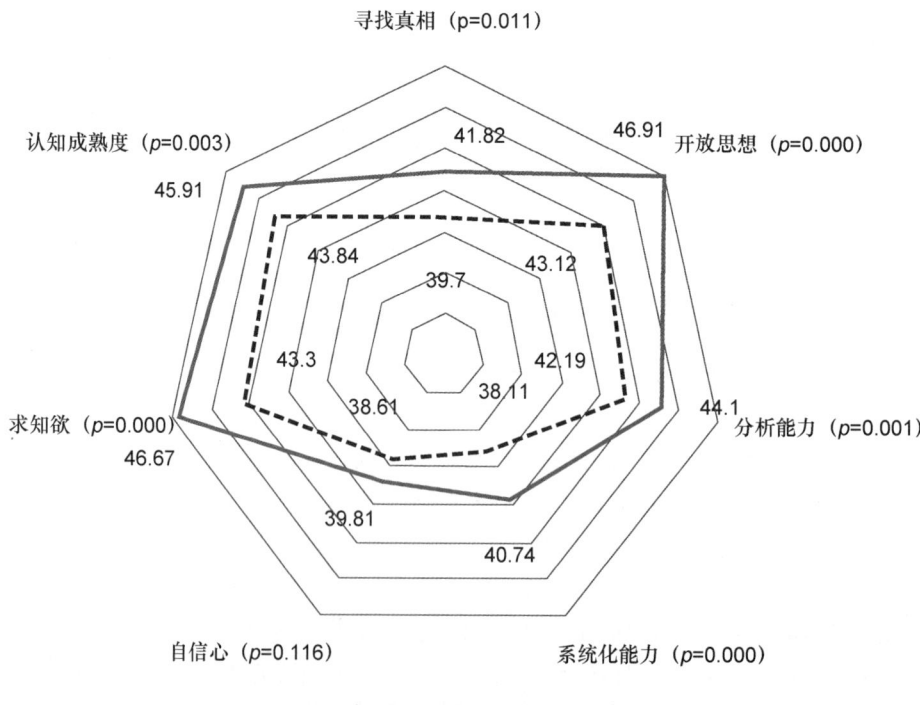

图 16.6　批判性思维能力前后测对比(杨苗 等,2017,p.110)

学生综述写作九个分项能力的均值是 3.9097,接近 4 分良好的评价。经重复测量检验,每个维度的三个项目得分间有统计学差异,说明在专业内容、语言能力和思维的每个评价维度里,学生在不同分项能力的得分有差异。两两比较的结果显示:每个评价维度中都是最大均值与最小均值之间有统计学差异。专业内容方面,学生恰当引用权威信息源并进行客观评估的能力(A3)较差;语言能力方面,语言使用的学术性(B3)也较弱;思维能力方面,学生论证的条理性和逻辑性(C3)得分偏低。对三大维度九个指标的得分进行相关分析的结果显示,有六对指标之间有较高的相关性(表 16.2),其中三大维度内部都各有指标相关,各维度之间主要是专业内容可信性(A3)与论据充分性(C2)相关,语言使用逻辑性(B2)与论证逻辑性(C3)相关。

表 16.2 综述写作九个分项能力相关分析结果(杨苗,林常敏,2017,p.110)

具有相关关系的指标	相关系数	p 值
A2 专业内容时效性 vs. A3 专业内容可信性	0.829	0.011
A3 专业内容可信性 vs. C2 论据充分性	0.800	0.017
B1 语言使用规范性 vs. B3 语言使用学术性	0.759	0.029
B2 语言使用逻辑性 vs. B3 语言使用学术性	0.730	0.040
B2 语言使用逻辑性 vs. C3 论证逻辑性	0.715	0.049
C1 论点明确性 vs. C3 论证逻辑性	0.911	0.0002

研究的初步结论是学生的批判性学术素养在经过一年多的课程学习之后得到提升,课程设置的培养目标得到实现。批判性学术素养三位一体的金字塔框架必须依托动态的专业信息管理过程来实现整合培养的目标。本研究还发现,学生在语言、专业信息管理和思维三大维度均有能力发展不均衡的问题。学生具备初步的文献检索与分析能力,但一旦涉及较高层次的思维,即批判性和创造性思维,如理解研究的论证过程和结论、对专业信息进行评价和综合、形成自己的观点等,学生就显得能力不足。所以学术英语课程要加强这些方面的教学与训练。

三、展望

本学术英语课程在试行三年,正式运行三年之后,于 2019 年和 2020 年分别在中国大学 MOOC(慕课)和学堂在线上线,成为在线开放课程。2018 年,我们完成校级精品资源共享课程后,就开始在校内实施线上线下的混合式教学,并于 2020 年获广东省教育厅认定为线上线下混合式一流本科课程。课程共包含 12 个单元 46 个教学视频,总长约 7 小时,与本书出版的 12 个教学案例(其中综述写作分成两章)一一对应。慕课视频主要为学生准备,本书的读者则是学术英语的授课教师。两种资源结合,我们希望这门课程能够在更多高校推广,使更多大学生受益。

展望未来,我们的课程将面向更多专业和层次的学生,我们将面临更多的挑战,其中最大的挑战就是大规模在线开放课程所带来的学生数量可能会影响教师针对个体的学习反馈,尤其是学术写作方面。为解决这个问题,需要在课程中强化同伴反馈和修改环节。但是同伴反馈和修改一直因受太多个人因素(Benson 及 DeKeyser,2019;Han,2017;Wu,2019)和环境因素(Han,2019)影响而效果欠佳。在学术写作的同侪反馈和修改中,学生对学术体裁的特征的理解和运用尤其重要，而这些单靠课程内的训练远远不够，需要通过大量阅读和分析原汁原味的专业文献习得，也需要批判性阅读和分析大量的学习者文本去发现问题、解决问题。未来学术英语课程的发展方向应该是借助现有或自建的专家学者或学习者的学术英语语料库，大力鼓励数据驱动式学习。学生通过语料库的检索获得语言使用的真实样例，并对照学习者的习作样例，进行发现式或者验证式学习，可以解决同侪反馈时语言信息不足和自信不足的问题，提高同侪反馈的效果。而教师则激励学生进行调查和思索，从真实材料中得出自己的结论。

我们期待本书能抛砖引玉，吸引更多的同行加入学术英语教学。我们也期待使用本书的同行能和我们交流，进一步改善课程，一起推动我国的学术英语课程研究。

参考文献

Benson S, DeKeyser R, 2019. Effects of written corrective feedback and language aptitude on verb tense accuracy. Language Teaching Research, 23: 702-726.

Charlies M, 2011. The routledge handbook of corpus linguistics. System, 39(1): 113-115.

Cronbach L, 1963. Course improvement through evaluation. Teachers' College Record, 64: 672-683.

Han Ye, 2017. Mediating and being mediated: learner beliefs and learner engagement with written corrective feedback. System, 69: 133-142.

Han Ye, 2019. Written corrective feedback from an ecological perspective: the interaction between the context and individual learners. System, 80: 288-303.

Johns T, 1991. Should you be persuaded: Two examples of data-driven learning. // Johns T, King P. Classroom concordancing. English Language Research Journal, 4: 1-16.

McConnell KD, Doolittle PE, 2012. Course-embedded assessment: Aligning Pedagogical Practices to Enhance Student Learning. // Secolsky C, Denison DB. Handbook on measurement, assessment, and evaluation in higher education. 2nd ed. New York & London: Routledge.

Scriven M, 1967. The methodology of evaluation. // Stake RE. Perspectives of curriculum evaluation. American Educational Research Association. Monograph series on curriculum evaluation No.1. Chicago: Rand McNally, 39-89.

Wu ZW, 2019. Lower English proficiency means poorer feedback performance? A mixed-methods study. Assessing Writing, 41: 14-24.

林颖怡,杨欣,周浩锋等,2020. 以医科生为主体的学术素养理论建模研究——批判性思维能力之重要性与培养模式探讨,教育教学论坛,27: 1-4.

杨苗,2017. 体裁教学法课程框架中的医学英语扩展式学习：一项基于批判性学习需求分析的介入研究. 北京: 高等教育出版社.

杨苗,林常敏,2017. 医学院校大学英语教学中依托信息管理的批判性学术素养培养实证研究. 复旦教育论坛. 15(4): 107-112.